KT-573-888

Terpsichore in Sneakers

Post-Modern Dance

Sally Banes

with a new introduction

Wesleyan University Press

Copyright © 1977, 1978, 1979, 1987 by Sally Banes
All rights reserved

This book was first published by Houghton Mifflin Company

Parts of this book have been previously published in *Dance Scope, Dance Research Journal, Village Voice, Dance Magazine* and *The Postmodern Moment*, ed. Stanley Trachenberg (Greenwood Press).

Grateful acknowledgment is made to the following for permission to use previously published material: Yvonne Rainer, Chart from "A Quasi Survey of Some 'Minimalist' Tendencies in the Quantitatively Minimal Dance Activity Midst the Plethora, or an Analysis of Trio A." Reprinted from Yvonne Rainer, *Work 1961-73.* (Halifax, Nova Scotia: Nova Scotia College of Art and Design; New York: New York University Press, 1974), by permission of the author, Steve Paxton, "Satisfyin Lover," Reprinted from *0 to 9*, no. 4 (1968), by permission of the author. Lucinda Childs, "Street Dance," from Lucinda Childs: A Portfolio." Reprinted from *Artforum 11 Excerpt*, reprinted by permission of the choreographer. Douglas Dunn, "Talking Dancing." Reprinted from James Klosty, *Merce Cunningham* (New York: Saturday Review Press, 1975), by permission of Douglas Dunn and E. P. Dutton.

Library of Congress Cataloging-in-Publication Data

Banes, Sally.
Terpsichore in sneakers.

Reprint. Originally published: Boston: Houghton Mifflin, 1980. With new introd.
Bibliography: p.
Includes index.
1. Modern dance. I. Title.
GV1783.B36 1987 793.3'2 86-7829
ISBN 0-8195-6160-6 (pbk.: alk. paper)

WESLEYAN UNIVERSITY PRESS
Published by University Press of New England, Hanover, NH 03755
Manufactured in the United States of America
Wesleyan Paperback, 1987

93 92 91 6 5 4 3

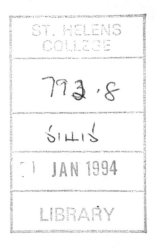

ST. HELENS
COLLEGE
793.8
61415
JAN 1994
LIBRARY

Our steps are so easy and familiar to us that they never have the honor to be considered in themselves, and as strange acts.

— Paul Valéry
Dance and the Soul

Contents

List of Illustrations

Acknowledgments

Many people aided me generously in the researching and writing of this book. Thanks go first to Noël Carroll for many valuable insights and criticisms in the course of long discussions and patient readings. I also appreciate the help of: Robert Alexander, Helen and Daniel Banes, Ann Beckerman, Byrd Hoffman School for Byrds, Ping Chong, Robert Cornfield, the staff of the Dance Research Collection of the Library and Museum of the Performing Arts (New York Public Library at Lincoln Center), Terry Curtis Fox, Carter and Sheldon Frank, Mimi Johnson and Performing Artservices, Deborah Jowitt, Michael Kirby, Kasper Koenig, Brooks McNamara, Curt Matthews, Ellen Mazer, David Moberg, Wendy Perron, Robert Pierce, Carole Pipolo, Richard Schechner, Jim Self, Marcia B. Siegel, Philip Taubman, Daniel Zwerdling, and at Houghton Mifflin: Janice Byer, Christina Rago, John Russell, and my editor, Jonathan Galassi. Without the kind cooperation of the choreographers this book would not have been possible.

Some of the chapters were published in part or in other versions in various publications. I want to thank my editors at those publications and at other publications where I have written about dance: Jack Anderson and George Dorris, *Dance Chronicle;* Tobi Tobias, William Como, and Richard Philp, *Dance Magazine;* Nancy Reynolds, Sally R. Sommer, and Dianne Woodruff, *Dance Research Journal;* Richard Lorber, *Dance Scope;* Tom Borek, *Eddy;* Bonnie Marranca and Gautam Dasgupta, *Performing Arts Journal;* Bob Roth, *The Reader;* Rob Baker, and Denise Martin, *Soho Weekly News;* and Burt Supree, *Village Voice.*

S.B.
December 1978

Preface to the Wesleyan Paperback Edition

I WROTE *Terpsichore in Sneakers* during the years 1973–78. When I began the book, the term "post-modern" was rarely used to categorize the kind of dance I was writing about, though by the time the book was done, the term was much more common in dance, as well as in other arts. However, since the book was published, in 1980, "post-modern" has become a term that obsesses critics and historians of culture generally.

I have chosen to let the original text stand, despite the fact that, especially in the introduction, I might now choose to state some matters differently. My research on the Judson Dance Theater over the past eight years has given me new perspectives as well as new facts on that phenomenon, but those have since been published in my book *Democracy's Body: Judson Dance Theater 1962–1964*. My thoughts about modern dance have become less polemical and more complex, but the treatment of historical modern dance as a series of avant gardes and its relations to various other dance cultures—not only post-modern, but also ballet, and folk and popular traditions, Western and non-Western—must be the subject for some future study. Further, I must retract my surprising statement that sneakers do not serve as symbols; the rest of the book certainly belies that claim. Now, the original introduction itself seems a product of the seventies, but that is partly why I have left it intact.

In order to inform the reader about my current perspective on post-modern dance and on new developments on the New York scene in the 1980s, I have added an introduction to this edition, in which I discuss the problems of defining post-modern dance in light of the term's use in the other arts and trace the development of the stages that, in retrospect, emerge more clearly in the history of post-modern dance.

At the end of the book, the general bibliography and chronology have been updated.

For their work on the second edition, I would like to thank Belinda Josey and Jeannette Hopkins, at Wesleyan University Press. I would also like to acknowledge Stanley Trachtenberg, Laurel Quinlan-Ryan, Anne Valois, and Allen Robertson for commissioning articles that led to the new introduction. Once again I am grateful to Noël Carroll for critical readings and debates.

Introduction to the Wesleyan Paperback Edition

When Yvonne Rainer started using the term "post-modern" in the early 1960s to categorize the work she and her peers were doing at Judson Church and other places, she meant it in a primarily chronological sense. Theirs was the generation that came after modern dance, which was itself originally an inclusive term applied to nearly any theatrical dance that departed from ballet or popular entertainment. By the late 1950s, modern dance had refined its styles and its theories, and had emerged as a recognizable dance genre. It used stylized movements and energy levels in legible structures (theme and variations, ABA, and so on) to convey feeling tones and social messages. The choreography was buttressed by expressive elements of theater such as music, props, special lighting and costumes. The aspirations of modern dance, anti-academic from the first, were simultaneously primitivist and modernist. Gravity, dissonance, and a potent horizontality of the body were means to describe the stridency of modern life, as choreographers kept one eye on the future while casting the other to the ritual dances of non-Western culture.[1] Though they were especially conscious of their oppositional role to modern dance, the early post-modern choreographers, possessed of an acute awareness of a historical crisis in dance as well as in the other arts, recognized that they were both bearers and critics of two separate dance traditions. One was the uniquely twentieth-century phenomenon of modern dance; the other was the balletic, academic *danse de l'école,* with its strict canons of beauty, grace, harmony, and the equally potent, regal verticality of the body extending back to the Renaissance courts of Europe. Rainer, Simone Forti,

Steve Paxton, and other post-modern choreographers of the sixties were not united in terms of their aesthetic. Rather, they were united by their radical approach to choreography, their urge to reconceive the medium of dance.

By the early 1970s, a new style with its own aesthetic canons seems to have emerged. In 1975, Michael Kirby published an issue of *The Drama Review* devoted to post-modern dance, using the term in print for one of the first times in regard to dance and proposing a definition of the new genre:

> In the theory of post-modern dance, the choreographer does not apply visual standards to the work. The view is an interior one: movement is not preselected for its characteristics but results from certain decisions, goals, plans, schemes, rules, concepts, or problems. Whatever actual movement occurs during the performance is acceptable as long as the limiting and controlling principles are adhered to.[2]

According to Kirby, post-modern dance rejects musicality, meaning, characterization, mood, and atmosphere; it uses costume, lighting, and objects in purely functional ways. At present, Kirby's definition seems far too limited. It refers to only one of several stages—analytic post-modern dance—in the development of post-modern dance, which I intend to trace here.

The term "post-modern" means something different in every art form, as well as in culture in general. In 1975, the same year the post-modern dance issue of *The Drama Review* appeared, Charles Jencks used the term to refer to a new trend in architecture that had also begun to emerge in the early sixties. According to Jencks, post-modernism in architecture is a doubly-coded aesthetic that has popular appeal, on the one hand, and esoteric historical significance for the cognoscenti, on the other.[3] In the dance world, perhaps only Twyla Tharp could have fit such a definition at the time, but her work was not commonly considered post-modern dance. (Much "new dance" of the eighties could also fit such a definition, but at this point it would be revisionist to call only eighties dance post-modern. It is, rather, as I discuss below, post-modern*ist*.) In the visual-art world and in theater, a number of critics have used the term to refer to artworks that are copies of or comments on other artworks, challenging values of originality, authenticity, and the masterpiece and provoking Derridean theories of simulacra. This notion fits some post-modern dances, but not all.

In dance, the confusion the term "post-modern" creates is further complicated by the fact that historical modern dance was never really *modernist*. Often it has been precisely in the arena of post-modern dance that issues of modernism in the other arts have arisen: the acknowledgment of the medium's materials, the revealing of dance's essential qualities as an art form, the separation of formal elements, the abstraction of forms, and the elimination of external references as subjects. Thus in many respects it is post-modern dance that functions as *modernist* art. That is, post-modern dance came after modern dance (hence, post-) and, like the post-modernism of the other arts, was anti-modern dance. But since "modern" in dance did not mean modernist, to be anti-modern dance was not at all to be anti-modernist. In fact, quite the opposite. The analytic post-modern dance of the seventies in particular displayed these modernist preoccupations, and it aligned itself with that consummately modernist visual art, minimalist sculpture.[4] And yet, there are also aspects of post-modern dance that do fit with post-modernist notions (in the other arts) of pastiche, irony, playfulness, historical reference, the use of vernacular materials, the continuity of cultures, an interest in process over product, breakdowns of boundaries between art forms and between art and life, and new relationships between artist and audience.[5] Some of the new directions of dance in the eighties are even more closely allied to the concerns and techniques, especially that of pastiche, of post-modernism in the other arts. But if we were to call sixties and seventies post-modern dance *post-modern* and dub eighties new dance *post-modernist,* the confusion would probably not be worth the scrupulous accuracy. Further, as I argue in the section on the eighties below, I believe the avant-garde dance of all three decades is united and can be embraced by a single term. And I continue to recommend the term "post-modern." The use of the word, however, deserves yet another caveat. Although in dance "post-modern" began as a choreographer's term, it has since become a critic's term that most choreographers now find either constricting or inexact. By now, many writers on dance use the term so loosely it can mean anything or nothing. However, since the term has been used widely for almost a decade, it seems to me that, rather than avoid it, we should define it and use it discriminately.

The 1960s: Breakaway Post-Modern Dance

The early post-modern choreographers saw as their task the purging and melioration of historical modern dance, which had made certain promises in respect to the use of the body and the social and artistic function of dance that had not been fulfilled. Rather than freeing the body and making dance accessible even to the smallest children, rather than bringing about social and spiritual change, the institution of modern dance had developed into an esoteric art form for the intelligentsia, more remote from the masses than ballet. The bodily configurations modern dance drew on had ossified into various stylized vocabularies; dances had become bloated with dramatic, literary, and emotional significance; dance companies were often structured as hierarchies; young choreographers were rarely accepted into an implicit, closed guild of masters. (Ballet, for obvious reasons, was not acceptable as an alternative to modern dance. So something new had to be created.) Although Merce Cunningham had made radical departures from classical modern dance, his work remained within certain technical and contextual restraints—that is, his vocabulary remained a specialized, technical one, and he presented his dances in theaters for the most part. Cunningham is a figure who stands on the border between modern and post-modern dance. His vertical, vigorous movement style and his use of chance (which segments not only such elements as stage space, timing, and body parts, but also meaning in the dance) seem to create a bodily image of a modern intellect. In his emphasis on the formal elements of choreography, the separation of elements such as décor and music from the dancing, and the body as the sensuous medium of the art form, Cunningham's practice is modernist; his work and the theories of John Cage, his collaborator, formed an important base from which many of the ideas and actions of the post-modern choreographers sprang, either in opposition or in a spirit of extension. In a sense, Cunningham moved away from modern dance by synthesizing it with certain aspects of ballet. Those who came after him rejected synthesis altogether.[6]

By breaking the rules of historical modern dance, and even those of the avant-garde of the fifties (including not only Cunningham, but also such choreographers as Ann Halprin, James Waring, Merle Marsicano, Aileen Passloff, and others),[7] the post-modern choreographers found new ways to foreground the medium of dance rather than its meaning. Their program fit well with a cultural trend given expression in Susan Sontag's *Against Interpretation,* a book of essays written between 1962 and 1965. In the title essay, Sontag calls for a transparent art—and criticism—that will not "mean," but will illuminate and open the way for experience. "What is important now," Sontag wrote, "is to recover our senses."

> We must learn to see more, to *hear* more, to feel more. Our task is not to find the maximum amount of content in a work of art, much less to squeeze more content out of the work than is already there. Our task is to cut back content so

that we can see the thing at all. . . . The function of criticism should be to show *how* it is what it is, even *that* it is what it is, rather than to show *what it means*.[8]

The dances by the early post-modern choreographers were not cool analyses of forms but urgent reconsiderations of the medium. The nature, history, and function of dance as well as its structures were the subjects of the post-modern inquiry. A spirit of permissiveness and playful rebellion prevailed, foreshadowing the political and cultural upheavals of the late sixties. The younger generation of choreographers showed in their dances that they departed not only from classical modern dance with its myths, heroes, and psychological metaphors, but also from the elegance of ballet and even from post-modern dance's closest influences. The breakaway period lasted roughly from 1960 to 1973. Within that time, the first eight years saw an initial bursting of forms and definitions, and several major themes of post-modern dance were set forth: references to history; new uses of time, space, and the body; problems of defining dance.

The first of these themes was, in a sense, a way of looking back, of acknowledging the heritage these choreographers had set out to repudiate. Through references to other dance traditions, often couched in ironic terms—such as Rainer's screaming fit in a pile of white tulle in *Three Seascapes* (1962), or David Gordon's instructions for how to make a successful modern dance in *Random Breakfast* (1963)—these pieces set themselves in dialogue with their own history.

The second and third set of themes looked at the present and the future, asking through practice what new dance could be. In works like Simone Forti's *Huddle* (1961), in which the performers take turns crawling over the huddled group for about ten minutes, or in Elaine Summers's *For Carola* (1963), which consisted of lying down very slowly, or in Paxton's *Flat* (1964), which included getting dressed and undressed in unhurried real time and striking frozen poses, or in Rainer's *Trio A* (1966), a catalogue of uninflected movements, time was flattened and detheatricalized, stripped of the dynamics of phrasing typical of modern dance and ballet: preparation, climax, recovery.

The use of space was explored both in terms of its articulation in the dance (i.e., the use of architectural details in the design of the dance or the exploration of a surface other than the floor) and in terms of place (i.e., art gallery, church, or loft as venue, instead of a theater with a proscenium stage). Forti, never a member of the Judson Dance Theater, presented her two earliest works, *Rollers* and *See-Saw* (both 1960), in an art gallery, and her evening of dance constructions (1961) in Yoko Ono's loft on Chambers Street, where the audience walked around the relatively static dances as if they were sculptures. Not only was her use of space a break from the practice of modern dance, but the particular places she used shifted the locus of her activity from the dance world to the art world and raised the choreographer's status to that of a serious artist. Trisha Brown danced on a chicken-coop roof and in a parking lot. Her Equipment Pieces set people walking down buildings and trees and on walls. The members of the Judson Dance Theater performed in the church's gym and in its sanctuary, as well as in a roller-skating rink in Washington, D.C., and in the tiny Gramercy Arts Theater, which had a proscenium stage so small that it reduced all the dances to minimum action. Paxton gave his *Afternoon* (1963) on a farm in New Jersey, and he and Deborah Hay performed on the grounds of a country club in Monticello, New York, in 1965. By the late sixties, entire outdoor dance festivals were being organized by producers; the impetus toward performing outside moved from the choreographer's aesthetic choice to the producer's marketing tactics. And also by the late sixties, galleries and museums had become the most common venue for post-modern dance performance. This was possible partly because visual artists moved away from making objects in the sixties, presenting performances or videotape installations, rather than things to be stationed on the walls or on the floor. In this context, dance events fit both aesthetically and practically into the programming of museums and art festivals both in the United States and in Europe.

Issues of the body and its powerful social meanings were approached head-on. The body itself became the subject of the dance, rather than serving as an instrument for expressive metaphors. An unabashed examination of the body and its functions and powers threaded through the early post-modern dances. One form it took was relaxation, a loosening of the control that has characterized Western dance technique. Choreographers deliberately used untrained performers in their search for the "natural" body. Another form was the release of pure energy, in dances such as Carolee Schneemann's *Lateral Splay* (1963), in which dancers hurtle through space until they meet an object or another person, and Brown, Forti, and Dick Levine's "violent contact" improvisations (1961). Yet another form was the use of nudity, in works such as Paxton and Rainer's *Word Words* (1963) and Robert Morris's *Site* (1964) and *Waterman Switch* (1965). A number of dances involved eating onstage, and several of Paxton's works used inflatable tunnels that were reminiscent of digestive tracts. Schneemann's *Meat Joy* (1964) and Rainer's "Love" duet in *Terrain* (1963) dealt with explicitly sexual imagery in different ways.[9]

The problem of defining dance for the early post-modern choreographers was related to the inquiries into time, space, and the body, but extended beyond them, embracing the other arts and asserting propositions about the nature of dance. Games, sports, contests, the simple acts of walking and running, the gestures involved in playing music and giving a lecture, and even the motion of film and the mental action of language were presented as dances. In effect, the post-modern choreographers proposed that a dance was a dance not because of its content but because of its context—i.e., simply because it was framed as a dance. This opening of the borders of dance was a break from modern dance that was qualitatively different than issues of time, space, and the body. To be nude was more extreme than to be barefoot, but it was still an action of the same sort. To call a dance a dance because of its functional relation to its *context* (rather than because of its internal movement qualities, or *content*) was to shift the terms of dance theory, aligning it with the contemporary "institutional" theory of art.[10]

The years 1968–73 were a transitional period in which at least three more themes were developed: politics, audience engagement, and non-Western influence. Political themes of participation, democracy, cooperation, and ecology, although often implicit in the early sixties, were now made explicit. As theater and dance became more political, the political movements of the late sixties—anti-war, black power, student, feminist, and gay groups—used theatrical means to stage their battles. A number of choreographers mobilized large groups in their dances. Rainer's pieces of this period included *WAR*, a version of *Trio A* for the Judson Flag Show, and a street protest (all 1970). Her *Continuous Project—Altered Daily* (1970) examined not only the stages and modes of performance, but also issues of leadership and control. Paxton's *Untitled Lecture, Beautiful Lecture, Audience Performances* (all 1968), *Intravenous Lecture* (1970), *Collaboration with Wintersoldier* (1971), and *Air* (1973) were didactic works that dealt more or less overtly with issues of censorship, war, personal intervention, and civic responsibility. The Grand Union, a collective for improvisation, formed in 1970 and the following year gave a benefit performance for the Black Panthers. A women's improvisation collective, the Natural History of the American Dancer, was formed in 1971. In 1972, Paxton and others began Contact Improvisation, which has evolved not only as an alternative technique, but also as an alternative social network. Contact

Improvisation is concerned with physical techniques of falling, with duet situations, and with physical improvisation, but its forms have social and political connotations. Its performance seems to project a lifestyle, a model for a possible world, in which improvisation stands for freedom and adaptation, and support stands for trust and cooperation.

The influence of non-Western forms and movement philosophies, although present from the beginnings of post-modern dance through the influence of John Cage and Zen Buddhism, became more pronounced in the late sixties, as dancers forsook regular dance classes for training in such forms as Tai Chi Chuan and Aikido and, in Rainer's case, found new sources for narrative in the epic mythological dramas of India. The American fascination with the Third World, expressed not only in post-modern dance and in a resurgent black dance movement, but also in cultural forms as diverse as kung-fu films, Hindu religious cults, Maoist political sects, and Oriental and African fashions in clothing, reflected the changing power relations of African and Far Eastern nations and the impact of the war in Vietnam. These political crises sparked conflicts between Eastern and Western values as basic as attitudes toward time and the body. New directions in political change suggested new models for dance forms—for instance, the prospect of millions of Chinese people rising early to practice Tai Chi Chuan for health and communal spirit. For complex historical and political reasons, the aesthetic and social functions of the black dance movement of the sixties diverged sharply from the predominantly white post-modern dance movement; although African dance became an important source for black choreographers in the sixties and seventies, several post-modern choreographers were drawn to Eastern forms.[11]

The 1970s: Analytic Post-Modern Dance

By 1973, a wide range of basic questions about dance had been raised in the arena of post-modern choreography. A new phase of consolidation and analysis began, building on the issues that the experiments of the sixties had unearthed. A recognizable style had emerged, one that was reductive, factual, objective, and down-to-earth. It is this style to which Kirby refers. Expressive elements such as music, special lighting, costumes, props, et cetera, were stripped away from the dancing. Performers wore functional clothing—sweatpants and T-shirts or casual everyday dress—and danced in silence in plain, well-lit rooms. Structural devices such as repetition and reversal, mathematical systems, geometric forms, and comparison and contrast allowed for the perusal of pure, often simple movement. If the dances of the first phase of post-modern dance were primarily polemical in their theoretical thrust—an assortment of all kinds of rejections of the then prevailing, constraining definition of dance—then the works of analytic post-modern dance were programmatic in their theoretical thrust. That is, the analytic post-moderns were committed to the goal of redefining dance in the wake of the polemics of the sixties. And, further, they had an idea of how such a definition should be pursued, that is, in terms of emphasizing choreographic structure and in terms of foregrounding movement per se. Their program was to make dance as such the locus of audience attention by making dances in which all the audience was given to see was structure and movement per se, i.e., movement without overtly expressive or illusionistic effects or reference. Rainer's *Trio A*, choreographed in 1966, was an early analytic exemplar. Lucinda Childs's *Calico Mingling* (1973), a work for four dancers composed only of forward and backward walking patterns in six-step phrases that trace semicircular or linear paths, is a paradigmatic analytic work, as are Brown's various Accumulation Pieces and Structured Pieces. Paxton's improvisatory solos of the seventies were a continuation of the analytic strand of his work present from his earliest investigations into walking in *Proxy* (1961).

In analytic post-modern dance, movement became objective as it was distanced from personal expression through the use of scores, bodily attitudes that suggested work and other ordinary movements, verbal commentaries, and tasks. Tasks were a way of producing impersonal, concentrated, real movement—goal-oriented in an immediate sense. All of these strategies had been used in the sixties, but in the seventies they became a dominant (although not exclusive) trend, and they were organized more and more programmatically. A number of choreographers continued to work in older post-modern modes (Carolee Schneemann, for instance, made performances involving issues of the female body) or moved in other directions (see, for instance, the discussion of the work of Deborah Hay and others below; Yvonne Rainer moved in that decade from dance to performance art to film).

The analytic dances called attention to the workings of the body in an almost scientific way. One noted the workings of the muscles in Batya Zamir's body, for instance, as she traversed her aerial sculptures. One scrutinized the particular configuration of a lift or a hold in a Contact Improvisation encounter. The anti-illusionist approach demanded close viewing and clarified the smallest unit of dance, shifting the emphasis from the phrase to the step or gesture. It combined low-key presentation and physical intelligence in a way that seemed to define a new virtuosity—a heroism of the ordinary. As I have noted, analytic post-modern dance was a style and approach that was consistent with the values of minimalist sculpture. It was also consistent with the values of baring the facts and conserving means that were the legacy of a post-Watergate, post-oil-crisis society. The energy of post-modern dance was literally reduced. One of the most obvious divergences from modern dance, ballet, and the black dance movement was the rejection of musicality and rhythmic organization. But also, the analytic choreographers dispensed with principles of dramatic phrasing, contrast, and resolution. The bodies of their dancers were relaxed but ready, without the pulled-up, stretched muscle tone of the ballet or classical modern dancer.[12] The analytic post-modern dances pulled the spectator into the process of choreography, either by direct participation or by baring devices. And although these dances were not meant to have expressive meaning—e.g., the psychological or literary significance of historical modern dance—they did, of course, mean something: the discovery and understanding of their forms and processes was one aspect of that meaning, and the striving toward objectivity, the down-to-earth style, the casual or cool attitude, the sense that "it is what it is" did not excise meaning, but, rather, constituted a crucial aspect of the dance's import.[13] In some ways, the Grand Union resembled the earlier period of post-modern dance as proposing a loose polemic. Nevertheless, its performances belong to analytic dance because it was so often involved in revealing conditions of performance, ranging from choreographic structures to the display of psychological chemistry between the performers. The Grand Union demystified theater even as the group produced it.

The 1970s: Metaphor and the Metaphysical

Although the analytic mode of post-modern dance dominated the early seventies, another strand developed out of related sources. The spiritual aspect of the same asceticism that led to the clarification of simple movements led in its way to devotional expression. The appreciation of non-Western dance led to an interest in the spiritual, religious, healing, and social functions of dancing in other cultures. The disciplines of martial-arts forms led to new metaphysical attitudes. Experiences of communal living gave rise to dance forms that expressed or even caused social bonds. Dance became a vehicle for spiritual expression. For instance, Deborah Hay's solos of the seventies included cosmic images that were reminiscent of Hindu temple dances, and Barbara Dilley's *Wonder Dances* used meditative movement explorations and explosive moments of ecstatic outpourings in performances informed by the choreographer's interest in Tibetan Buddhism. Dance also became a vehicle for expressions of community with spiritual overtones, as in Meredith Monk's theatrical, mythic works such as *Education of the Girlchild,* a portrait of a tribe or family of heroic women. The works of Laura Dean and Andy deGroat—especially their spinning dances, resembling Sufi dances—fell somewhere between images of private and communal devotion. Deborah Hay's Circle Dances were like folk dances that were instructions for dancing with friends to popular music, dispensing with spectators. Anna Halprin's "rituals" were intended for physical and psychic healing and for creating instant communities; using Esalen-type techniques, she guided large groups of dancers and nondancers to form their own structures for dancing together in individual ways. Kenneth King's use of dances as metaphors for technology, information and power systems, and the mind itself fall into the metaphoric category; for instance, *The Telaxic Synapsulator* (1974), performed simultaneously with *Dance Spell* (1978), included a reading of excerpts from Marie Curie's *Radioactive Substances,* slides projecting information about the destructiveness of radioactivity, dancers performing movements that seem to describe processes of breaking down chemical elements, and a marvelous machine with gleaming and spinning parts. Robert Wilson's theater of images, often incorporating dances by other choreographers, including Kenneth King, Andy deGroat, Lucinda Childs, and Jim Self, also falls into this category.

Where analytic post-modern dance is exclusive of such elements, metaphoric post-modern dance is inclusive of theatrical elements of all kinds, such as costume, lighting, music, props, character, and mood. In this way, and in its making of expressive metaphors and representations, this strand of avant-garde dance resembles historical modern dance. But it also differs from historical modern dance in such important, basic ways that it seems more useful to include it as another category of post-modern dance than to consider it modern dance. These dances draw on post-modern processes and techniques. The key post-modern choreographic technique is radical juxtaposition. But also, these dances often use ordinary movements and objects; they propose new relationships between performer and spectator; articulate new experiences of space, time, and the body; incorporate language and film; employ structures of stillness and repetition. Metaphoric post-modern dance also counts as post-modern because it participates in the distribution system—the lofts, galleries, and other venues—that has become the arena for post-modern dance. That is, it presents itself as post-modern dance.

The 1980s: The Rebirth of Content

Since 1978 or so, avant-garde dance has taken a number of new directions. Some of these directions stand apparently in direct opposition to the values of analytic post-modern dance, making the very use of the term "post-modern" problematic for current dancing. Perhaps we should reserve the term for use only in reference to the analytic mode of the 1970s, just as the strictest definition of modern dance restricts us to the late 1920s through the 1950s. Then the breakaway choreographers of the 1960s could be called the forerunners of post-modern dance, just as Isadora Duncan, Loïe Fuller, and Ruth St. Denis are sometimes called the forerunners of modern dance. And the new dance of the 1980s could be called post-modern*ist*. But as I have already made clear, I want to argue for an inclusive use of the term "post-modern," one that applies to the breakaway dances of the sixties, the analytic and metaphoric dances of the seventies, and the new dances of the eighties, because all of these currents are related, principally because they set themselves apart from mainstream theatrical dance in ways that are not simply chronological.

The current generation of post-modern choreographers (and the current work of the older generation) reopens some of the issues that concerned historical modern dance. Thus it seems to depart from the concerns of its immediate predecessors. But it would be ahistorical to call the current generation modern dance; we would intuitively recoil, I think, from placing the modern dance choreographers Jennifer Muller and Norman Walker in the same camp as post-moderns Wendy Perron, Johanna Boyce, or Bill T. Jones. The views and practices of the current generation are not simply a return to an older style or method. They build on and, in their turn, depart from the redefinitions and analyses, as well as the techniques and anti-techniques, of the post-modern inquiry into the nature and function of dance. The shift is an obvious reaction by a new generation of choreographers to the concerns of their elders; by the end of the 1970s, the clarity and simplicity of analytic post-modern dance had served its purpose and threatened to become an exercise in empty formalism. Dance had become so shorn of meaning (other than reflexive) that for a younger generation of choreographers and spectators it was beginning to be regarded as almost meaningless. The response was to look for ways to reinstall meaning in dance.

The post-modern choreographers of the 1960s and 1970s saw their work as part of a continuing debate about the nature and function of theatrical dance. From the breakaway years of the early sixties, especially during the time of the Judson Dance Theater, when every rule was questioned, to the consolidation of the analytic and metaphoric streams of post-modern dance in the late sixties and seventies, when earlier experiments grew into recognizable styles, choreographers have been asking, "What is dance?" and "Where, when, and how should it be performed?" and even "Who should perform it?"[14] While the "new dance" choreographers of the eighties still enthusiastically enter into that mediumistic debate, one of the most striking features that sets them off from their post-modern forebears (which sometimes even includes themselves at an earlier time) is the question "What does it mean?" For reasons that have to do with both the history of the avant garde and the temper of our times, the eighties are witnessing an urgent search to reopen the question of content in all the arts, and dance is no exception. But beyond the question of emphasis on form and function versus content, the two "generations" diverge on such fundamental issues as technical virtuosity, permanence of repertory, elements of theatricality, the use of other media, the relationship between dance and music, the influence of mass culture, and even on such seemingly external features as venue.

A noticeable shift in the style of post-modern dance, which in retrospect marked the beginning of new dance in the 1980s, took place in 1979 with a number of key works by established post-modern choreographers. For Trisha Brown's *Glacial Decoy,* Robert Rauschenberg designed the elegant costumes and décor, adding layers of translucent nondance material to the liquidity of the choreography. Lucinda Childs's *Dance,* a collaboration with composer Philip Glass and visual artist Sol LeWitt, both extended Childs's analytic rigor—LeWitt's décor included a series of stringent geometric backdrops, each one lit in turn in a primary color, alternating with films of the dance that invited contrast and comparison between the larger-than-life images of the performers and their live actions, and Glass's music was built upon repetitive phrasing—and simultaneously added an element of celestial expressivity, as both the film and the music buoyed the dancers with a sense of monumentality and harmony. Laura Dean, whose use of folk dance style and structure had for some time depended on strictly patterned musical accompaniment, presented *Music,* in which, as choreographer and composer, dancer and pianist, she made herself a human emblem of the fusion of music and dancing. Steve Paxton, who for years had worked, in a down-to-earth style, primarily with either Contact Improvisation formats and techniques or in solo performance improvising with percussionist David Moss, in the same year presented a collaboration with Lisa Nelson, *PA RT,* in which both took on humorous, vague character roles to the recorded music of Robert Ashley's mantralike, chanted, Midwestern inner monologues, *Private Parts.* In *Foot Rules,* Douglas Dunn explored the conventions of the pas de deux and changed brightly colored costumes with a vengeance. In *An Audience with the Pope, or This Is Where I Came In,* David Gordon introduced a unified narrative conceit.

But also, in 1979–1980 a new group of younger post-modern choreographers began to emerge quite visibly. Eric Bogosian, the enterprising curator of dance at The Kitchen, presented among other events in that season Molissa Fenley's *Mix,* Johanna Boyce's *Pass* and other works, Karole Armitage's *Do We Could,* short pieces by Cesc Gelabert, and Charles Moulton's *Thought Movement Motor.* In early 1980, the Grey Gallery, at New York University, sponsored a series of young choreographers, including Jim Self (who had made dances in Chicago in the mid-seventies but, since arriving in New York in 1976, had temporarily given up choreography to dance with Merce Cunningham), Ton Simons, a Dutch dancer studying at the Cunningham studio, Fenley, Boyce, and Armitage. Later in 1980, Fenley, Boyce, and Moulton presented new works, and Bill T. Jones and Arnie Zane performed the third installment of their trilogy *Hand Dance/Monkey Run/Blauvelt Mountain.* Wendy Perron and Susan Rethorst presented a joint concert, which included Perron's punk/androgynous *A three-piece suite,* with a group of women dressed in men's suits performing eccentric, at times violent moves, and Rethorst's neoclassic *Swell.* In the fall of 1980, Tim Miller began his weekly performance art-cum-dancing serial *Me and Mayakovsky,* a synthesis of autobiography and political outcry, and shortly thereafter he and John Bernd organized "Men Together," a festival of dances on gay themes. Despite their stylistic and philosophic differences (Fenley, for instance, was fascinated with the virtuosity of speed and endurance, while Boyce reveled in game structures and the quotidian qualities of the untrained performer, and Miller worried about war and set things on fire), all these choreographers shared a new, raw, almost shocking energy, in sharp contrast to the serene dances of the previous generation of analytic post-modern choreographers and their followers.

Almost all of the currents in the new dance of the eighties in New York—the new directions of both the earlier generation of post-modern choreographers and their descendents—find a source in that historic season. Some, such as

Fenley's interest in certain kinds of virtuosity, are threads those younger choreographers continue to work out in the course of their ongoing oeuvre; others, such as Tim Miller's political commentary, or Laura Dean's interest in musicality, have been followed by larger waves of activity among other choreographers.

One kind of meaning in dance has always been the skills and complexities of sheer virtuosity. In the sixties, the impulse of the post-modern choreographers was to deny virtuosity and to relinquish technical polish, literally to let go of bodily constraints and inhibitions, to act freely, and also, in a spirit of democracy, to refuse to differentiate the dancer's body from an ordinary body. The level of dance technique in both ballet and modern dance had steadily risen (and continues to rise) in the United States since the 1930s. As in other periods in Euro-American dance history when technique seemed all-important, the choreographers of the 1960s protested. But unlike, for instance, the Romantic choreographers of the 1830s and 1840s, their response was not to emphasize expression over technique; rather, they dropped out of the technical arena altogether. The notion of letting go also manifested itself metaphorically in the "one-night stand"—a refusal to hang on to dances and to store them in a repertory, an acknowledgment of dance's ephemeral nature—and, further, in the method of improvisation, in which the dance is created for the moment and instantaneously disappears. In the 1980s, this impulse has reversed. The spirit is one of survival. Dances are preserved on film and videotape. One of Trisha Brown's recent works (*Opal Loop*) includes material improvised in performance by Steve Paxton that Brown's dancers Lisa Kraus and Stephen Petronio learned by watching a videotape of Paxton's performance. Now post-modern choreographers have companies—for instance, the David Gordon Pick-Up Company, the Trisha Brown Company, the Lucinda Childs Dance Company, Kenneth King and Dancers—and their companies perform works from the repertory. I suspect that this is partly a response to economic demands set down by touring commitments, producers, and granting agencies; but certainly it is also part of the process of becoming an established choreographer. Now choreography demands strength, skill, and endurance. The more a dance has in it, the more it seems worth—contra the "less is more" philosophy of analytic post-modern dance. Virtuosity becomes the subject in dances by choreographers such as Charles Moulton, whose works build on a vocabulary of athletic moves; Elizabeth Streb, whose dances quote circus acrobatics; and Molissa Fenley, whose pieces are "walls of dance" that operate at top speed, and whose dancers rehearse wearing weights. These dances border on the physical feats of the athlete/gymnast, while in the world of gymnastics, figure skating, and other sports, the form has become more dancerly. Ironically, as more and more Americans take up athletic pastimes, from jogging to weight lifting, what it means to have an ordinary body has changed over the past decade. Now everyone is an athlete, and sports are no longer fun to do, but, for some, a daily grind and even a source of injury. In social dancing (beginning with the disco routines of the seventies but continuing with forms such as new wave, robot dancing, break dancing, and electric boogie), "doing your own thing," as in the sixties, was gradually replaced by actions of physical dexterity, complicated timing and partnering, and acrobatic embellishment. The ante has been upped for post-modern choreographers. In the virtuosic works of the eighties, the significance of the dance is the refinement of bodily skills, and yet, in light of the previous generation's renunciation of bravura, the current dances also seem to establish themselves as another installment of the debate on the subject.

If in the sixties and seventies we were content to let artworks simply be, rather than mean, and to let criticism describe, rather than interpret, in the eighties we want to find substance and order in an increasingly recalcitrant world. We can no longer afford the permissiveness of the sixties. The modest thriftiness of seventies retrenchment has given way to values in every aspect of American life more suited to the drastic economic cutbacks of Reaganism. Ours is an age of artifice, specialization, conservation, and competition. As in the 1930s, the contradictions between rich and poor are great, but even those with less money to spend are willing to spend it with a vengeance on elegant clothing and entertainment, immediate pleasures that will partly compensate for inflation, debt, and unemployment. In this milieu, the current values in post-modern dance of virtuosity, elegance, and ornament are not surprising.

Perhaps the most striking overall shift in new dance since the seventies is what Noël Carroll has called "the return of the repressed"—i.e., expression.[15] The search for meaning in art finds a parallel in current critical writing, just as the artists' refusal to manufacture specific meaning in an earlier generation was accompanied by a spate of descriptive criticism, of the kind Susan Sontag called for in "Against Interpretation." The recent intellectual infatuation with structuralism and post-structuralism, symptomatic of our present rage for meaning and order, is in turn perhaps a symptom of our national, indeed global, sense of insecurity and doom. Scholars in every field turn to linguistic analysis and the new jargon of literary criticism and French psychoanalysis in attempts to make tidy sense of the messiness of experience. Artists, at times following the theorists, incorporate ready-made sign systems and arch commentaries on other artworks in their works.

While the critical community in dance has not rushed to embrace semiotics and post-structuralism with the fervor found in other fields, choreographers (though not necessarily motivated by deeply theoretical concerns) have been exploring some of the implications of this perspective. There are many kinds of meaning in current dancing, and many ways of making meaning as well. To eschew content beyond the dancing per se is in itself a kind of expression, but much of the new dance choreography seeks content external to the dance medium. One method of installing meaning in dance, the most nonverbal of the arts, is in fact to appropriate language and languagelike systems. A number of choreographers make dances based on the hand gesture, an emphasis unusual for Euro-American dance. Dana Reitz, for instance, makes improvisations in which the movements and static shapes of the hands are foregrounded; the open palms or wavelike gestures, rooted in movements of Tai Chi Chuan, remind us of the powerfully emblematic use of the hands in daily life, but in the dance they do not serve as signals. The "language" of gesture emerges in a different form in Wendy Perron's highly personal system of arm and hand movements. Remy Charlip uses the conventional gestures of American Sign Language for the deaf, often juxtaposed to verbal texts—dreams and stories and, notably, the song "Every Little Movement (Has a Meaning All Its Own)." Jane Comfort and other younger choreographers have also used sign-language translations of spoken texts as movement vocabularies in their dances, much like closed-caption television. David Gordon since the late seventies has elucidated the mysteriously shifting correspondences between verbal behavior (often embellished with puns) and gesture as illustration, as emblem, as feedback, and simply as an abstract movement pattern.

Not surprisingly, the interest in verbal language has been accompanied by a rekindling of interest in narrative structures. Where the previous generation of post-modern dancers either repudiated literary devices altogether, preferring the radical juxtaposition of movement over logical connections, or, in the case of Meredith Monk, whose works might be said to add up to some kind of story, made fragmented, rather than linear, tales, in yet another cyclical development so typical of dance history, the narrative, whose death seemed a certainty in the sixties and seventies, has been reborn in the eighties. Yet this development is not simply a return to older values or even techniques, for the new narrative finds exposition in ways that take into account the entire history of the post-modern choreographers' deliberate dismantling of literary devices.[16]

One important way the new narrative departs from the stories of classical modern dance is in its use of verbal language, rather than movement, to tell the story. As in *Peter and the Wolf,* the narration takes place on two simultaneous levels—oral (or, occasionally, written) commentary and dancing. (Arnie Zane in fact choreographed a punk version of *Peter and the Wolf* in 1985 that raised questions of gender and linguistic confusion and sexual extremes.) It is striking that the folktale, an exemplary case of literary narrative structure, has attracted several younger new dance choreographers (as it did, for different reasons, the Romantic choreographers of the 1830s and 1840s), for instance, Ralph Lemon in his *FolkTales* and Hope Gillerman in *The Princess Story* (both 1985). The renewed fascination with the workings of narrative and with language as the domain of the choreographer parallels the revival of a new orientation toward the verbal in the avant garde generally, after the previous generation's mistrust of the word. And this also fits with the rise of semiotic theory.

One outgrowth of the revival of the narrative is an emphasis on the genre of autobiography, a result, perhaps, of the synthesis of new narrative concerns with the personal, intimate mode of performance that emerged in the work of Grand Union and other early post-modern choreographers, as boundaries between performer and spectator, art and life were challenged. The public display of the personal was partly a political gesture in the style of the New Left, and thus it is not surprising that several of the choreographers who work in the genre of autobiography often work in the arena of political dance as well: Boyce, Miller, Jones and Zane, Perron, Bernd, Ishmael Houston-Jones and Fred Holland, among others. They use the intimate revelation of personal details as occasions to meditate on larger issues: war, racism, sexual politics. But even where their dances remain specifically private, that very act of confessional revelation seems to take on political meaning. Autobiography also provides an anti-sentimental twist on the practice of narrative; it imbues a plot with tension by mixing the suspense structure of a story with the direct, factual quality of intimacy that relates to earlier post-modern dance.

Beyond narrative meaning, the new dance strives to express other features that the analytic dancers tried to purge from their work, such as character, mood, emotion, situation. Jim Self's dances, such as his 1982 solo *Lookout,* in which, as the program explains, "a man watching television tries to sort the mistaken identities of two intruders," or his 1985 cinedance *Beehive*, a humorous exploration of the dancing language of bees, suggest character and plot, but in oblique ways, with a kind of soap-opera plot line. Eric Barsness's *Blood on the Keys* is a tragicomic view of the life of Chopin. Mary Overlie's *Adam and Eve* is a dance about love and marriage. Judy Padow's *Complex Desires* (1981) uses certain signals of emotional expression, but decontextualized in such a way that the emotions resist categorization, as the title suggests. Susan Rethorst's works approach descriptions of femininity. Pooh Kaye, Yoshiko Chuma, and Jo Andres all, in their separate ways, evoke a new primitivism. These dances are different from modern dance, however, because in important ways they *present* the nondance information (i.e., plot, character, situation), rather than *represent* it. They are not seamless theatrical illusions, productions of fictional worlds (à la Martha Graham or Doris Humphrey). The movement vocabulary is only partially expressive; it also remains partly abstract and it resists definitive interpretation. The emotional or narrative content remains elusive and fragmented, and the meaning of the dance is played out in several, not always corresponding, dimensions.

One of the devices for bearing the new expression, as may be seen from some of these examples, is the use of popular genres and allusions to popular performance styles, including vernacular dance. This interest in itself constitutes an entire stream of new direction in new dance (although it has roots in the Pop Art sensibility of the early sixties). Tharp's use of jazz and blues music and her quotations of Afro-American dance in the early seventies foreshadowed this tendency, which by now cuts across all genres of theatrical dance (e.g., in 1983, both Les Grand Ballets Canadiens and the New York City Ballet presented new dances quoting from Fred Astaire). Marta Renzi's proto-MTV dances, set to rock-and-roll, create cartoonlike images of young lovers; Gail Conrad mixes tap dancing with surrealistic situations and objects; Lisa Fox recently collaborated with tap dancer Camden Richman; Charles Moulton used tap dancing and other vaudeville techniques in his *Variety Show;* M. J. Becker included real acrobats as foils for her own dancerly contortions in *Break Out;* Elizabeth Streb's handling of objects and constructions resembles circus acts; Barbara Allen makes dances that resemble B movies and Harlequin romances; Karole Armitage, Fox, Fenley, the group Kinematic, Andres, and others work in a punk/new wave style. In 1981, The Kitchen presented two programs of teenage street dancing as part of its dance series. The effect on post-modern audiences and choreographers remains to be measured; Perron, for instance, choreographed part of her *Dancing to Good Bands . . . As Revealing as Self Portraits* (1982) by using as a score a photographic contact sheet of electric boogie, shot by Paula Court at one of The Kitchen concerts, and a spate of other choreographers have made reference to break dancing. And a wing of new dance/performance art called "new vaudeville" includes the mime Bill Irwin and the juggler Michael Moschen. The merging of "high art" and popular traditions is one of the characteristics of post-modernism, and yet in the history of the avant-garde arts it is nothing new; vanguard artists have perennially turned to folk, popular, and exotic art as sources for breaking with mainstream values as well as for "new" materials and techniques. Perhaps what makes the current version of this practice particularly post-modern is that it is enveloped in an acute historical self-consciousness, making quotation a laminating process across both historical periods and current geographical, social, and stylistic divisions.

Another way of installing expression in dance is the use of multiple channels of communication, the proliferation of media that the analytic choreographers of the seventies staunchly renounced. The rigor of Childs's work of the seventies has softened into an elegant expressiveness in her recent collaborative works: *Dance* (1979; LeWitt/Glass), *Relative Calm* (1981; Wilson/Gibson), *Formal Abandon* (1982; Riesman), and *Available Light* (1983; Gehry/Adams). At the same time, she has embellished her earlier, austere choreography with dips, rises, hops, and pirouettes that recall the pulsing musicality of Baroque style. Similarly, Trisha Brown's collaborations *Glacial Decoy* (1979; Rauschenberg), *Opal Loop/Cloud Installation #72503* (1980; Nakaya), *Son of Gone Fishin'* (1981; Judd/Ashley), *Set and Reset* (1983; Rauschenberg/Anderson), and *Lateral Pass* (1985; Graves/Zummo) assert the liquidity of her recent choreography on many levels: the slipperiness of the movement as well as the transparent or even watery imagery of the décor and costumes. A number of choreographers have set their dancers changing costumes throughout a work, as though they were using a manual for the semiotic analysis of clothing. New dance once again opens itself to music, special lighting, film, and new technologies such as video and computers.[17]

Perhaps the key means for bearing expression in dance, as choreographers have always known, and the major, most obvious shift from the previous generation's values, is the use of music. The evocative use of music can instantly create an entire mood; for example, the nostalgia of rock-and-roll "oldies" or the currency of punk music, as suggested above, and the recent rise of MTV shows a general cultural fascination with visualizing music through dance. But, more generally, the association of new dance with music—often, the very closest correspondence, "dancing to the music"—signals a radical shift in the history of twentieth-century avant-garde dance, which until the eighties had been systematically separating itself from music. The new musicality is more closely related to social dance practice than to the development of modern dance in the twentieth century. Where Isadora Duncan and Ruth St. Denis made their dances visualizations of symphonic music, Mary Wigman, a generation later, preferred to use simple percussion; Cunningham makes dances that do not correspond structurally to the music at all (except by accident); the analytic post-modern choreographers often danced in silence. Meredith Monk's "operas," Laura Dean's collaborations with Steve Reich (inspired by various non-Western traditions), and Twyla Tharp's use of Afro-American social dance style were early examples of the new fusion of music and dance. Fenley intensified this trend, making dances to the polyrhythms of Afro-Caribbean music that were inspired, in part, by the ritual and social dancing of West Africa and the high energy of new wave music, but that also reflect a commitment to a search for an original movement vocabulary. The interest in popular entertainment clearly reinforces this direction, both in new dance and in new music. But an equally powerful recent interest by post-modern choreographers in choreographing for the ballet also reinforces the new musicality.[18] This new relationship between music and dance has practical results: where in the sixties and seventies post-modern dance became part of the visual-art world, sharing its theories and structures as well as its venues, in the eighties dance has moved into the music world, taking place in clubs and cabarets, rather than galleries and museums. In the eighties, the worlds of avant-garde music, avant-garde visual art, performance, and popular music have begun to merge, and the post-modern choreographers have joined them, and the music scene in New York has replaced the visual-art world in providing a new context for post-modern dance. For reasons of its own, the visual-art world is less conducive to providing that context. Visual artists have returned to making commodities that will last, and the gallery system is no longer inclined to deal in live performance. The underlying impulse of Conceptual Art—to undermine the status of the art object as a means of investment—is obviously spent; in times of economic distress, people want to buy objects rather than finance ideas or actions. The changing social life of the avant garde also reflects the next context. In the sixties, artists and dancers went out social dancing after concerts; the avant-garde of the eighties programs performance into the social scene, selling beer at intermissions or presenting art dance at discotheques and clubs in late-night performances, especially on the Lower East Side, where a cabaret scene has joined the new gallery scene. Thus, on the one hand, post-modern dance has built its own special audiences and circuits, and on the other hand, it seeks new audiences in the wider network of popular music and dance culture.

The downtown dance world has by now established its own institutions for showing new dance. In the eighties, one can place oneself in the post-modern camp simply by choosing (or being chosen) to perform in a post-modern venue. There are at least six centers for post-modern dance in New York: The Kitchen (formerly in Soho, now in Chelsea), Dance Theater Workshop (in Chelsea), Danspace at St. Mark's Church, P.S. 122 (both on the Lower East Side), P.S. 1 (in Long Island City, Queens), and the Brooklyn Academy of Music. Although choreographers and companies are fairly mobile, switching venues from season to season, some have become identified with one theater or another. For instance, the more established Brown, Childs, and Dean have each appeared at Brooklyn Academy of Music on a regular basis (and for the past several years BAM has presented entire rosters of older and younger avant-gardists on its Next Wave series), and P.S. 122, the newest of the venues, often produces very young, little-known choreographers (as well as group programs mixing dance and performance, older and younger artists), whereas The Kitchen produces seasons and also runs a touring program that produces Self, Moulton, Fox, and Barsness outside New York (and in the past has produced tours for Rethorst and Fenley); Dance Theater Workshop presents modern as well as post-modern choreographers. These places are institutions with curators, rather than convenient places to show work (as, for instance, Judson Church had been). Thus there is a demand for post-modern choreography by producers, and their taste partly determines who counts as post-modern. But besides these "alternative" institutions, post-modern dance is performed at countless lofts, a few churches, and universities, as well as the more recent club or cabaret. The institutionalization of downtown dance was marked in 1984 by Dance Theater Workshop's establishment of the New York Dance and Performance Awards (The Bessies), the dance equivalent to the *Village Voice*'s Obie awards for Off-Off Broadway theater.

Perhaps the new musicality in post-modern dance is partly responsible for another great shift, the recent emergence of a group of black post-modern choreographers.[19] Gus Solomons stood practically alone in the previous generation of avant-gardists; today, the roster of choreographers who identify themselves as both black and post-modern, including Jones, Houston-Jones, Holland, Lemon, Blondell Cummings, Bebe Miller, and many others, is long enough for acknowledgment on both fronts: an entire festival at St. Mark's Church took place in 1984, and the Dancemobile Black History Month sponsored a post-modern night in 1985.

But this shift is also part of the new political expression in post-modern dance. In a broad sense, the fascination with popular entertainment and mass media is another manifestation of an anti-elitist impulse. But more specifically, the past five years have seen a rash of dances and festivals with explicit political content, from the "Men Together" festival to the black post-modern series to the wide-ranging programs in "Frontline: Dance and Social Commentary" at P.S. 1 in 1984 that included current work by Craig Bromberg, Sally Silvers, Kenneth King, Viveca Vazquez, and others, as well as reconstructions of leftist dances of the 1930s. Stephanie Skura's dances comment ironically on dance-world politics. And beyond the political content of the performances themselves, the past several years have seen dancers organize around various political issues, notably disarmament and U.S. involvement in Central America.

As I stated earlier, the new dance of the 1980s often seems to diverge so drastically from the post-modern dance of the 1970s—in particular, the analytic wing—that at times it seems pointless to include it in the same conceptual category. However, it seems to me that despite all the differences explored or suggested here, the connections still remain. For one, the very people involved in new dance in the eighties comprise not only the students and younger colleagues of the previous generation of post-modern choreographers, but also those earlier choreographers themselves; for another, these artists see themselves as sharing as well as extending the same post-modern heritage.

Outside New York

Post-modern dance does not, of course, happen only in New York, although in the United States New York serves as a center, as it does in the dance world generally. There is activity on the West Coast, in particular; in Minneapolis, where the visionary programming by Suzanne Weil and her successors at the Walker Art Museum since the early seventies fostered a strong post-modern inclination; in Chicago, where the Columbia College Dance Center and later MoMing produced in- and out-of-towners; in Austin, where Deborah Hay now lives and works; and in numerous other locales. The Contact Improvisation network traverses the nation, as well as Canada and parts of Europe.

For reasons that I have outlined above and elsewhere,[20] post-modern dance has largely been a United States phenomenon. However, over the past twenty years, post-modern choreographers and dancers have toured extensively, performing and teaching at arts festivals and in theaters all over Canada, Great Britain, the Continent (especially in Holland, France, and Italy), and Japan. Also, the situation in dance internal to various countries—reactions to ballet and modern dance—has resulted in distinctive national avant-garde movements paralleling though not imitating the American experience of the sixties and seventies. At the same time, American influence increases as European companies commission dances from American post-modern choreographers. Americans Mary Fulkerson and Steve Paxton have been teaching at Dartington, in England, since the early seventies, contributing to a New Dance movement that has taken firm hold in England. The London Dance Umbrella, organized by Val Bourne, has since the late seventies fostered an exchange of ideas between American post-modern choreographers and a growing community of similar-minded choreographers and dancers from Europe, with an annual festival of dance concerts, lectures, exhibitions, and workshops on music, design, and criticism, as well as its activities during the rest of the year as a producing agency and information center. The major venues for new or post-modern dance in London are Riverside Studios and ICA. British exponents of new dance include Richard Alston (now working primarily for ballet companies), Rosemary Butcher, Laurie Booth, Michael Clark, Siobhan Davies, Libby Dempster, Maedée Duprès, Fergus Early, Jacky Lansley, Sue MacLennan, Ian Spink, and the American-born Mary Fulkerson. In Montreal, the center for the new-dance activity, called *danse actuelle*, is the performance space Tangente; the journal *Parachute* covers new dance and performance. In Germany, where the tradition of modern dance flowered briefly between the two World Wars, greatly influencing the style of American modern dance, the younger avant-garde choreographers seem more influenced by imagistic avant-garde theater than by either German or American dance traditions. Pina Bausch and Susanne Linke are two of the dominant new choreographers, and both of them are expressionist rather than analytic. Various other experimental choreographers in West Germany constitute an alternative to opera-house ballet (the major form of German dance), called the Poor Dance movement. In Japan, what we might call post-modern dance is called *butoh* (short for *Ankoku Butoh,* or "dance of darkness"), a term used at first as a catchall for postwar avant-garde dance that departs from both classical Japanese dance-theater forms and the Western dance imported to Japan, but that now denotes a particular dance-theater theory and technique.[21] All of these currents in new dance outside the United States have, in turn, had their influence here through tours and exchanges, such as a tour by the British group Second Stride in 1982, New Dance from France in 1983, the New York–Montreal Dansèchange in 1984, visits by the Butoh group Sankai Juku, Pina Bausch's group, and others to the Los Angeles Arts Olympics in 1984, and the influx of new German dance during the 1985 Next Wave Festival at the Brooklyn Academy of Music.

NOTES

1. For an explication of traditional modern dance structures, see the three bibles of modern dance composition: Louis Horst, *Pre-Classic Dance Forms* (New York: The Dance Observer, 1937; reprint ed., Dance Horizons, 1972); Louis Horst and Carroll Russell, *Modern Dance Forms* (San Francisco: Impulse Publications, 1961); and Doris Humphrey, *The Art of Making Dances* (New York: Rinehart, 1959; reprint ed., Grove Press, 1962); see also the many reviews and histories of modern dance, including those cited in notes to the introduction to the first edition of this book.

2. Michael Kirby, "Introduction," *The Drama Review* 19 (T-65; March 1975): 3.

3. Charles Jencks, *The Language of Post-Modern Architecture* (New York: Rizzoli, 1977).

4. Noël Carroll unraveled some of these complexities with particular clarity in his lecture on post-modernism in the arts and in culture generally at Jacob's Pillow, Becket, Massachusetts, 16 July 1985.

5. Jerome Rothenberg discusses some of these aspects of post-modernism in "New Models, New Visions: Some Notes Toward a Poetics of Performance," in Michel Benamou and Charles Caramello, eds., *Performance in Postmodern Culture* (Madison, WI: Coda Press, 1977). In "Postmodern Dance and the Repudiation of Primitivism," *Partisan Review* 50 (1983): 101-121, Roger Copeland argues that modern dance strove for synthesis in terms of form and unity in terms of the audience's experience of the work. A mistrust of language underlies the primitivist longings of the modern dancers. Here and in a second article, "Postmodern Dance/ Postmodern Architecture/Postmodernism," *Performing Arts Journal* 19 (1983): 27-43, Copeland makes some useful observations about post-modern dance. However, his definition is much more narrow than the one I propose here, although he does suggest the possibility of two different camps of post-modern dance (in "Postmodern Dance/Postmodern Architecture/ Postmodernism," p. 33).

6. For descriptions and analyses of Cunningham's work, see Merce Cunningham, *Changes: Notes on Choreography,* ed. Frances Starr (New York: Something Else Press, 1968); Sally Banes and Noël Carroll, "Cunningham and Duchamp," *Ballet Review* 11 (Summer 1983): 73-79; Roger Copeland, "The Politics of Perception," *The New Republic* (17 November 1979).

7. On the avant-garde of the 1950s, see Jill Johnston, "The New American Modern Dance," in *The New American Arts,* ed. Richard Kostelanetz (New York: Collier Books, 1967), pp. 162-

193, and Selma Jeanne Cohen, "Avant-Garde Choreography," *Criticism* 3 (Winter 1961): 16-35, reprinted in three parts in *Dance Magazine* 36 (June 1962): 22-24, 57; (July 1962): 29;31, 58; (August 1962): 45, 54-56.

8. Susan Sontag, "Against Interpretation," *Against Interpretation* (New York: Farrar, Straus, and Giroux, 1966), p. 14.

9. These and many of the following dances are described in the body of *Terpsichore in Sneakers* and in Sally Banes, *Democracy's Body: Judson Dance Theater 1962–64* (Ann Arbor: UMI Research Press, 1983). Also, accounts of many of the dances mentioned in this essay may be found in the works by choreographers and critics listed in the bibliographies.

10. On the institutional theory of art, see George Dickie, *Art and the Aesthetic* (Ithaca: Cornell University Press, 1974).

11. On black dance in the sixties, see Lynne Fauley Emery, *Black Dance in the United States from 1619 to 1970* (Palo Alto: National Press Books, 1972; reprint ed., Brooklyn: Dance Horizons, 1980).

12. Two short films exist that show these stylistic features very clearly: Childs's *Calico Mingling* and Rainer's *Trio A.*

13. On meaning and expressiveness in post-modern dance, see Noël Carroll and Sally Banes, "Working and Dancing: A Response to Monroe Beardsley's 'What Is Going On in a Dance?,' " *Dance Research Journal* 15 (Fall 1982): 37-41, and Noël Carroll, "Post-Modern Dance and Expression," *Philosophical Essays in Dance,* ed. Gordon Fancher and Gerald Myers (New York: Dance Horizons, 1981), pp. 95-104.

14. In addition to the various books and articles about post-modern dance cited above, the films *Making Dances* (Michael Blackwood) and *Beyond the Mainstream* (Merrill Brockway for Dance in America), show works in both the analytic and metaphoric veins of 1970s post-modern dance.

15. Noël Carroll, "The Return of the Repressed: The Re-Emergence of Expression in Contemporary American Dance," *Dance Theatre Journal* Vol. 2 no. 1 (1984): 16-19, 27. Deborah Jowitt writes differently about the same phenomenon in "The Return of Drama," *Dance Theatre Journal* Vol. 2 no. 2 (1984): 28-31.

16. See, for instance, Marcia Pally, "The Rediscovery of Narrative: Dance in the 1980s," *Next Wave* Festival Catalogue, 1984.

17. See Noël Carroll, review of The Public Theater's FilmDance Festival, *Dance Magazine* 58 (March 1984): 52-54, 90-91, and his review of The Moving Camera: A Series of Performance and Video Collaborations, *Dance Magazine* 59 (March 1985): 93-94, 98, for specific descriptions of cinedances and live dances using video, and for analyses of this trend. Also, see the various essays by artists and critics in the catalogue (ed. Amy Greenfield) for the FilmDance Festival, a project of the Experimental Intermedia Foundation, 1983.

18. The appeal of ballet to the new generation of post-modern choreographers (as well as to the older ones) is a complex phenomenon that deserves closer study. In certain ways, the formalist values of contemporary ballet have more in common with post-modern dance than with modern dance. But, also, many post-modern dancers began to use the study of ballet technique as an antidote to the personal style of teaching in modern dance; others had first studied ballet as children and found in its vocabulary yet more material for their pluralistic view of dance. If anything can be used in a dance, why not the Western high-art-dance tradition as well as social dance, non-Western dance, and nondance moves?

19. The divergence of black and white vanguard dance in the sixties and seventies is of course a matter of politics as well as aesthetics. For the majority of black choreographers, issues

of black power and identity were much more compelling than the questions that preoccupied the white post-modern dancers; the black dances expressed political and cultural concerns and often were inspired by African or Afro-American style and function. One of the key elements of traditional Afro-American style is the inextricable connection between music and dancing.

20. In Sally Banes, "Icon and Image in New Dance," *New Dance U.S.A.* Festival Catalogue (Minneapolis: Walker Art Center, 1981), pp. 7-21.

21. The catalogue for Festival International de Nouvelle Danse (Montreal, 19-29 September 1985), published by *Parachute,* includes articles on new dance and dancers in the United States, Japan, Canada, England, Germany, Belgium, and France. Dance Umbrella literature also gives information on new dance from Europe, Japan, and the U.S.A.

Introduction: Sources of Post-Modern Dance

To Americans today, modern art already seems old-fashioned. By the middle of the twentieth century, the modern novel, painting, sculpture, and music had reached their heights, and a new generation of writers, artists, and composers — as well as of critics — was facing a crisis of form and content at the very root of the arts. The same was true of modern dance — a term that encompasses a range of individual styles and idioms which had already, since its beginnings at the turn of the century, suffered a multitude of changes, splits, and variations. We still use the term modern dance to refer indiscriminately to an enormous variety of concert art dance that is not rooted in the *danse d'école* (i.e., ballet). Modern dance identifies itself as aesthetic, whereas revue and musical theater dancing know themselves to be entertaining.

I want here to trace briefly the development of modern dance to show why in the 1960s a genre we now call *post-modern* dance inevitably arose. It began as an underground current, and although it now flows closer to the surface in the public eye, it remains a branch outside the mainstream of modern dance.

Nineteenth-century America never developed a sustained ballet tradition, although it had raised home-grown performers, and provided appreciative audiences for visiting stars like Fanny Elssler and Marie Bonfanti. But it was an American, Loïe Fuller (1862–1928), working in Paris in the 1890s, who was to begin to lay the groundwork for modern dance. Presenting dances borrowed from a popular entertainment style in a serious, high art context, Fuller set forth two hallmarks of modern dance: freedom of movement and the solo form. Exaggerating the size of the dancer's skirt, and using brilliant lighting effects (which she invented and patented) to transform herself and her props and costumes into moving sculptures of light and color, Fuller (who had been an actress, playwright, manager, and dancer) made radical changes in art dance. Many of them would be rejected by early twentieth-century choreographers, and would remain latent until the 1960s: for instance, Fuller eschewed the projection of emotion or personality of the performer, virtuosic dance technique, and even the appreciation of physical beauty in the dancer. Instead, she made the central focus of the performance the image — an object she created with fabrics, sticks, lights, and shadows. The movement that was required to create the desired visual effect was the correct movement. There were rarely narratives in Fuller's dances; the text of the performance was the physical creation of an objective presence. Fuller wore neither tights nor corset, and her feet were either bare or shod in flat slippers. When she danced with a group, she planned the dances so that the individual differences between the ways the dancers moved would be preserved. She often used untrained dancers in her works, and she gave her performers a wide range of movement choices within the preset, imagistic frameworks she created.[1]

Isadora Duncan, a Californian born fifteen years after Loïe Fuller, was another American dancer who triumphed in Europe. Even before she saw Fuller's marvelous organic shapes in Paris in 1899, Duncan had been inspired by the motions of natural things — waves, trees, the cycles of the seasons — to find a "natural" movement expression in the human body, outside the restricting codes and costumes of the ballet. She danced barelegged, barefoot, in loose robes, using the fluid, simple movements suggested by figures on Greek vases, inspired by the profound emotions aroused by the music of serious composers like Beethoven, Schubert, and Chopin. She built simple dances with elemental, repetitive structures and the most basic of locomotor steps. Duncan (who first toured Europe under Fuller's auspices) emphasized the personal in dance, in both the format of her concerts, which were often solo, and their meaning, which was expressive of deep, individualized emotions.

Duncan believed that the source of human movement and emotion lay in the solar plexus, a principle that dictated the use of the whole body in dance, from the center outward, in contrast to the balletic, peripheral deployment of the arms and legs. Apparently Duncan's choreography was not improvised, but followed a fixed plan. But surely her charismatic stage presence imbued the spare dances with much of their legendary power. Her ideas about the possibilities of human freedom and personal expression in life, as in dance, her unabashed love for the human body, her rejection of the rigidity imposed by an academic approach to movement — these attitudes (rather than the actual skeletal choreography that survives) are her most important legacy.[2]

Ruth St. Denis, born in 1879, had — like Duncan and Fuller — grown up on the professional stage. She had danced solo acts in variety houses and acted in touring companies since adolescence. Like Duncan, she saw Fuller in Paris, and she was also impressed by the performances of Sada Yacco and her Japanese theater troupe at Fuller's theater at the Paris Exposition of 1900. St. Denis, unlike the other two American forerunners of modern dance, worked primarily in the United States. But ironically, what she presented for American audiences was a spiritual vision filtered through a personal interpretation of Oriental forms: her impressions of East Indian, Egyptian, and Japanese dance styles. The seriousness of her spiritual endeavor raised her exoticism to high art, although the troupe she established with her husband Ted Shawn after 1914 often performed on vaudeville circuits. The training that St. Denis and Shawn provided at their Denishawn Schools from 1915 through 1930 was an eclectic blend of fundamental ballet, Delsartean exercises, Indian, Javanese, Chinese, and Japanese dance techniques, as well as St. Denis' "music visualizations." (These were dances that mirrored the structures of musical compositions in terms of mood, as well as notes and phrasing.) Denishawn is historically significant not because of its lavish productions (which look dated today), nor because of its analysis of movement (St. Denis and Shawn formulated no coherent theories), but because it provided for the next generation of modern dance choreographers intensive training in a wide-ranging variety of styles, continuous professional performance experience, and a definite aesthetic — exotic and extravagant — against which its students rebelled during the late 1920s.[3]

As a corrective to the Denishawn dances, which they considered superficial, frivolous, ornamental — a showcase for individual skill rather than serious expression — Martha Graham with her music director Louis Horst, and partners Doris Humphrey and Charles Weidman approached form, technique, and subject matter schematically. Graham urged that American choreographers concern themselves with American, not Eastern dances, with themes that recognized the serious issues of the day, with modern life and not faraway times or places. Even when her heroines were mythological, as Jill

Johnston points out, they were heroines of a twentieth-century "self-conscious recognition, confrontation, and resolution."[4] Both Graham and Humphrey (and Mary Wigman, working in Germany) used space theatrically to express their thematic concerns. Both used an abstraction, or distortion, of the natural breath cycle — on which they built complex superstructures of dance vocabularies and syntax. For Graham, the breath could pull the body into contraction and release, extreme positions dramatizing psychological connotations of pain and ecstasy. For Humphrey, the breath pulled the body out of two possible kinetic and symbolic "deaths" — the stable positions of standing upright and lying down — into fall and recovery, creating an asymmetric arc that both traced theatrical designs of interest and signified the social triumph of humankind over inertia. The costumes used by both of these choreographers were relatively austere, but still expressive. The dances exploited gravity, instead of attempting ballet's illusion of transcending it. Their rhythms were the angular, jagged, percussive rhythms of an age fascinated by jazz and the potential wonders and horrors of machines.

Graham's musical director, Louis Horst, advocated choreography based on the thematic coherence and variation of preclassic dance forms. These were the court dances developed in the fifteenth through seventeenth centuries, such as the majestic yet simple pavane, the "hot and hasty" gigue, and the sparkling, brisk gavotte.[5] Each mood had its form, and the rhythmic structure in combination with the symbolic, dramatic requirements of the content of the modern dance built up a vocabulary which eventually became codified into a grammar of Graham technique.

For Humphrey, the contrasts of visual design, rhythm, dynamics, and motivations and gestures were the structuring forces of a dance. As she looked to the kinetic danger of the constant fall and recovery of equilibrium as a movement analogue to the states of social existence, so the asymmetry required in her four aspects of dance structure corresponded metaphorically (and in theatrical terms, as well) to the uncertainty and variety of modern life. To Humphrey, the worst sin for a choreographer was to make a dance that was too stable, monotonous, or symmetrical. She analyzed the architecture of natural forms, but always expressed them in terms of human usage. Although stylized enough to look symbolic, her gestures seemed more like exaggerations of the naturally expressive movements our culture readily associates with certain emotional states, than the highly specific, symbolic gestures of the Graham vocabulary, which must be "read" in order to grasp the meaning of the dance.[6]

The emphasis on the personal in American modern dance made the course of its history entirely different from that of ballet. Classic theatrical dancing has evolved over the past four hundred years — and no doubt will continue to evolve — through an abstract, codified, impersonal vocabulary, but one that is directly transmitted from teacher to pupil. Based on the fundamental principles of the five positions through which the body always passes, and the turnout from the center, the system alters gradually during the complex historical process of transmission, in minor ways: refinements, development of strength and skill, shifts of style occur. Deviations from the basic line and look also occur, but always return to the standard, reaffirming their roots in the classic tradition. Individual dancers also lend their own particular meanings and style to the standard vocabulary. But in ballet, changes in materials, method, and style take place within the context of a conservative, academic tradition. That tradition is resilient enough to absorb innovation.

Since the modern dance was predicated so heavily on personal, often intimate, formats, on subjective content, and on individual quests for movement styles that would express not only the physicality of the choreographer, but also his or her thematic concerns and theories of movement, every slight shift in technique or theory from teacher to student came to mean not further refinement but further revolt. The history of modern dance is rapidly cyclical: revolution and institution; revolution and institution. The choices for each generation have been either to enter the new academy (but, inevitably, to dilute and trivialize it in doing so), or to create a new establishment. In this system, the importance of the choreographer over the dancer is obvious. The "tradition of the new"[7] demands that every dancer be a potential choreographer.

The late 1940s and early '50s were not creative years in modern dance. The political and artistic tumult of the early years had dissipated. As Jill Johnston, writing in the '60s, put it, a new modern dance was desperately needed, since "the old was really beginning to look its age."[8] Neither the subjects nor the techniques of the dances proliferating from the next generation of choreographers (those who came from Graham and Humphrey-Weidman, as well as from Hanya Holm, Tamiris, and Lester Horton) were new. The death of the WPA Federal Dance Project, the Second World War, and then the cultural conservatism of the Cold War years seemed to sap the next generation of revolutionary spirit, both politically and artistically.

But even during this period Merce Cunningham, a soloist in Martha Graham's company from 1939 to 1945, offered a fresh approach to dance in his own work. Beginning in 1944, he gave dance concerts that departed radically from the by-then traditional modern dance. His innovations in dance paralleled those of his friend and colleague John Cage in music. Essentially, he made the following claims: 1) any movement can be material for a dance; 2) any procedure can be a valid compositional method; 3) any part or parts of the body can be used (subject to nature's limitations); 4) music, costume, decor, lighting, and dancing have their own separate logics and identities; 5) any dancer in the company might be a soloist; 6) any space might be danced in; 7) dancing can be about anything, but is fundamentally and primarily about the human body and its movements, beginning with walking.

For Cunningham, the basis of expression in human movement is inseparable from the body, and it comes from the fact that everyone walks differently. You don't need externally expressive features to create significance in a dance when movement already is intrinsically significant, "in its bones."[9] Although a Cunningham dance is made out of movements performed by technically skilled dancers doing complicated steps, it is as inherently expressive and distinctive as the action one might see on a city street. And each dance has its own qualities and features, just as one would never mistake Times Square for Piazza San Marco or Michigan Avenue.

Often the different components in an evening of Cunningham's dances have appeared together for the first time on opening night — the music, for example, surprising the dancers as much as the audience. This is both because of a lack of time and for theoretical reasons: for Cunningham, the different sensory channels are autonomous, a situation that reflects the arbitrary correlation of sensory events in life. It also frees the dancing from slavishly following or contrasting with the music. Yet, without corresponding directly in rhythm, tone, color, or shape, the expressive elements that coexist simultaneously in the dancing, music, and décor do create an overall effect. Cunningham, whose collaborators have included composers John Cage, David Tudor, David Behrman, Christian Wolff, Pauline Oliveros, and La Monte Young, and visual artists Robert Rauschenberg, Jasper Johns, and Andy Warhol, isn't interested in making sure the audience puts the elements together to "get" a particular message from the dance event, but rather in presenting a variety of experiences — aural, visual, kinetic — which the spectator is free to interpret, select from, or simply absorb.

Modern life requires that we live by our wits rather than by rules. Things rarely turn out as we have planned them, and to live at any given moment means to change plans at the last minute, to hear one thing and see another, to try to make some kind of personal order out of the bewildering chaos of sensory and mental experience. Cunningham's dances decentralize space, telescope or stretch time, allow for sudden unison activity, repetition, and rich variety and dispersal. They do away with the familiar comfort and predictability of dance movement that follows either a musical structure, a story, a psychological structure, or the demands of a proscenium stage frame.

Yet by staying within a dance-technical system while relinquishing certain kinds of control, Cunningham preserves physical logic and continuity in his works. He may use chance methods like tossing coins or dice or picking cards at random to determine the order of movements in a phrase, the sequence of phrases in a dance, the places to put the dancers on stage, the number of dancers in a section, or the parts of the body to be activated. Chance subverts habits and allows for new combinations. It also undermines literal meanings attached to sequences of movements or combinations of body parts, since the next time the sequence or combination may be totally different. But Cunningham's program has rarely allowed for improvisation by the dancers or spontaneous determination of the phrases. The speed and complexity of his movements would make certain situations physically dangerous. Once determined, the paths and positions of the dancers must be exact. Still, the look of his dances is not rigid but flexible. Flexibility applies to so many aspects of the dancing itself: his elastic use of space and time, of the feet and spine, of the shape and order of the dance phrases. It also applies to logistics, for with his Events, beginning in 1964, Cunningham has invented a portable dance mechanism that can be reassembled on site with very little notice.

Unlike the post-modern choreographers, inspired by Cunningham's ideas or critical of his method, who would carry his theories further, however, Cunningham remains entrenched in a dance-technical idiom. It is an idiom that he invented, combining the elegant carriage and brilliant footwork of ballet with the flexibility of the spine and arms practiced by Graham and her contemporaries. Added to this synthesis of styles were Cunningham's own contributions: clarity, serenity, sensitivity to a wide range of speeds and sustainment in deploying steps and gestures, and the unusual qualities of isolation derived from chance combinations. The technical inventions and freedom of choreographic design create a style of dancing that seems to embody flexibility, freedom, change, and — especially in Cunningham's own solos — pleasure in the idiosyncratic drama of individuality.

There were other dance avant-gardists in the early 1950s who influenced the post-modernists of the '60s, either because their own ideas about dancing departed drastically from the mainstream, or simply because they offered performing and choreographing situations for young dancers. James Waring (1922–1975) was a choreographer and designer whose dances sometimes looked like Cunningham's — with their decentralized use of space, collage formats, disconnected structures but balletic carriage — but his method was based on intuition rather than chance. Waring abandoned narrative and dramatic structure in the mid-1950s, creating atmospheres (often nostalgic), referring lovingly and archly to variety dancing and ballet, and mixing musical as well as dancing styles (including ordinary and idiosyncratic gestures). Waring was a gentle humorist, sometimes parodying other dance genres, often close to camp. Never able to support a full-time company, he nevertheless gave concerts of his work regularly from 1954 to 1969. Among those who performed with him were Toby Armour, Lucinda Childs, David Gordon, Deborah Hay, Fred Herko, Yvonne Rainer, and Valda Setterfield. In the late 1950s, Waring gave composition classes and organized concerts of choreography by his students at the Living Theater in 1959 and 1960.

Aileen Passloff, Waring's contemporary, appeared in some of his works and shared a studio with him at times. She began choreographing in the late 1950s, often to avant-garde music, including works by La Monte Young and Richard Maxfield. She used such dancers as Setterfield, Gordon, Armour, Barbara Dilley Lloyd, Louis Falco, and Burt Supree, and sets and costumes by Waring, Remy Charlip, and Claes Oldenburg. Some of her dances are, like some of Waring's, nostalgic tributes to great memories of ballet, or folk dance. Others were resolutely modernist. "Closer to calisthenics than choreography," sniffed a *Time* magazine critic in 1960.[10] Critics complained because Passloff's body looked too short and thick to be dancerly. But Yvonne Rainer remembers that when she saw Passloff perform *Tea at the Palaz of Hoon* at the Living Theater in 1960, she realized that there was a multitude of possibilities for the look of dancers' bodies, and that her own "chunky construction" might do well.[11]

Although Ann Halprin worked primarily on the West Coast after 1955, she had a far-reaching impact on choreography in New York through her students. Halprin had studied kinesiology, anatomy, and improvisation with her teacher Margaret H'Doubler at the University of Wisconsin in the early 1940s.[12] Halprin's use of improvisation, tasks, and slow or often-repeated movements influenced Simone Forti, who studied and performed with Halprin for four years, and her other students, including Yvonne Rainer, Trisha Brown, and Robert Morris. Halprin collaborates with visual artists and musicians, and her early works were deliberate, spontaneous, joyous confusions of life and art. Her workshops have been important foci of exchange for young dancers, musicians, poets, and artists on the West Coast. As Halprin incorporated information from Gestalt therapy, body alignment work, altered states of consciousness, and the creative process (as analyzed by her husband, architect Lawrence Halprin) her work has moved away from training artists, and toward finding the artist within ordinary people. She and members of her company now lead sessions with community groups as well as ad hoc groups to "create a common language through movement experiences" and "collectively create rituals and ceremonies out of life situations" with the hope of recycling the values of intense group rituals into daily life.[13]

But sources outside dance were equally important for the revolutionary notions of the post-modern choreographers, who found structures and performance attitudes in new music, film, the visual arts, poetry, and theater—especially in Happenings, Events, and Fluxus (a neo-Dada group), where the borders between the art forms blurred and new formal strategies for artmaking abounded. Repetition; alogical structures; simultaneous events; the primacy of the visual in theater, noise in music; real objects surfacing in paintings; and the detritus of the quotidian world that provided material for Happenings could all be translated by the young choreographers into dance terms. They were members of an artistic community, partly by virtue of the situation at Halprin's workshops and Cunningham's studio in the Living Theater building, two places where rich exchanges of ideas and actions blossomed. Exchanges of personnel took place too, since some of the young choreographers performed in Happenings and the painters, poets, composers, and sculptors often appeared in, or even made, the dances. These nondancer friends of the choreographers were convenient personnel when dances required large casts, but also the aesthetics of the new dance proposed, as had Happenings, that untrained bodies appear in performance.

John Cage's multimedia event at Black Mountain College in 1952 (where Merce Cunningham improvised a dance, a film was projected, Cage lectured, David Tudor played the piano, M. C. Richards and Charles Olson read their poetry, Robert Rauschenberg showed his paintings and played recordings of his choice on an old gramophone — all within strict time brackets) had created a paradigm not only for the later Happenings but also for the entire avant-garde for the next twenty years or so. Cage was inspired by Antonin Artaud's theatrical ideas, Marcel Duchamp's use of chance operations, and the Zen philosopher Huang-po's doctrine of nonevaluation. Cage synthesized the avant-garde strains of Futurism (especially *Bruitisme*, or "noise music") and Dadaism to create an American avant-garde that generated new forms of music, theater, dance, painting, poetry, as well as the less definable categories of Happenings, Events, and Fluxus.[14]

Allan Kaprow's Happenings set precedents for breakdowns between art and life experiences; Robert Whitman's Happenings skillfully mixed media and manipulated ordinary objects into fantastic transformations. Jim Dine used objects as performers, building collages of textures and images. Claes Oldenburg set objects in motion, transformed scale or material with comic results, emphasized details of the work over the composition of the whole, and used an associative, rather than narrative, structure in his works.

The new theater, like the new visual art, was in a process of dematerialization. When a live sculpture or painting dissipated the traditional permanence of the art object, it dissolved the commodity aspect of the work as well. A sense of immediacy and concreteness combined with spontaneity and an interest in the work process, rather than the finished product, to repudiate the romantic notion of the artwork as a fixed instance of the artist's expression. Strategies of monotone and repetition undercut values of craftsmanship and composition. The use of human scale and ordinary, at times industrial, materials brought an earthly, workaday quality into painting, sculpture, theater, and also into dance. As visual art edged toward theater (setting itself at war with modernist art, according to Michael Fried[15]), the corresponding movement in dance, while also focusing on the spectator's perceptions and shifting points of view, seemed to contradict Fried's argument by both repressing the theatrically expressive elements of the form and thrusting it closer to an objective identity.

Merce Cunningham inspired much of post-modern dance by serving both as an inspiration for further innovation and as an authority to be criticized. What Cunningham did to spawn the new movement was to have Robert Dunn teach a composition workshop at Cunningham's studio. Dunn, married then to Judith Dunn who danced in Cunningham's company and friendly with James Waring, had studied music composition with John Cage at the New School. He brought Cage's ideas, especially those concerned with chance procedures, into his dance composition class. He also analyzed Erik

Satie's repetitive time structures, recommending them for use in choreography. The students in the workshop during the first year, 1960 to 1961, were Paul Berenson, Simone Forti, Marnie Mahaffey, Steve Paxton, and Yvonne Rainer. Later, Ruth Allphon, Judith Dunn, and Ruth Emerson joined. The second year the class was given, starting in fall 1961, there were many more participants, including Trisha Brown, David Gordon, Alex and Deborah Hay, and Elaine Summers.[16]

Judith Dunn recalls:

> As a teacher Bob Dunn was outrageous. He allowed interminable rambling discussion, which often strayed wildly from the opening point. He permitted class members to deal with whatever hit their fancy. To examine, consider and present any object, dance collection of words, sounds and what have you in answer to problems he had given for study. He posed questions arising out of the most basic elements — structure, method, material . . . Evaluation, in terms of "good or bad," "acceptable-rejected," were eliminated from discussion and analysis replaced them. (What did you see, what did you do, what took place, how did you go about constructing and ordering. What are the materials, where did you find or how did you form them, etc.) There was no formula to be filled. Initially this caused some anxiety. What he asked was that invention take place and that work continue to be produced economically and practically.[17]

For the members of the class, many of whom had studied composition with Louis Horst and Doris Humphrey at Connecticut College, the freedom from evaluation and prescribed formulae was unprecedented. But they had varying reactions to Dunn's approach. Some only showed up for class to present dances they had worked on independently. David Gordon remembers that he, for instance, always tried to find the loopholes in what he perceived as a paradoxically rigid attitude toward chance.[18]

Robert Dunn organized the first concert at the Judson Church, after his students had found the place where they could show the work they had made in his class. The concert, given on July 6, 1962, began with a projection of films as the audience was being seated — "chance-edited footage by Elaine [Summers] and test footage that [John Herbert McDowell] made, all of which was blue-y," [19] and a clip from W. C. Fields' *The Bank Dick*. The films dissolved into the first dance on the program, Ruth Emerson's *Shoulder*. The program also included *Once or Twice a Week I Put on Sneakers to Go Uptown* by Fred

Herko (who died in 1964); *Transit* and *Proxy* by Steve Paxton; *Helen's Dance* and *Mannequin Dance* by David Gordon; *Rain Fur* by Deborah Hay; *Divertissement, Ordinary Dance,* and *Dance for 3 People and 6 Arms* by Yvonne Rainer. There were dances by William Davis, John Herbert McDowell, Gretchen McLane, Carol Scothorn, and Elaine Summers; a collaboration by Alex Hay, Deborah Hay, and Charles Rotmil; and music by John Cage.[20] Yvonne Rainer, who along with Steve Paxton and Ruth Emerson had "auditioned" for the use of the church, recalls:

> The first concert of dance turned out to be a three-hour marathon for a capacity audience of about 300 sitting from beginning to end in the un-airconditioned 90° heat. The selection of the program had been hammered out at numerous gab sessions, with Bob Dunn as the cool-headed prow of a sometimes over-heated ship . . . I remember Fred Herko on roller skates; I remember John Herbert McDowell with a red sock and mirror; I remember Deborah Hay hobbling around with something around her knees; I remember doing my own *Ordinary Dance;* I remember being in Steve Paxton's *Proxy* with [lighting designer] Jennifer Tipton. We were all wildly ecstatic afterwards, and with good reason. Aside from the enthusiasm of the audience, the church seemed a positive alternative to the once-a-year hire-a-hall mode of operating that had plagued the struggling modern dancer before. Here we could present things more frequently, more informally, and more cheaply, and — most important of all — more cooperatively.[21]

Those on the program who had shown their own choreography before (as had Rainer, for instance) had either appeared on James Waring's program at the Living Theater, or had followed the two standard routes: hiring a hall or auditioning for the annual concerts of work by young choreographers given at the YM-YWHA on 92nd Street.

In August, Elaine Summers organized a concert by the group in Woodstock, New York. The dances were by Summers, Elizabeth Keen, and Ruth Emerson; and Laura de Freitas, June Ekman, and Sally Gross contributed a structured improvisation.[22]

When fall came and Dunn did not resume his workshop, Paxton and Rainer called for weekly meetings at Rainer's studio. Later, the new collective workshop transferred to the Judson, where a third concert was held on January 29, 1963, and a fourth program on the following night. In April, Rainer gave her evening-length *Terrain.* In May, seven members of the group — by this time, Robert Rauschenberg had joined them — were invited by the Washington Gallery of Modern Art to give a concert in Washington, D.C., where they performed in a roller-skating rink. In June, a concert of eleven dances and two plays was given at the Pocket Theater in New York.[23]

From the time of the first concert, the group included "choreographers" who were not trained dancers, but artists, composers, and writers. Although many of the choreographers were also accomplished dancers who had performed with Cunningham, Waring, Passloff, and others, some of the dancers had never choreographed their own works. The informality and flexibility of the workshop permitted the use of nondancers in dance pieces, as well as the presumption by nondancers that they could not only dance but even choreograph. "People who came around simply got sucked in," as John Herbert McDowell put it. He saw the Judson situation as a meeting of artists as important historically as Paris in the 1920s, pointing out that it was the explosion of interacting ideas from a variety of fields that opened up new attitudes about what dance could be.[24]

And the audiences were also artists, painters, musicians, dancers, writers, film makers, intellectuals, people who lived in the neighborhood of the church, in Greenwich Village. It was an audience acutely aware of the crises in modern art and knowledgeable about the history of alternatives to art traditions, eager to be surprised, shocked, provoked. Except for sympathetic reviews by Allen Hughes at the *New York Times,* the press generally ignored or disapproved of the goings on at the Judson, at least in the early years. Another notable exception was Jill Johnston at the *Village Voice,* an enthusiastic partisan who championed the cause of the revolution and explained it in her columns in the *Voice,* reviews in *Art News,* panels, talks, and "action-lectures."[25] Johnston organized concerts out of town for her friends, and she even choreographed and performed herself on occasion. When she favored one choreographer over another in public, inevitably competition and resentment arose. But "whatever she wrote, her columns were the greatest single source of PR since Clement Greenberg plugged Jackson Pollock."[26]

At first the Happenings makers stayed away from the Judson. But after Rauschenberg became involved, the schism narrowed somewhat. However, other tensions grew, because with Rauschenberg's participation came changes in audiences and a new sense of stardom and rank within the group. One wing — including Trisha Brown, Lucinda Childs, David Gordon, Alex Hay, Deborah Hay, Robert Morris, Steve Paxton, Yvonne Rainer, and Robert

Rauschenberg — consolidated. They were invited to perform out of New York, they were favored by Johnston, and were seen as the major proponents of a Judson aesthetic. Some participated in the Yam Festival in May 1963 (at the Smolin Gallery, New York City, George Segal's farm in South Brunswick, New Jersey, Hardware Poet's Playhouse in Manhattan, and various other locations), along with members of Fluxus and makers of Happenings and Events. They traveled to New Paltz, New York, in January 1964 and appeared at the Once Festival in Ann Arbor, Michigan, the following month. In February and March 1964, Steve Paxton organized the Surplus Dance Theater series at Stage 73 in New York, and the following year in May he produced the First New York Theater Rally, with revivals and new dances by Carolyn Brown, Trisha Brown, Lucinda Childs, Judith Dunn, Gordon, Alex Hay, Deborah Hay, Tony Holder, Morris, Paxton, Rainer, and Rauschenberg. At the rally there were also Happenings, performances, and music events by Oyvind Fahlstrom, Claes Oldenburg, Karlheinz Stockhausen, the Once Group, and Robert Whitman, and an exhibition curated by Lewis Lloyd.[27]

In 1964, Robert Dunn offered a composition course again. But by then the rules of dance had changed. The initial surge of experimentation at the Judson, having momentarily consolidated, nevertheless resisted institutionalization as dance activity proliferated. Yet the weekly workshops had lost their value for those choreographers who found performing opportunities elsewhere, or whose ambitions led them on to major independent work. Teaching jobs outside New York City separated the group geographically, and bonds were further loosened by outside engagements, solo concerts, and a constant influx of new choreographers at the Judson. According to Jill Johnston, the original momentum of the core group was dwindling by the end of 1963.[28] By 1965, Meredith Monk, Kenneth King, and Phoebe Neville were emerging as the leaders of a "second Judson generation." Concerts continued to be given at the Judson Church until 1968, but they also abounded in art galleries, lofts, other churches, and various other nonproscenium spaces.

But it was not only artists who provided fruitful areas of exchange for choreography. The new dance both simplified itself and complicated itself with technological experiments. Technology offered an objective rigor that was a welcome antidote to the subjectivity of dramatic dance, and a logical extension of a concern with methodology. In October 1966, Experiments in Art and Technology (EAT), a foundation partly organized by Rauschenberg, sponsored a series of performances in which artists collaborated with engineers from Bell Telephone Laboratories. Nine Evenings: Theater and Engineering, as the series was called, included works by Childs, Alex Hay, Deborah Hay, Paxton, Rainer, and Rauschenberg, as well as by John Cage, Oyvind Fahlstrom, David Tudor, and Robert Whitman. The events, held at the 69th Regiment Armory (where the famous New York Armory Show of 1913 was held) were partly disastrous, encountering many technical problems and leaving several of the pieces to some extent unrealized.[29]

In the late 1960s and early 1970s, when political unrest pervaded the country, several choreographers made dances with political themes, either explicit or implicit. Rainer, for instance, danced *Trio A* in a convalescent condition and called it *Convalescent Dance* on a program of works protesting the war in Vietnam during Angry Arts Week in 1967; choreographed a march through Soho based on her *M-Walk* to demonstrate against the invasion of Cambodia and the Kent State killings in 1969; arranged a dance for the Judson Flag Show in 1970; and the same year made a piece called *WAR*. Steve Paxton's dances during that period (including *Intravenous Lecture, Beautiful Lecture, Collaboration with Wintersoldier,* and *Air*) treated specific issues of censorship, the war, and political corruption. More general themes of political organization were expressed by embodying communal forms in large, simply structured group pieces like Paxton's *Satisfyin Lover* and *State* and Deborah Hay's increasingly informal group dances. (See Paxton and Hay.) The use of nontrained dancers by many post-modern choreographers, appropriate in a general context of antiauthoritarianism, receded conspicuously in the late 1970s.

The experiments and adventures of the Judson Dance Theater and its offshoots laid a groundwork for a post-modern aesthetic in dance that expanded and often challenged the range of purpose, materials, motivations, structures, and styles in dance. It is an aesthetic that continues to inform the most interesting work in dance today.

Originally reacting against the expressionism of modern dance, which anchored movement to a literary idea or musical form, the post-modernists propose (as do Cunningham and Balanchine) that the formal qualities of dance might be reason enough for choreography, and that the purpose of making dances might be simply to make a framework within which we look at movement for its own sake. But there are other purposes post-modernism claims for dance. One is that a dance can formulate or illustrate a theory of dance, as in Rainer's *Some Thoughts on Improvisation,* in which her taped voice posed questions about the choreographic process and the nature of "spontaneous determination" of movement design, while she in fact improvised; or as in Douglas Dunn's *101* which proposed that stillness can constitute a dance. Another purpose, partly inspired by phenomenological philosophers and writers, is to embody different perspectives on space, time, or orientation to gravity, as Trisha Brown did, for example, with her Equipment Pieces. The breakdown of the distinction between art and life (not in the sense that life becomes more artistic but that real life is both subject and material for art), the clarification of individual, discrete movements, the isolation of the essential characteristics of dance, have all become valid purposes for making a dance. So has the option of making a dance for the pleasure of the dancer, whether or not the spectator finds it pleasing, or even accessible. The very question of what it means to create a dance can generate choreography: is writing a score (as Simone Forti has done) an act of choreography? Is dance-making an act of construction and craft or a process of decision making? In post-modern dance, the choreographer becomes a critic, educating spectators in ways to look at dance, challenging the expectations the audience brings to the performance, framing parts of the dance for closer inspection, commenting on the dance as it progresses.

A variety of organizational strategies have been employed in order to achieve these aims. One crucial step was the use of actual time, rather than artificial meter. That is, actions were no longer fitted to the temporal structures dictated by musical accompaniment, but simply took the time they would take off-stage. Another was the use of repetition to emphasize the passing of time. Uninflected phrasing, which Rainer made paradigmatic in *Trio A*, had the effect of flattening the time structure so that dynamics no longer participated in the design of the dance over time. Not only can the body be relaxed in post-modern dance (in contrast to both ballet and modern dance), but time, in the sense of suspense, is also relaxed.

Whether the prevailing structure is a mathematical system for using space, time, or the body; or arbitrary assemblage; or fragmentation, juxtaposition, the deliberate avoidance of structure by improvisation; or the constant shifting of structures by chance methods, there is always the possibility, in post-modern dance, that the underlying form will be bared. The anti-illusionist stance dictates that seams can show, and that part of the aesthetic pleasure in watching the dance derives from learning its structure by examining the seams: watching mistakes occur in improvisation, witnessing fatigue, danger, awkwardness, difficulty; watching movement being marked and learned.

Watching systems being built and dismantled. Refusing to be seduced by mere skill.

One way to draw attention away from matters of virtuosic technique is to demystify it by making dances that acknowledge their own process of being made. Another is to simplify the choreography so drastically that technique is bypassed, and related to such simplification is the use of natural movements. Natural movements present the body concretely, showing the body engaged in the kind of casual, everyday postures that one associates with ordinary actions. Thus anything, from doing somersaults to standing still, from combing one's hair to walking to eating to telling stories, can become material. What makes a movement a part of a dance, rather than simply an ordinary movement, is that it is installed in a dance context. The use of objects (carrying or otherwise manipulating them), improvisation, spontaneous incidents, tasks, games, and relaxed time structures all engender new possibilities for dance movements, especially natural movements. When the forerunners of modern dance, Loïe Fuller and Isadora Duncan, spoke of "natural" movement, they referred to gestures that imitated or represented forms in nature — for Fuller, flowers and butterflies; for Duncan, the movements of waves and trees. In the 1920s and '30s, Graham and Humphrey looked for "natural" movements based on breathing, by which they meant gestures connoting the expressiveness of psychological or social realities by means of body tension. For the post-modern choreographers of the 1960s and '70s, "natural" means something quite different. It means action undistorted for theatrical effectiveness, drained of emotional overlay, literary reference, or manipulated timing. A jump, fall, run, or walk is executed without regard to grace, visual appeal, or technical skill. The action has exactly the amount of abandon and rough edges and takes exactly the length of time it might take outside the theater. The body is no more pulled up or tense than it is in daily life. This new sense of casual activity rooted in concrete experience is typified in the covering of the foot, the basic tool of dance. If ballet clad the foot in satin slippers, concealing the surface of the body and its workly strength behind a covering that stood for soft, graceful femininity, and if modern dance brazenly bared the foot to symbolically secure its contact with the earth, the muse of post-modernism wears sneakers, symbolizing nothing, providing the speed and lightness of pointe shoes but also comfort, maintaining a cool, human distance from the earth while keeping the feet firmly on the ground.

The post-modern aesthetic is not a monolithic one, and in it one can find many contrasting concerns and methods. There are those groups and choreographers, such as Grand Union, Simone Forti, and Douglas Dunn, who often practice a kind of choreographic relativity, letting their performers range over time and space at different rates. Then there are others like Lucinda Childs, Kenneth King, Laura Dean, and Andy deGroat, who usually operate as geometers, tracing distinct designs in a well-controlled space. There is one class of choreographers that draws the spectator's attention to complex movement designs, and another that simplifies or complicates movement in order to emphasize the bodily operations of the particular dancers making the designs. And in Steve Paxton's Contact Improvisation and Deborah Hay's Circle Dances, the primary focus in the dance is the dancer's physical sensation and awareness, a focus that threatens to remove the work from the realm of art altogether, by making the spectator obsolete.

In the '70s, once the issues of technique and expression had been identified, tested, and resolved in a variety of ways, and once dance had been reduced to its essential features, a new expressionism arose in the work of Meredith Monk, Kenneth King, and others. Narrative was reinstalled in dance, but one that was distanced by techniques of alienation and reflexiveness, as in Rainer's later work, some Grand Union performances, and David Gordon's recent work. And even virtuosity once again surfaced in the dances — a virtuosity of inventiveness, skill, and endurance, as in Douglas Dunn's graceful, symmetrical constructions, Lucinda Childs' obsessively precise dances, and David Gordon's elegantly witty works. Batya Zamir's adventures on aerial sculptures and Trisha Brown's Equipment Pieces are examples of dances that require a new set of physical skills.

I have chosen ten choreographers and one group to write about here. Many other dancemakers were actively involved in the creation of the post-modern dance aesthetic, not only dancers like Judith Dunn, Elaine Summers, and Rudy Perez, but also, as I have noted, composers such as John Herbert McDowell and Philip Corner and visual artists including Alex Hay, Robert Morris, Robert Rauschenberg, and Carolee Schneemann. However, those I have considered here have worked consistently in dance, many of them at least since the beginning of Judson Dance Theater, and also their work is representative of various themes and issues that have concerned all the post-modernists.

Several choreographers who could be considered part of the post-modern movement have not been included here for a number of reasons. Some, such as Laura Dean, Andy deGroat, Batya Zamir, Judy Padow, David Woodberry, Wendy Perron, Kei Takei, Sara Rudner, Mary Overlie, Pooh Kaye, and others, have been working for less than a decade or in styles that are still evolving. Twyla Tharp, on the other hand, whose work bears lengthy analysis, has been excluded from this study even though many of her early interests and methods were closely intertwined with those of the post-modernists. Tharp's aspirations have changed, or so her recent work seems to say, and rather than using popular dance forms in an avant-garde context, she works seriously in mainstream forms: ballet and movie musicals.

Among these ten choreographers and one group, nearly every theoretical and practical position in the post-modern aesthetic is represented. These are the dancemakers who have acquired the status of a new academy, according to the cyclical model of modern dance history proposed above. And yet, in many ways this group has succeeded in breaking that cycle and transcending it. Although younger choreographers certainly draw inspiration from the theories and dances discussed here, the post-modernists reject a hierarchical position of authority for the most part. Their break with tradition carries with it the explicit notion that there need be no more academies; that rules are not sacrosanct but can be either useful or unnecessary. If it is a new establishment, post-modern dance is so pluralistic that it inaugurates a new type of establishment: one that tolerates invention and welcomes change.

Simone Forti: Dancing as if Newborn

THE ORDINARY ADULT body is a creature of habit, unconscious responses to physical stimuli, unadventurous routines. For the most part, we travel in a kinesthetic rut, never even noticing the remarkably intricate changes that happen when we walk or run, reach up, sit, or lie down. We rarely experiment with these familiar actions, once we have mastered them. To take notice or to run experiments in everyday life would crowd our consciousness with details, making us nearly dysfunctional.

Play and art have often been regarded as related activities that allow us to ignore the exigencies of daily existence and spend time concentrating on the pleasures, skills, and powers that our bodies — or other bodies — possess. Two aspects of the play-as-art theory concern dance. The first is that, as both Konrad Lange and Karl Groos held, art resembles the illusion-making process of symbolic games.[1] Lange considered art a mature version of make-believe, a deliberate and sophisticated illusory construction. The other aspect, a corollary to the first, is the traditional aesthetic of dance which explains that only by the "play" of bodies more skilled and graceful than our own do we find excitement and beauty.

Through her dances Simone Forti proposes a different theory of dance art, one that accepts and values both the real and the commonplace. The simple presymbolic games of children, as well as the activities of animals and plants provide her with movement material that when performed on the adult body makes it a "defamiliarized" object.

Forti, who has also choreographed under the names Simone Morris and

Simone Forti and Peter Van Riper in a performance of *Big Room*. Photograph © Babette Mangolte, 1976.

Simone Whitman, was born in Florence, Italy, in 1935, the child of an Italian Jewish family. In 1939 her family escaped to Switzerland and then moved to the United States. She grew up in Los Angeles and went to Reed College in Oregon, majoring in psychology and sociology. In 1956, she and her husband, Robert Morris, dropped out of school and moved to San Francisco. There she discovered that she wanted to be a dancer.

For four years Forti studied and performed with Ann Halprin, learning principles and methods that would influence her own work for the next two decades, although not always explicitly. In a sense, Forti began choreographing with an advantage: her body was not ingrained with any one technique or theory of dance, in part because she started dancing at the age of twenty-one, and in part because her teacher was Ann Halprin. Halprin had broken with conventional modern dance just a year before, substituting for academic codes of specialized movements a tolerant, inquisitive, open attitude toward the body's capabilities, in the service of self-expression and spatial architecture. Holding classes on a huge outdoor platform at the foot of Mount Tamalpais, Halprin encouraged improvisation, not as a blind flood of expression but as a means to set loose all conceivable movements, gestures, and combinations of anatomical relationships, ignoring connotation, and bypassing habit and preference. Halprin approached improvisation analytically. The body's operation as an instrument was the primary focus of her investigations. She might explore, for example, what happens when the position of the spine changes while running, or ask her students to notice how, when holding two rocks, the added weight and momentum changed the relationships among body parts. When Forti studied with Halprin, the mornings were devoted to these sorts of explorations and the evenings to improvisations arising more often from imagery than from kinesiological analysis. The important thing was to work free associatively, trying not to compose or to judge the movements, or to create any overview, but simply to be "very strict about letting out whatever flickered through."[2] For herself, Forti recalls vividly, improvisation was often involved with "crawly, underground ant-tunnel imagery."

The Dancers' Workshop (Halprin's group) also worked together on performance projects, often in collaboration with the other artists who gathered at Halprin's studio in Kentfield, California — including composer La Monte Young, actor John Graham, dancer A. A. Leath, painter Jo Landor, and Halprin's husband, architect Lawrence Halprin. One project on which Graham, Ann Halprin, and Forti (then known as Simone Morris) worked together was a set of improvisations involving language that had its source in Graham's concerns as an actor. Forti came to call these experiments the Nez plays:

> I felt that we were working out of a Zen state. But it wasn't Zen, so we took the word Nez. Sometimes I would say things as contrasts, like apple-green. It would come out of a sudden image, or a need, for tartness or for something as plain as a color. There'd be long dialogues, and a lot of juxtaposition.

Since high school, when Forti and a friend discovered a movie theater that showed surrealist films, she had been intrigued by fantastic juxtapositions. By the time she worked with Halprin, Forti had read Kurt Schwitters' Merz scenarios, which may have provided another source for her own title. Schwitters, making junk collages, poetry, environments, and performances, began in 1920 to label his entire oeuvre Merz, preferring to use his own fortuitous title (it had appeared in one of his collages, a fragment of the word komMERZiell) to avoid identifying totally with the Dadaists.[3] Schwitters envisioned a Merz drama that totally fused all the art forms, using objects as principal actors, and employing both everyday and improbable materials in illogical combinations:

> Even people can be used.
> People can even be tied to backdrops.
> People can even appear actively, even in their everyday position, they can speak on two legs, even in sensible sentences . . .
> And now begins the fire of musical saturation. Organs backstage sing and say, "Futt, futt." The sewing machine rattles along in the lead. A man in the wings says: "Bah." . . . A water pipe drips with uninhibited monotony . . .[4]

Schwitters was never able to stage his Merz dramas. But the influence of his vision on later avant-garde theater, especially the Happenings in the 1960s, is obvious.[5]

Halprin also had a gift for evoking deep concentration, for helping her students arrive at what Forti now calls a "dance state," a "state of enchantment." At the workshops, one learned that such a state could be voluntarily induced:

> Sometimes it would be a matter of doing an activity that would set you up or help you induce the dance state. It could be just walking around in a circle

and focusing on the sensations in your body. The sensation of one part moving against another. Of momentum — of different parts, of the mass. And being satisfied to stay focused on those sensations for — oh, fifteen minutes. And then a lot of impulses start to come.

The use of natural movements has informed Forti's work since her studies with Halprin. The movements are "natural" in the sense that they came out of a relaxed state and without preparation but instinctively, organically — in contrast to movements characterized by the tension of both ballet and modern dance. Every movement has a distinctive quality, Halprin taught, and discrimination against different possibilities of movement experiences can only be restricting.

But after four years of improvising, Forti found the chaos of total freedom and the continuing floods of imagery disturbing. She feels that there was a correlation with the impasse that abstract expressionism reached at about the same time. Morris, who had been painting abstract expressionist works during those four years — and encouraging Forti to paint too — gave up painting when they moved to New York in 1959, she recalls.

In New York, Forti took classes briefly at the Martha Graham and Merce Cunningham studios. But she "*would not* hold [her] stomach in" at the Graham classes, and she found the speed and fragmentation of the Cunningham style bewildering. She felt that Cunningham was brilliant at articulating the adult, isolated condition, but that "the thing I had to offer was still very close to the holistic and generalized response of infants."[6] She taught at a nursery school, where the meaningfully repetitive movements of the children captured her attention, and she listened often to the reductive music of La Monte Young, whose use of simple, clear, sustained tones impressed her deeply. After seeing Robert Whitman's Happening *E.G.* in 1960, she felt that she had discovered an aesthetic close to her own. Later that year, she worked with Whitman on his *The American Moon.*[7] Another influence on her at this time were reports on the activities of the Gutai group in Japan. (Michael Kirby suggests that their action works were one important inspiration for Happenings.)[8] A group of artists in their twenties and thirties experimenting with unusual media, their "paintings" included sheets of tinfoil scratched with a blue-inked pen, and a vinyl canvas covered with paint by means of a brush attached to a toy tank. They held exhibits of their works out-of-doors in a pine grove, and they presented action works as well as finished objects. In a piece by Koichi Nakahashi and Yasuo Sumi, paper balls dipped in paint were thrown at a white wall, after which ladles full of colored water were thrown at a cellophane wall that separated the artists and the audience.[9] Forti had seen photographs of Gutai's work before she left San Francisco.

The same year, Forti joined the Robert Dunn composition class taught at the Cunningham studio. She says that she enjoyed the use of chance techniques gleaned from John Cage's music scores, seeing aleatory methods not as a relinquishing of control but as a means of evoking in performance the original events and structures at the moment of composition. She appreciated Dunn's stress on working quickly, and on clarifying the concept behind each dance. Yet for someone who had already been experimenting for four years with Halprin and other artists on the West Coast, the Dunn class must have been frustrating at times. The rest of the students were discovering a new world of dance, but Forti already inhabited it. In the summer of 1960, Forti had returned to Halprin's workshop with Morris for the summer, bringing a New York friend — Yvonne Rainer — with her.

In December 1960, Forti was invited to participate in a group evening at the Reuben Gallery, which had been the site of several Happenings. Forti contributed *See-Saw* and *Rollers* to a program that also included *A Shining Bed* by Jim Dine and *Blackouts* by Claes Oldenburg. Both of Forti's pieces were games for adults based, with very few changes, on children's playground equipment. The structure of each piece showed the operations of the adult body in a situation that is ordinary for children, but rare for adults. Skills of balancing and adapting to momentum were tested in a systematic examination of the processes of equilibrium.

See-Saw began when Robert Morris set an eight-foot plank on a sawhorse fulcrum, attaching it to two walls by elastic cords at either end. A toy that made a mooing sound when moved was fixed to one end of the seesaw. Morris removed the coat he had been wearing and, dressed in a sweater and shorts, sat on one end of the plank while Yvonne Rainer, identically dressed, got on the other. They seesawed for a while, creating zigzag patterns with the plank and elastic, and then made a series of movements that forced the balance to fluctuate radically. Rainer shrieked and threw herself around (an improvisation based on Forti's having thrown a ragged jacket onto the floor, saying "Improvise that!"[10]); Morris read in a flat voice from *Art News*, then together they stood in the center of the plank, gently shifting it back and forth while Forti, stationed at the lighting board, sang a nonsense song. Yvonne

Rainer has stated that *See-Saw* influenced her own work: she was impressed by the use of the seesaw for its physical properties, and the resulting demands it made on the performers. But she was especially affected by the episodic, unconnected structure of the piece. "One thing followed another. Whenever I am in doubt I think of that. One thing follows another."[11]

In *Rollers*, two shallow wooden boxes mounted on wheels, each containing a singing performer, were made to careen madly by means of three ropes attached to each wagon, manipulated by members of the audience. The wild movement of the boxes "produces an excitement bordering on fear, which automatically becomes an element in [the] performance."[12] The fear was immediately evident both in the voices and in the physical adjustments of the performers as they adapted or surrendered to the increasing momentum of the wagons.

These two dances, billed as Happenings, were as different from conventional dance concerts as could be imagined. The performers wore street clothes instead of leotards. In *See-Saw*, the man and the woman were dressed exactly alike. In *Rollers*, the spectators were called on to participate. And although the activities for each piece were planned in advance, the outcome of the specific movements was indeterminate. The dances took place in a gallery, not on a stage, and, rather than framing special movements requiring the technical skill of trained dancers, these pieces simply required ordinary movements that permitted the performers to meet the demands of the equipment. Neither illusion, story, mood, place, nor character were "created." The performers were not making believe, but simply executing certain commonplace actions.

For her next concert, part of a series at Yoko Ono's loft on Chambers Street, which included an environment by Morris; music by Philip Corner, La Monte Young, and Richard Maxfield; and poetry by Jackson MacLow, Forti made an evening called "Five Dance Constructions and Some Other Things." Almost all of the pieces, which were done at different sites in the loft, have been performed at later concerts.

One construction, *Slant Board*, for three or four people, takes place on a wooden ramp slanted at a 45-degree angle to the floor, and leaning against the wall. Five or six ropes, knotted at one-foot intervals, are attached to the top of the ramp, and the performers are instructed to move constantly and calmly, from top to bottom, and from side to side, on the incline. They may rest during the piece, but must remain on the board for its duration — about ten minutes. The steepness of the incline turns the task into a strenuous one, testing the endurance of the performers at its limits.

Huddle, another dance construction, provides a human structure for the performers to climb. Six or seven people form a strong web by facing each other and bending forward, planting their feet firmly, keeping the knees slightly bent, and putting their arms around each other's waists and shoulders. One person separates from the structure (which tightens in compensation), climbs over the huddle slowly and calmly, finding available foot- and handholds supplied by the other bodies, and rejoins the huddle on the other side. There is no particular order for climbing, but by the shifting of balance and readjustment of center that takes place when one person withdraws to start the climb, the group can immediately feel one person's intention to ascend. *Huddle* lasts for about ten minutes and is meant to be walked around and examined by the audience like a sculpture. As a structure it frees the body from a standing position and allows for new movements and positions. Like *Slant Board,* it is a cooperative game which requires its performers to formulate ad hoc, intuitive and consensual rules in order that the individual plans progress smoothly. In *Huddle,* laughing is permitted, as is the occasional possibility of two people climbing at once.[13] At times, *Huddle* has been used to proliferate second-generation huddles, when the performers from the original group find audience members to join them in the game.

The evening also included *Hangers,* in which five people stand passively in long rope loops suspended close together from the ceiling, while four people walk in and out of the cluster, causing the hangers to turn, bump, and sway. As in *Rollers,* the motivation for a performer's movement is totally removed from his or her control. The material of the dance consists in the operations of the performer's weight in relation to gravity and the chance collisions of the walking performers. In *Platforms,* a man and a woman get under two separate platforms, whistle for fifteen minutes, then emerge. The man wears a wristwatch to time the duet.

In *Accompaniment for La Monte's "2 sounds" and La Monte's "2 sounds,"* one person stands in a long rope loop, which another person winds up completely, after turning on the tape recording of La Monte Young's "2 sounds," a twelve-minute piece of tape music. The person standing in the rope unwinds and rewinds, driven by momentum, and finally, reaching a still point, hangs there listening until the tape ends. The movement is secondary to the sound, literally a movement accompaniment to a music performance. *From*

Instructions gave conflicting tasks to two men: one was instructed to lie on the floor for the duration of the piece, and one told to tie the first man to a wall (which could be done because there were pipes running along the wall). *Censor* was another competition, pitting one person shaking a pan of nails against another person singing a song. The object was for the two to find a balance at high volume. *Herding* was a game with the audience, in which the performers politely herded the spectators back and forth in the loft until they became rather resentful. But by that time they were in place to see the final piece, *See-Saw.*

By spreading the locales of the constructions and "other things" around the loft, Forti both changed the spectator's physical relationship to the dance and eliminated time-consuming scene changes. The performance became a straightforward presentation of activities, almost as if those activities were objects, arranged the way objects might be in a gallery, where the spectator is free to move closer or farther away. Where preparation was necessary, it was simply incorporated into the activity, without any attempt to mask it. In *Accompaniment to La Monte's "2 sounds,"* for example, one performer's role was to turn on the tape and wind up the other performer's rope, and in *Platforms* the man helped the woman under her platform and then got under his own.[14]

Forti's game structures were antidotes both to the symbol-laden narratives of the traditional modern dance choreographers and to the limitless improvisation of Halprin. In all of Forti's games, from the fairly rudimentary sensory-motor pieces such as *Accompaniment, Hangers,* or *See-Saw,* to the more socially complicated rule games such as *Slant Board* and *Huddle,* to the competitions *Censor* and *From Instructions,* there is a strong, basic structure for motivating movement. The fundamental elements of dance — balance, weight, momentum, energy, endurance, articulation of body — are explored in the most direct and economical manner. What matters is not so much the movements themselves, but the *range* of movements, from very relaxed to very tense, that can be generated in an orderly manner, according to the rules of the game but without a restrictive movement aesthetic. Games have a specific order supplied by their particular rules. But games also allow — indeed, promote — individualized solutions to the rules. In the language of psychologist Jean Piaget, play allows for pure assimilation without accommodation; that is, one can digest information about the world during play without having to adjust to the real world's demands. One exercises and enjoys one's own categories of understanding and one's own physical capabilities.[15]

Often, play is a very serious activity, and to make dances out of games does not mean that either the activity or the choreography is frivolous. For Forti, the play format was a way of examining natural movements and presenting them to an audience in appropriate ways in a dance situation. Movement could be isolated for aesthetic enjoyment, but not by the structure of the performance itself — rather, by the mental processes of the spectator. That is, Forti did not abstract and rearrange the movements in the games into a new, artistic composition. Her role as a choreographer was to invent the structure of the game. By then presenting the entire process of the activity in a performance framework, she implied that the goal of the onlooker while watching the movements would be a different one than if he or she watched such activity outside of a performance. But perhaps Forti also hoped that the spectators would carry a new awareness of kinesthetic forms with them out of the performance. Although the movements did not conform to any single stylistic code, their overall appearance was of raw, comfortable movement, functional and unpretentious, devoid of elaboration through unnecessary gestures.

During 1961, Forti also worked with Trisha Brown and Dick Levine on improvisations using rule games. One of her favorite rule games, which she has often used in improvisations and workshops since, is *Over, Under, and Around.* Each performer follows two sets of rules: one, a privately determined sequence for the three actions (going over, under, and around the other performers), cued either by hearing a particular letter on the radio, or by personal choice; the second, a particular sequence for carrying out the interactions with the other performers. Since some of the rules are known and some secret, the results can be both chaotic (as when two people try to go over each other at the same time) and harmonious.

Forti operated like an explorer, finding dance everywhere in the commonplace as well as making concert frameworks for dissecting ordinary movements. In 1963, she published "dance reports" and instructions for some of the dance constructions, in La Monte Young and Jackson MacLow's *An Anthology.*[16] The reports were minute analyses of physical processes evident in the sprouting of an onion, which cause its weight to shift, and in the action of children rolling snowballs down a hill.

Though Forti might naturally have been involved in the Judson Dance Theater, which grew out of Robert Dunn's composition class in 1961–1962, she never joined it. By 1962, she had married Robert Whitman, and during their marriage, from 1962 to 1966, she made no dances, but devoted herself to helping him with his Happenings, including *Flower, Hole, Water, Night Time*

Sky, and *Prune/Flat.* There was some tension between the makers of the Happenings and the Judson choreographers at first, and the Whitmans rarely went to the early Judson concerts. During those years, however, Forti's dance construction *Huddle* was performed by Fluxus, a group (centered around George Maciunas, Nam June Paik, Dick Higgins, Alison Knowles, Robert Filliou, George Brecht, and others) that regarded itself as neo-Dadaist. They took *Huddle* with them to Europe as part of the Fluxus Festorum of new music, performing the dance in Paris, Copenhagen, and Dusseldorf as an example of "non-instrumental action music."[17] In 1966, Forti worked as administrative assistant and documentor for Experiments in Art and Technology (EAT), leading up to Nine Evenings: Theater and Engineering, at the 69th Regiment Armory. She produced and directed a television program on EAT, and wrote an article on Nine Evenings for *Artforum.*[18]

In 1967, Forti began to choreograph again. She presented three new works at the School of Visual Arts, on a program that also included dances by Trisha Brown and Steve Paxton. Although her new pieces — *Face Tunes, Cloths,* and *Song* — also had qualities of play, they focused more on the sound than on the movement aspects of performance. For *Face Tunes,* Forti invented a simple machine which she used to interpret a score of seven faces drawn in profile on a long scroll. As the machine rolled the drawings, Forti played their shapes on a slide whistle. *Cloths,* which Jonas Mekas called "a sort of underground opera," had unseen performers crouching behind three frames, tossing cloths over the frames.[19] During the ten minutes the piece lasted, each performer flipped four or five cloths and sang two or three songs, which overlapped with taped songs Forti had collected from various friends, interspersed with silence. In *Song,* Forti sang an old Tuscan folksong in counterpoint to the Beatles' "Fool on the Hill," played on a record player.

The next year, for a concert at the Cornell University School of Architecture, she made two pieces that consisted of slides accompanied by sound: *Book,* a set of thirty-five Brownie snapshots projected in pairs, accompanied by *Song;* and *Bottom,* four slides projected one at a time for five minutes each, accompanied by 1) frenetic drumming, 2) a single, constant chord sung by La Monte Young, Marian Zazeela, and Forti, 3) a vacuum cleaner, and 4) a simple, whistled, repeated melody. *Fallers* exploited the physical environment of the performance space, a seventeenth-floor penthouse, with a terrace. Several performers jumped from the penthouse roof to the terrace, shocking and delighting the audience inside with a vision of free falling bodies. That year, she gave a concert in Rome that began the animal studies that would occupy her for the next ten years. In the winter of 1969, Forti worked in Turin with an experimental theater group, The Zoo. She came back to Italy in the summer to participate with other artists in the Festival of Music, Dance, Explosions, and Flight in Rome.

Joining half a million people at the Woodstock Festival later that summer, Forti "perceived a set of mores regarding the sharing of space and fate which seemed to form a whole integrated way. I fell in love with that way, and remained with it for a year."[20] She stopped thinking of herself as a dancer, trying simply, in the countercultural idiom, to "be me." She traveled, learning "hippie protocol," staying at communes, always studying the changes and movements in her own body and in the processes around her. For example, she speaks of a small dance of balance she discovered while standing on a rock and holding another rock on her head, of watching a rock wall crumble slowly and then standing on the wall to test its movement, of the intensity of physical sensations while on drugs. Her dancing and movement observations were part of a communal vision in which everyone was a dancer, a musician, a cook, a guest, a host. When eventually she felt the unity of that communal vision disintegrating, she returned to New York and for a short time studied singing with Pandit Pran Nath, an Indian master and teacher of La Monte Young. Then she went to California where she practiced Tai Chi Chuan, occasionally substituting for Allan Kaprow and leading open sessions of dance and music jams, which she named "Open Gardenia," at California Institute of the Arts. Beginning to collaborate with musician Charlemagne Palestine, she developed the three cornerstones of her subsequent work: crawling, animal movements, and circling.

Since 1974, when Forti presented *The Zero* and *Crawling* at Sonnabend Gallery on a program of old and new works, almost all of her dances — including *Big Room, Red Green,* and *Planet* — have been built on these three movement themes. Whether they are solos, duets, small or large group pieces, whether they are accompanied by her own taped voice reading scientific-sounding reports on animal movements, or by Peter Van Riper's circular music improvisations on saxophones, percussion instruments, flutes, bullroarers, tapes, and toys, the dances are constructed on these primary blocks of movement activity.

In the crawling explorations, one sees an analytic intelligence at work as Forti examines each term in the sequence, making us aware by watching, as

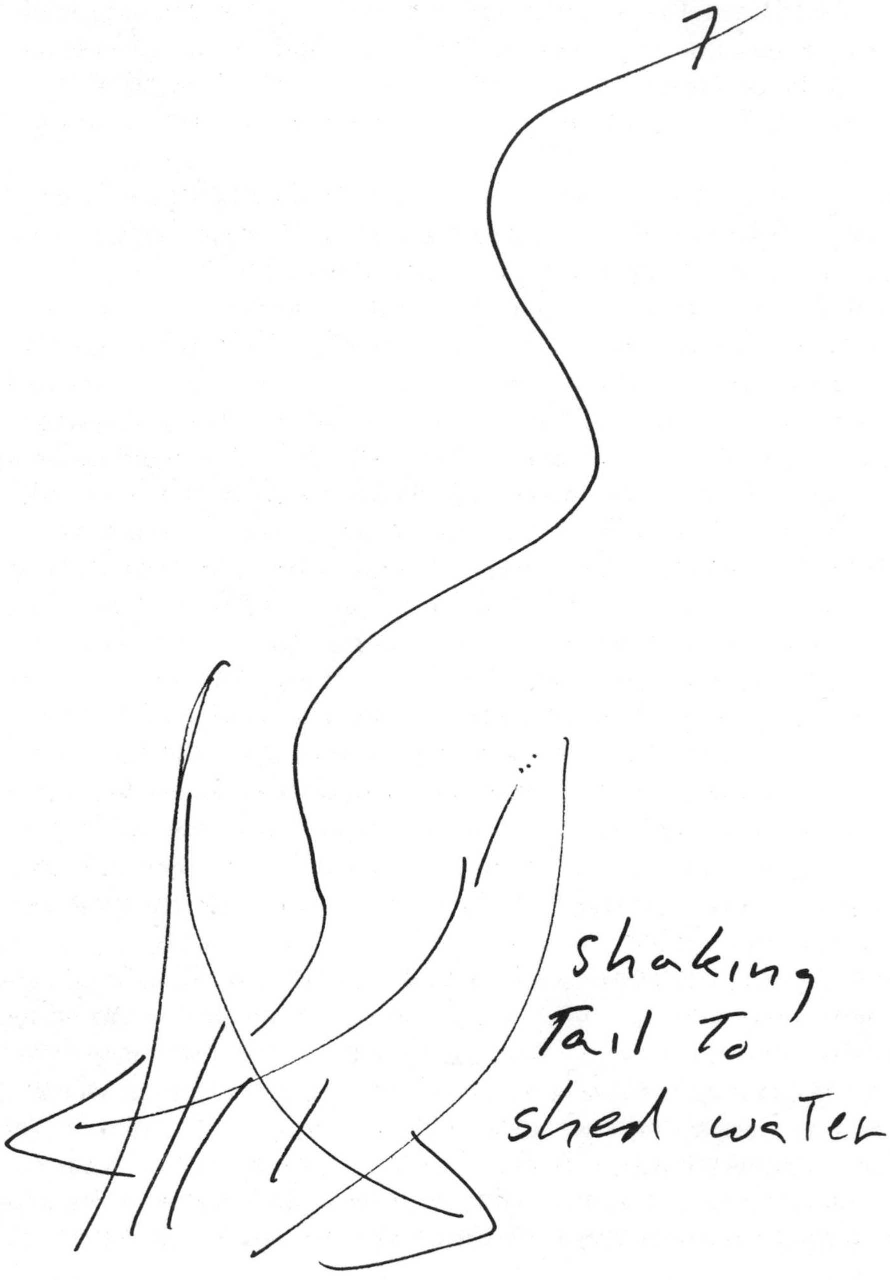

Duck Drawing: Shaking Tail to Shed Water (Simone Forti)

she is by feeling, of the minute shifts of weight that happen as the hand reaches forward, of the necessary curve in the spine that allows one knee to advance. It could be the migration of a baby or of an animal. In the dance called *Crawling,* she combines the crawling explorations with specific kinds of animal creeping and other animal movements.

Forti had begun her studies of animal movements at the zoo in Rome in 1968, using two of the studies — flamingoes sleeping while standing on one leg, and polar bears swinging their heads — in *Sleepwalkers.* In these "zoo mantras" Forti empathizes with, rather than imitates, the animals.[21] She tests their actions on her own, differently structured body, pinpointing the differential between human and animal movements. A violent swing of the neck and head, gleaned from the polar bear, propels an efficient turn while traveling on all fours. A symmetrical bounding from a crouch, so simple for a rabbit, makes stringent demands on a person's lower back, hips, and thighs. In order to approximate the sleeping situation of the flamingo — standing on one leg with the head tucked under the wing — Forti found that trying to go to sleep while leaning far backward produced an equivalent problem for a human.

In *Crawling,* Forti's voice tells stories about a bee and fly confronting each other, the rabbit's method of locomotion, the wrestling of brown bears, the actions of a crow, an elephant, a snake. And she crawls. The crawling is the base of the dance, out of which the other activities arise and back to which they always return. Although her movements never correspond exactly to the situations described in the tape, they correlate in terms of the precise, penetrating attention to the mechanics of animal motions.

From crawling, she suddenly yet deliberately drops the weight into one hip, and finds herself pivoting to sit, facing another direction, as the hip meets the floor. Then she crawls and sits, crawls and sits, the way an infant experiments with a chance change. The sudden acts of sitting become more and more frequent, and then the legs straighten, the back straightens, until she is crawling in an almost vertical position, and finally, until she walks. Next those walking to crawling to walking transitions are explored. Then she stands in place, testing a contraction and release of her upper back that brings her arms into a forward and backward sweep reminiscent of wings. She squats on arched feet, still testing the thrust of her arms, then sits suddenly, crawls, stands, squats again, and bounds forward, covering a long space at a low level, reminding one of the rabbit her schoolmarmish voice had described in the tape. Now she goes on to the polar bear action, using violent swings to shift the direction of the crawl, standing low, touching the floor gently, her hands coming up off the floor momentarily as the head rolls back. Next she stands and strides in a figure eight, again leaning more and more steeply into the center of each circle, one arm up like an axis centering her in relation to the ground, her head nestled against it, the other arm held against her face protectively. She bends and crouches as the circles diminish in size, and again she is on the floor, crawling, this time with arms and legs splayed out like a crab's, her movements very heavy as the impulse comes from the center of the body, rather than from the joints. "The embrace is arboreal," her voice concludes.

Forti is concerned about how particular movements fit into the ecosystem of the mover:

> I find that when I look to see what is that system by which I survive, the question boggles my mind. With the animals in the zoo I have at least the illusion of understanding the limits and nature of the life system in which they find themselves. An animal walking in a cage is a different thing than is an animal walking in the grasslands. And yet it's not.[22]

The separation of aspects of the self that Forti feels comes with captivity brings the animal's "dance behavior," as she calls it, into sharp relief. The observations she makes of the animals' dance behavior clarify aspects of her own dance behavior, both privately and in performance:

> The strongest clue I have to why I've again and again returned to the zoo is the feeling state that I'm sometimes in when I find myself looking eye to eye with a particular animal. Often I find that at that moment there's a flood of warmth that seems to pass between us and that I'm held spellbound.[23]

This sense of connection is related to Forti's concept of the "dance state." She also observes that the animals, in their ritual behavior produced by the physical environment in the cage, regularize matrices out of which they improvise variations. This too is related to the "dance state," the state of enchantment out of which Forti feels she moves.

> Maybe I could compare it to certain meditational states, or states in which you arrive at a certain concentration and then it's not an effort to do what you're concentrating on doing, because your whole system is flowing in that

direction. You're acting almost — I wouldn't say in a state of no-mind, but your system is geared to *performing.* It could be adrenalin, it could be theta waves, it could be what Castanedas writes about: a state the warrior can be into where his powers are awakened. Enchantment comes from the root *to chant.* I think of it as a musical state, a state in which the musical centers of the mind are in focus, in operation, and all your motor intelligence is blossoming.

The excitement of so many games, Forti says, is that they bring the player into such a dance state. And the problem she has found with so many conventional dance classes — which leads to problems in performance — is that dancers are taught how to "go through all kinds of numbers but you're not dancing because you're not in a dance state."

In her circling and banking studies, Forti traces circles and ellipses with a walk that speeds up, her weight leaning into the center of the orbit, until she seems caught in a suddenly tapped whirlpool of momentum, yielding to it passively. She switches into figure eights, spinning new circles in new directions. The geometric design of the circling has much in common with the repetitive, elemental constructions of minimalist sculpture. But actually it is better understood in relation to Forti's animal and infant themes. All three investigate different sensations and body states. In the circling, the elemental repetition and the giving in to momentum induce an altered consciousness, as they do in the dances of choreographers who work primarily with spinning. Forti's fascination with the circles is not simply kinesthetic, but rooted in mystical numerology, in her belief that in the "seven circles which form the basis of the Star of David" one also finds shapes of the Arabic numerals, and in her idea that depending on the location of the center of movement along the spine, "the body has a different geometry and measures differently in time."[24]

Big Room (1975), *Red Green* (1975), and *Planet* (1976) all use these basic blocks of movement materials, but intersperse them with other themes. *Big Room,* a collaboration with musician Peter Van Riper, permits each to do solos and both to work together. He plays repetitive, circular patterns on the kalimba, simple melodies on several pitches of saxophones, he whirls plastic hoses (bullroarers) to make a whistling sound. Forti does plant studies, lying awry on one shoulder with legs and arms spiking up into the air, or finding different places on the floor to lie quietly on her side. At one point she performs what seems to be a ritual of marking out the space. She runs from the corner, falls on her back in the center of the room and slides back a little, pulling her legs up close to her body and jabbing them sharply in and out. Then she begins from the next corner, running and, at the center, hopping with arms straight up, falling back, sliding, kicking. And so on until all four corners have been marked. When Van Riper whirls the bullroarers, she backs up into the corridor of space the hoses form, until she stands pressed against him, leaning her back against his chest. The structure of *Big Room*, with its blocks of music and movement material put into gear in different orders and combinations — sometimes with nonverbal signals, as when one starts a certain sequence with the expectation that the other will follow, or sometimes simply when one calls out to the other the name of the desired bit — creates a sense of mutual play between the two, a sense of trust and shared exploration, relying on preferences of the moment while paying attention to the present needs of the partner. To the audience, sitting in a horseshoe surrounding the dance, the actions seem to consecrate a special space for the dance's unfolding.

Red Green is an improvisation with Van Riper, Forti, and dancers Pooh Kaye and Terry O'Reilly. Like *Big Room* it comprises several basic blocks of activities, which are improvised in terms of timing, sequence, and the spatial relations between the dancers. The movement material includes walking and banking in figure eights and circles, crawling, rolling slowly in a flat prone position, walking into running, falling, bounding, and perching in a kneeling position, and popping off the floor. Forti also sits and then falls off balance, rolling on rounded back to sit again in a new direction. Each activity is explored for a stretch of time, backed by the rhythmic texture of the corresponding music block. Then the dancing switches to a new section of activity. Crawling and rolling remain themes that thread through the entire piece, but for the most part the sections are discrete. When the new action begins, the dancers drop what they were doing and begin the new movement, in a way that reminds one of a child reaching for a newly sighted toy and dropping the present one without regrets.

Planet is a large group piece that begins with about forty performers crawling, sitting, taking the crawl up to a walk and going back into the crawl. Then several performers did animal movements — including a bird (Pooh Kaye), a lion (Forti), an elephant (Sally Banes), a monkey (David Appel), three young bears (Anne Hammel, David Appel, Pooh Kaye), and lizards (Terry O'Reilly, David Taylor). Other actions for the smaller group include a *Huddle,* balancing and falling, running while singing high-pitched ululations, crawling and sitting. Finally, when the small group begins circling and banking, the large group gradually joins them until the entire auditorium, a former gym at Project Studios One in Long Island City, Queens, is filled with circling, leaning figures. The accompaniment is *Plumbing Music,* a sound tape by Van Riper.

Perhaps *Fan Dance* (1975) shows most clearly in theatrical terms Forti's sense of awe and closeness with the world of nature, with its mysteries and shadows. She enters the space, dressed in a black sweater and pants, holding two rattan fans which are natural-colored on one side and black on the other. In the space there is a plant (a fern on a stepladder, in the first version I saw), in front of a folding screen. As Forti moves in and out of heavy shadows, approaching the plant, she twirls the fans slowly, moving her arms so that at times she disappears completely in darkness, at times her presence is signaled with the light side of the fans. Music that sounds almost like crickets (Van Riper's *Three from Piru*) fills the air intermittently. She crouches by the plant, fans it with strong arms, walks in circles becoming visible and invisible. Suddenly Forti appears holding a rabbit-doll, which seems to be manipulating the fan in its paws. Like a Japanese puppeteer, she is invisible by convention as the tiny rabbit flaps the fans. Now the rabbit is gone, and Forti stands by the plant in profile, revealing and concealing her face alternately with the twisting fans. She fans the plant again, almost as if in ritual worship, and then falls back suddenly, somersaulting back, kneels and falls again, all the time continuing her ministrations to the fern. She begins to revolve around her own axis, spiraling her arms up around her face, and expanding the revolutions until they wobble in circles around the plant. She stops to stand in the shadow, watching the plant, then suddenly is gone.

Forti is a dancer who is emblematic of a moment in cultural history when a new naturalism daily seeks to uncover the secrets of the body and of various ecologies. She is a polemicist of a generation that investigates the border between nature and culture with curiosity and awe, and which promises comfort with each return to the basic. With her studies of caged animals, house plants, the geometries of the body, and discoveries of the maturing infant; with her compact body formulating and articulating comfortable shapes and movements, natural looking but riveting to watch; Forti makes dance another instrument in the ideology of organic living.

Simone Forti, Animal Stories[25]

Two chimps in a cage have a system worked out. A kind of music and dance which keeps them shifting around within earshot out of each other's way, a song and dance of protocol. There's pounding but never more than one hit or two at once, swinging from above arm over arm, changing location from the outside cage to the inside, and out again by turns avoiding each other, one calling the shots and playing its cage made instrument, a strong twig held in the teeth and twanged with a finger, never more than one twang or two at the time, then an arm swing and swing, pound, drop, change cages, pound, out again respecting protocol, the one calling the shots twanging once again and on.

A lion imprisoned, lethargic, accustomed to iron and concrete, roared a whole set to the rhythm of sawing, his belly like a bellows.

The rabbit locomotes by gathering all his energy at once; bounding.

Brown bear walk: front limb steps and whole side contracts to pull back limb into place. Boom, boo-boom. Boom, boo-boom. Boom, boo-boom. Giraffe. Back limb steps, crowds front limb which steps ahead: Boom-boom. Boom-boom.

The grizzly bear throws the weight of his great head up and around to wrench his whole frame into a sudden turn.

I saw an elephant who had perfected a movement with which he passed the time of day. It was a walking backwards and forwards, six or seven steps each way, with at either end a slight kick which served to absorb the momentum and to reverse the direction of travel of that great and finely balanced bulk.

The embrace is arboreal.

Yvonne Rainer: The Aesthetics of Denial

YVONNE RAINER was the most prolific and polemical of the Judson Dance Theater choreographers. She was championed by Jill Johnston as the exemplar of post-modern choreography, and frequently, to her own displeasure, the post-modern movement with all its diversity of interests, styles, and methods was collapsed by the public into a single enterprise with Rainer in the lead. After Judson, she choreographed large group works using both professional and nonprofessional dancers in the late 1960s, explored the relationships between different aspects of the performance process during the performance itself, and gave more and more freedom to her performers in regard to choosing the sequence of material in the dance. By the early 1970s, she had extricated herself from the leadership of Grand Union, the group that partly developed out of her own piece *Continuous Project — Altered Daily* (see chapter 11), and resumed a directorial role in dances increasingly concerned with narrative and personae. Her changing concerns in subject matter and focus led to the use of film, and in 1973, Rainer stopped choreographing to devote her time to film making.

Rainer was born in San Francisco in 1934. She wanted to be an actress, and did some performing in California before moving to New York in 1956. The following year, feeling dissatisfied with her acting classes, she took some dance classes at a friend's suggestion. She began her studies with Edith Stephen; soon she decided to seriously train to become a dancer, and took classes at the Graham studio twice a day, and ballet classes once a day. She recalls that at the Graham studio, "I was the worst in the class, very slow to learn about my body, very unmusical, always off the beat, had to follow the

Yvonne Rainer in a studio shot of *Trio A*. Photograph © Jack Mitchell, 1982.

person in front of me."[1] But still, she got the impression that her teachers thought there was something special about her dancing. "To me Graham was the only important person around then. I wasn't too aware of what Cunningham was up to. It had to do with Graham as a woman and an innovator."[2]

In 1960, on Simone Forti's recommendation, she returned to San Francisco for the summer to take a workshop with Ann Halprin. There she met Trisha Brown, La Monte Young, A. A. Leath, and John Graham. She was impressed by Halprin's use of movement while holding objects, but she was especially interested in the other people in the workshop.[3] Returning to New York that fall, Rainer shared a studio with Forti and Robert Morris, and she performed in Forti's *See-Saw.* She took classes at the Cunningham studio, including Robert Dunn's composition workshop. After the second year of the Dunn workshop, she was instrumental (along with Steve Paxton and Ruth Emerson) in organizing the Judson Dance Theater. From 1961 to 1965 she also danced with James Waring.

In her early dances (those of the first half of the 1960s), Rainer's style was eclectic, theatrical, almost surrealistic. Sounds and movements were often juxtaposed in arbitrary combinations. The chance methods embraced by Cunningham and then Robert Dunn led Rainer to use streams of movements connected alogically, but movements that were of a different ilk than those used by Cunningham. They included not only dance-technical steps and gestures, but also quirky motions like twiddling the fingers in front of the face (*The Bells,* 1961), drawing lines on her body with her finger (*Three Satie Spoons,* 1961), and having a screaming fit with a winter coat and a length of white gauze (*Three Seascapes,* 1962). Within the aleatory structure she used a great deal of repetition. Her dances also used noises that emanated, like the gestures, in an apparent stream of consciousness from her body: barks, wails, squeaks, beeps, grunts, mumbles, shrieks.

Soon she became concerned with the investigation of the everyday. *Ordinary Dance* (1962) repeated simple movements while Rainer recited a poetic autobiography. In *We Shall Run* (1963), twelve people in street clothes, not all of them dancers, ran for seven minutes in various floor patterns to the "Tuba Miram" of Berlioz's *Requiem.*

An important turning point in her choreography came in 1964 with a performance of *Room Service,* a piece generated by a game structure. Three teams of people, playing follow-the-leader in an environment created by sculptor Charles Ross, lugged furniture, among other activities. The game structure, task-oriented movements, and manipulation of objects converged to strip the movements of their expressive qualities. The use of objects altered both the types of movements used and the manner of performance. Both became functional, direct, natural in the sense that they were not stylized. The objects removed the drama from the dance performance, substituting a purposive, directed concentration. For Rainer, to lug a mattress in and out of the theater "seemed to be so self-contained an act as to require no artistic tampering or justification."[4] Movement itself became like an object, something to be examined coolly without psychological, social, or even formal motives. Like Alain Robbe-Grillet calling for a new novel without character, story, or commitment, Rainer proposed a new dance that would recognize the objective presence of things, including movements and the human body. Partly in reaction to her own early theatricality, partly in repudiation of the practice of most modern dance then current, and influenced by the theories of phenomenologists and visual artists, Rainer opted for neutrality, refusing to project a persona or make a narrative. She might have said of dance, as Robbe-Grillet said of the novel:

> Let it be first of all by their *presence* that objects and gestures establish themselves, and let this presence continue to prevail over whatever explanatory theory that may try to enclose them in a system of references, whether emotional, sociological, Freudian or metaphysical. . . . We had thought to control [the world around us] by assigning it a meaning, and the entire art of the novel, in particular, seemed dedicated to this enterprise. But this was merely an illusory simplification; and far from becoming clearer and closer because of it, the world has only, little by little, lost all its life.[5]

Descriptive activity, rather than an attempt to probe beneath surfaces for mysterious, "deeper" meaning, was the corrective for the crisis of modern literature Robbe-Grillet offered, the antidote Rainer recommended for modern dance. In 1965, she formulated a strategy for demystifying dance and making it objective. It was a strategy of denial:

> NO to spectacle no to virtuosity no to transformations and magic and make-believe no to the glamour and transcendency of the star image no to the heroic no to the anti-heroic no to trash imagery no to involvement of performer or spectator no to style no to camp no to seduction of spectator by the wiles of the performer no to eccentricity no to moving or being moved.[6]

What was left for the choreographer and dancer? Something that was neither drama, nor the imagery of Happenings, nor the assault of spectator participation. Something that perhaps could only be fully realized in the imagination, the reduction of dance to its essentials.

The reductions continued. With *Trio A,* Rainer created a paradigmatic statement of the aesthetic goals of post-modern dance. The short dance, or long phrase (depending on one's perspective), exemplifies a new way of making and looking at dance, one that would influence a whole genre for at least twelve years. Because I believe that *Trio A* is the signal work both for Rainer and for the entire post-modern dance, I will devote the rest of this chapter to an analysis of it.

In 1966, Rainer made *Trio A,* intending to remove objects from the dance but hoping to retain the workmanlike attitude of task performance. She set out to systematically test her concerns regarding the distribution of energy, phrasing, and repetition (both as organizational strategies and as agents of style). Her theoretical groundwork was laid out in her essay, "A Quasi Survey of Some 'Minimalist' Tendencies in the Quantitatively Minimal Dance Activity Midst the Plethora, or an Analysis of *Trio A.*"[7] Her chart in that article (see p. 55) draws parallels between her own reductionism in dance and that of the minimalist sculptors who were her friends and colleagues. Without entirely restricting post-modern dance to the rigid categories suggested by the chart, she notes the salient points of divergence with conventional dance aesthetics. For phrasing, development and climax, variation, character, performance, variety, the virtuosic feat and the fully extended body, Rainer would substitute energy equality and "found" movement, equality of parts, repetition or discrete events, neutral performance, task or tasklike activity, singular action, event, or tone, and human scale.[8]

Yet at the same time Rainer operated dialectically in making *Trio A,* in regard to dance technique if not style or structure. Violating nearly every canon of classic dance conventions (both ballet and modern), she brought classical lines and gestures into conflict with their own subversions, to create an entirely new mode of dance. After *Trio A,* the choreographic terrain looked different. The boundaries of dance had burst open. Certain actions, certain postures, certain attitudes now became possible, and eventually familiar, parts of the vocabulary.

Trio A was a four-and-one-half-minute phrase originally performed as a set of three simultaneous solos by Yvonne Rainer, Steve Paxton, and David

Gordon at the Judson Church on January 10, 1966. It was then called *The Mind is a Muscle, Part 1.*

As Rainer points out in her essay on the work, "Dance is hard to see. It must either be made less fancy, or the fact of that intrinsic difficulty must be emphasized to the point that it becomes almost impossible to see."[9] Here Rainer clearly sets forth the two alternative solutions for the choreographer concerned with surmounting the ultimate difficulty the ephemeral nature of dance provokes: one can drastically simplify — as Lucinda Childs and Deborah Hay, for example, have chosen to do — or one can complicate the dance so that its instant disappearance becomes the subject of the choreography — as did Rainer in *Trio A,* Steve Paxton in his solo improvisations, and Douglas Dunn in *Gestures in Red. Trio A* is not fancy, but it is certainly not simple. It is a difficult, demanding work to watch. The entire four-and-one-half-minute series of constant changes in motion is performed as a single phrase with an uninflected distribution of energy, giving the appearance of a smooth, effortless surface. Yet obviously many of the movement events are quite complex and strenuous. The fact that there are no pauses between the events increases the scope of the effort. The paradox of the dance's appearance is that what looks easy and natural is actually very exacting. The movements have been carefully dissected, and in order to create the uninflected rhythm even the "natural" phrasing that nondance movements have in real life — i.e., the preparation, climax, and completion that seem to come with our breath cycle — has been flattened, equalized. Transitions come to appropriate equal time and weight to that of a handstand or balance on one leg. But the opposite side of the paradox is that those aspects of movement conventionally de-emphasized, like transitions or awkward moments, suddenly gain in stature. The difficulty of balance, for instance, is heightened rather than concealed or surmounted when the torso twists back and forth while the single supporting leg bends deeply. The dance fluctuates between letting the labor of its execution appear and disappear.

There are virtually no repetitions in the movement series, except certain strings of repetitions that constitute discrete events, e.g., four low swings of the arms in front and in back of the body, which begin the dance; ten taps of the foot, repeated on each side, that make a stuttered rond de jambe about a minute into the dance; a series of backward kicks interspersed with crouches and lunges near the end. That is, aside from the internal repetitiveness of some event modules, the modules themselves are not repeated or varied or developed in other ways. Each module is a distinct activity, and the dance is the chain or list of those modules. (Some locomotor transitions, however, like walking in a circle or part of a circle, are repeated throughout.) Yet so many of the actions look similar that one gains an overall impression of repetition in the midst of the insistent proliferation of unrelated movement material. There are rotations, twists, and circles of different parts of the body; relaxed swings, squats, lunges, and rolls of the head; a deeper rhythm, under the monotone, of the recurrent collapse and stretch of the body. The homogeneity of the execution masks the utter disjunctiveness of the series.

Thus on the first viewing of *Trio A* the undeviating effort (i.e., distribution of energy) acts like glue, making the phrase look like one coherent object, composed of similar actions. One notices primarily the salient features of a particular style, of a whole rather than the details of its parts. It is a style that diverges noticeably from classic dance. Overall, the stance is rather narrow, a quotidian stance, neither turned out as in ballet, nor extremely narrow as in the Graham school, nor a stylized openness as in Humphrey-Weidman technique, nor the elegant tension between turned out and parallel of the Cunningham style. There are some wide moments, creating occasional stark contrasts to the unemphatic vertical. Three body parts are equally conspicuous as loci of activity: the arms, the whole torso, and the feet. They are often set in motion either simultaneously or in close canon, so that the effect is of three unconnected activities happening in three different parts of the body. It is, on reflection, a redoubling of the feat of patting one's head and rubbing one's stomach. The head is also frequently brought into motion. But from time to time, the whole action is simply centered in the legs and feet, the arms hanging down relaxed, the rest of the body quiet. The body reaches the full stretch typical of ballet and modern dance only at the points of transition. Thus whenever the eye finds a familiar "line" to rest on, that line is disrupted and the spectator's comfort subverted. The dancer's gaze is never directed toward the audience. It is either averted by looking down or to the side when facing front, or it is directed away from the spectators because of the facing of the body away from front. The step style is generally low. Though there are some small jumps and leaps, as well as skips, overall the feet stay close to the ground. The foot is relaxed, rejecting both the arched tension of ballet and Cunningham, and the flexion typical of Graham and Humphrey. The most common method of locomotion is an ordinary walk, with some sliding and gentle tapping. For the most part the body level, too, is in the middle range. There are descents to the floor, and frequently, actions on the floor — a continuous prone roll toward the back of the stage, a cross-legged sit seguing into a backward somersault, a cumbersome hoist and flip of the entire body while partly kneeling. But despite this constant up and down activity, the overall look is that of action taking place at a medium level. There is very little work that goes into the air, above standing level. The space seems relatively unimportant, even though the actions trace a clearly discernible floor plan. The performer's attitude toward weight is neither buoyant and light, nor extremely strong or heavy. Generally, what emerges is a weight effort that looks "actual," that seems to correspond to the kind of effort one expends unconsciously on everyday actions.

In sum, the movement style is factual (matter-of-fact, direct, nonillusionistic), unexaggerated, unemphatic. Neither weight, nor time, nor space factors are noticeably stylized or emphasized. The one factor that is obviously altered and manipulated is the flow of movement. This is the device that makes the other factors recede.

But on subsequent viewings of *Trio A*, one notices not the congruence and similarity of the movements, but their diversity and wealth. Rainer herself refers to the deliberate attempt which "dealt with the 'seeing' difficulty by dint of its continual and unremitting revelation of gestural detail that did not repeat itself, thereby focusing on the fact that the material could not be easily encompassed."[10] The dance is a kind of catalogue of movement possibilities and combinations for the human body. There are ways the arms are held, the leg is turned, the head is lowered, the chest is sunk, the body squats, the ankle is grabbed, and different actions are put together, that seem to happen for the first time in the dance. Because her concern in the work was to do away with what she called the "preening" look of virtuoso dancing, Rainer could find and use awkward, unusual, or unexpected movements, without turning the piece into an idiosyncrasy. Instead, the cataloging looks systematic — though it is a system one would find difficult to predict — because so many movement possibilities are analytically tested. The sense of systematic invention comes, too, from the impersonal performance presence, and from the conscious criticism of Western dance embedded in the actions, a generative denial of the aesthetics of elegance, brilliance, *ballon*,* and virtuosity.[11] Of course, the early modern choreographers had rejected that aesthetic in the 1930s, going to the earth to get down from the aerial pointe work that was ballet's triumph, casting away their shoes to re-establish contact with the

* A ballet term for a light, elastic quality during jumps.

ground, giving in to gravity with the fall, recovering from the fall with a surge of breath, making movements that look harsh and weighty. But Rainer worked at a time when that revolution had faded, when even Graham's movements were becoming softer, when her epigones and the followers of Humphrey-Weidman had sweetened and smoothed the fruits of the rebellion, and when even the radical Cunningham had restored grace and elegance to the dance. And Rainer's awkward or weighty movements are different from those of the "black woolens" period of the 1930s: they are neither emphasized nor abstracted, but resemble "found" movements, autonomous, seeming to take their own time rather than fitting into the structured time slots of a dance's design, seeming to appropriate their own effort and proportion of the body's weight. There is no effect or design they are meant to contribute toward. And finally, Rainer's compositional structure deviates radically from the symmetries and musical forms of modern dance, depriving each movement of a secure position in a hierarchical arrangement of parts.

So it is not surprising that *Trio A* broke ballet conventions over half a century after modern dance set itself the task of repudiating ballet. Yet it is significant that in refusing the conventions of modern dance it builds on that earlier repudiation. It creates a world in which there are no longer two possibilities for movement but a multitude. It is a stringently antiballetic work. The turnout and carriage typical of ballet (and later, typical of Cunningham) are constantly achieved and then abandoned during the flow of the dance: one recognizes them only fleetingly, for they disappear instantly, and the red thread of subversion runs through every one. The head is turned, or one hand is held in a fist, or a shoulder rises sharply, or the arms swivel in the shoulder sockets. Some body parts at times seem to have the "correct" look, but rarely in alignment with all the other body parts at once. The lack of plot development in the phrasing, the antivirtuosic baring of workliness in certain of the movements — as when the back is rounded and dropped forward toward the floor while one foot is held just off the ground, so that the problems of balance are made the object of attention as the hands and head approach ground level; or when the dancer changes from one sitting position to another, leaving the leg in the same place so that suddenly it is bent outward and backward — and the straightforward angles of presentation of the body, and the fact that at the beginning of the dance the performer faces to the side and the dance ends with the performer's back to the audience: all these features drastically violate the canons of classic theatrical dancing.

The focus of the spectator's vision is led to the individual movement unit by several interlocking aspects of the dance: the attitude of involvement, the task orientation, the uninflected rhythm, and the discreteness of the units. This reorientation of vision and attention continues and expands Cunningham's achievement, which was to focus attention on the phrase.

The history of dance theory has been the repeated conflict between those who value technique and those who value expression. Those who followed Rameau and those who followed Lully at the turn of the eighteenth century, the fans of Marie Camargo and Marie Sallé, the Petipas versus the Fokines, the balletomanes against the modern dance advocates in the early twentieth century, the Cunninghamites and the Grahamites — all these conflicts have pitted technique against expression in cycles for centuries. With Rainer's *Trio A* the cycle is at last broken. The debate is made irrelevant. The possibility is proposed that dance is neither perfection of technique nor of expression, but quite something else — the presentation of objects in themselves. It is not simply a new style of dance, but a new meaning and function, a new definition of dance, that has appeared.

In thinking about *Trio A,* I have found Martin Heidegger's essay, "The Origin of the Work of Art," useful. Here the philosopher reflects on the artwork's source, rejecting the idea that it originates in the artist. He identifies the "thingly" and "workly" characteristics of works of art, showing how the work is neither a mere thing, nor an equipmental thing that uses up its material:

> In fabricating equipment — e.g., an ax — stone is used, and used up. It disappears into usefulness . . . By contrast the temple-work, in setting up a world, does not cause the material to disappear, but rather causes it to come forth for the very first time and to come into the Open of the work's world. The rock comes to bear and rest and so first becomes rock; metals come to glitter and shimmer, colors to glow, tones to sing, the word to speak. All this comes forth as the work sets itself back into the massiveness and heaviness of stone, into the firmness and pliancy of wood, into the hardness and luster of metal, into the lighting and darkening of color, into the clang of tone, and into the naming power of the word.[12]

Admittedly, Heidegger's interpretive writing seems more "expressive" than the aesthetic this particular text suggests. Still, we might extend his reflection to dance in regard to the unique, essential materials of its work: mind, muscle, and movement. For Heidegger, the origin of the work of art is in art, because "art is by nature an origin: a distinctive way in which truth comes into being, that is, becomes historical."[13] The artwork, making creative strife between "world" and "earth" — i.e., between the social world or the set of relations between humans, tools, natural things, and the natural realm or that which remains secluded, impenetrable, concealed — finds a way to bring the earth into the open without violating it. "In setting up a world, the work sets forth the earth."[14] The work shows itself to have been created, and by this workly aspect provides a framework for the thingly nature of its material. It lets the "unconcealedness," the truth of being, shine forth, at the same time that it protects the self-contained nature of its material. And in this process, "the artist remains inconsequential as compared with the work, almost like a passageway that destroys itself in the creative process for the work to emerge."[15]

In *Trio A* there is, in Heidegger's terms, a conflict between the refusal and dissembling of concealment. "At bottom, the ordinary is not ordinary; it is extra-ordinary, uncanny."[16] In the dance Rainer shows us ordinary movements as strange, at the same time making strange movements fall into place next to the extraordinary ordinary uses of the body.

Another ambiguity is the contradictory sense that there is a depersonalization of movement and the body, and a simultaneous zeroing in on the ways of the body. The personal disappears into the general. The role of the artist's hand, a stamp of personal style or idiosyncrasy, fades. In the same way, the distinctive performance presence of the dancer is obliterated, blotted out by the workly concentration and withdrawn face in much the same way that in Rainer's *New Untitled Partially Improvised Solo with Pink T-Shirt, Blue Bloomers, Red Ball, and Bach's Toccata and Fugue in D Minor* (1965) she eliminated personal projection by painting her face black. Yet at the same time that the artist and performer fade into the background of *Trio A*, the special qualities of hands, palms, arms, legs, joints, the head, the spine, the chest, all the ways of moving the body, all the varieties of posture and carriage "shine forth." The dance seems to make a clearing in which the spectator is freed to notice the extraordinary aspects of both mundane and dancerly movement. Now the tension of an extended leg is called to our notice, now the remarkable logistics of turning the body over itself and shifting weight, which results in a somersault. Now we focus on the particular angle of the pelvis, as it rocks in and out of its ordinary position, or on the way the hands stretch to meet behind the back, or the variety of ways the arms can circle in relation to the rest of the body. The process of isolation makes each movement pronounced, but at the same time the structure of the dance is covertly complex. The articulation of each discrete gesture, twist, circle, shift, or step occurs in an intricate chain of other, simultaneous and multifarious events. What appears to be a string or line of object/movements is, in fact, a braid. But the braid is so tightly secured by the monotone rhythm that it forms itself in the spectator's vision and memory as a single, long, indivisible figure. It is too long and dense and variegated to hold on to. Yet one experiences it as something that unrolls smoothly and seamlessly, even while the seams are showing.

Lincoln Kirstein refers to the development of the pirouette as the apogee of dance. "It displays in simultaneous plasticity all aspects of the turning column of the dancer's body. It is an ultimate emphasis of its tri-dimensionality. An audience cannot encircle the dancer; hence, the dancer revolves, presenting himself in completeness to his audience."[17] In the pirouette, developed and perfected by the virtuosic male dancers of the pre-Romantic ballet, the arrest, emblematic of the dancer's uprightness, provides a clear contrast, a sudden immobility, which stands against the whirl of movement that had preceded it. *Trio A* is a post-modern answer to the pirouette, a denial of classic dance that is also its expansion. In *Trio A* also the body constantly revolves, circling back on itself in physical and spatial configurations, presenting every aspect and angle of the body to the spectator. But what a difference in presentation: the body never stops, never conceals its up and downness, in and outness, emphasizing a continuum of motion over the sharp contrasts of eighteenth-century style. The beauty of *Trio A* lies not in ideas of grace, elegance, dramatic expression, or even of nature, but in the material truth of its coexistent presence and distance.

Trio A was performed for the first time in 1966 as *The Mind is a Muscle, Part 1* at the Judson Church. It was done twice, to the "musical" accompaniment of wooden slats thrown regularly, one at a time, from the church balcony. In a longer but still not complete version of *The Mind is a Muscle,* also performed at the Judson, in May 1966, Rainer created a special version of *Trio A* for Peter Saul, a balletic version with a pirouette or jump inserted "wherever possible."[18] That version, a solo, was titled "Lecture." The final version of *The Mind is a Muscle* was performed at the Anderson Theater on April 11, 14, and 15, 1968. In it, *Trio A* was danced once as a trio by three men and once as the solo "Lecture." It was the nucleus of an eight-part evening, with nine interludes of music and dialogue, which also included *Trio B*, a unison sequence of traveling movements for three women, and *Trio A*[1], a sequence of three male dancers taking turns hoisting each other while traveling diagonally between two mattresses. Peter Saul could not appear in the final version of the piece to do "Lecture"; Rainer remembers,

> I had grandiose fantasies of Jacques D'Amboise appearing at the end from nowhere to perform a bravura *Trio A*. Next in line (in my fantasy dance) was Merce Cunningham. I became obsessed with this idea and eventually proposed it to him at a party. He laughingly declined. I finally did it myself in tap shoes (minus the balletic furbelows) with the slats shot in from a ladder in the wings, and with a wooden grid that filled the proscenium space descending in the middle of the solo. It stayed down for one minute, then ascended out of sight.[19]

Trio A became a Rainer emblem, appearing in seven of her works besides *The Mind is a Muscle.* In 1967, at Angry Arts Week protesting the war in Vietnam, Rainer, recovering from a recent operation, danced *Trio A*, calling it *Convalescent Dance.* She thinks of that performance as the most perfectly realized version of the sequence, since her convalescent state suffused her performance with exactly the right quality of lightness.[20] In *Performance Demonstration no. 1* (September 1968), *Trio A* was performed in several different versions: once by Steve Paxton, which was "made splendidly flamboyant by virtue of his bare chest and *In the Midnight Hour* of the Chambers Brothers"[21]; once by Frances Brooks, the first nonprofessional (untrained) dancer to perform the sequence; once by Becky Arnold, who learned the phrase onstage while Rainer corrected her, the first of many rehearsal moments installed in Rainer's performances.

In *Rose Fractions* (February 1969), performed at the Billy Rose Theater, among other activities *Trio A* was done to "In the Midnight Hour." (During her "slot" in that performance, part of an avant-garde dance festival, she gave space to Deborah Hay who presented *26 Variations on 8 Activities for 13 People and Beginning and Ending.* This gesture was another protest against the cult of personality in the dance world.)[22] In *Performance Fractions for the West Coast* (April 1969), it was again taught during performance, and also danced to the Chambers Brothers' song. And in *Connecticut Composite* (July 1969), at the American Dance Festival in New London, Connecticut, *Trio A* was performed continuously in one room of the college gym, while a continuous lecture on the dance played on tape in another room, and films, a "people wall," "people plans," an "audience piece" (*Chair-Pillow*), and the germinal *Continuous Project — Altered Daily* were all going on in other rooms.

Rainer was invited to participate in the Judson Flag Show in November 1970, a protest by various artists of the arrests of people charged with desecrating the American flag. Her contribution was a version of *Trio A* danced twice by six people who wore only an American flag tied like a bib around the neck. And even in her last performance, the complex narrative *This is the story of a woman who . . .* (March 1973), a mix of slides, films, stories, dances, and personae, *Trio A* was included, "marked" once, and then danced to Grieg piano pieces.

Rainer conceived of the dance in populist terms:

> When I first began teaching *Trio A* to anyone who wanted to learn it — skilled, unskilled, professional, fat, old, sick, amateur — and gave tacit permission to anyone who wanted to teach it to teach it, I envisioned myself as a post-modern dance evangelist bringing movement to the masses, watching with Will Rogers-like benignity the slow, inevitable evisceration of my elitist creation. Well, I finally met a *Trio A* I didn't like. It was 5th generation, and I couldn't believe my eyes.[23]

Thus the spread of *Trio A* reached not only into Rainer's own works but also into other performances. When Grand Union began its improvisatory evenings, David Gordon recalls, he fell back on doing the sequence whenever he felt he might run out of things to do.[24] Other dancers and choreographers worked *Trio A* into their concerts and compositions, including Pat Catterson who performed it in retrograde in 1971, and incorporated part of it into her *Serial II* (1975).

"In setting up a world, the work sets forth the earth." *Trio A* tells us of a world in which people use their bodies with skill, intelligence, coordination, and economy. The skill it embodies is an unpretentious one which, though it requires effort and concentration, does not demand any special status or training for its proper performance. The dance speaks of a healthy, direct joy in the body's capabilities, in its powers of memory and organizational faculties, as well as "its actual weight, mass, and unenhanced physicality."[25] It also speaks of the profound pleasures of work, of a productive intellect guiding and being guided by physical ingenuity. Frequently in *Trio A* parts of the body lead the rest of the body into a new movement, seemingly predicting or causing that new branch of motion. The process is a metaphor for the intelligence of the human body. The organism is not merely a marvelous machine with levers of bone, gears and pulleys of ligaments and muscles, the dance tells. We are creatures made of mind and muscle, inseparable from each other. The fully conscious moving body is one that is fully alive. It is one that needs to work. And it is one that is capable of exerting both control and ease.

William B. Yeats wrote that

> Samuel Butler was the first Englishman to make the discovery that it is possible to write with great effect without music, without style, either good or bad, to eliminate from the mind all emotional implication and to prefer plain water to every vintage, so much metropolitan lead and solder to any tendril of the vine.[26]

The achievement of *Trio A* is its resolute denial of style and expression, making a historical shift in the subject of dance to pure motion. Not even posture or architecture enter into its projection of what dance finally is, at rock bottom.[27] In its neutrality, complexity, fleetingness and ongoingness, *Trio A* sets up a world of thoughtful activity that sets forth the earthly, intelligent body.

Yvonne Rainer, Chart from "A Quasi Survey of Some 'Minimalist' Tendencies in the Quantitatively Minimal Dance Activity Midst the Plethora, or an Analysis of *Trio A*"[28]

Objects	Dances
eliminate or minimize	
1. role of artist's hand	phrasing
2. hierarchical relationship of parts	development and climax
3. texture	variation: rhythm, shape, dynamics
4. figure reference	character
5. illusionism	performance
6. complexity and detail	variety: phrases and the spatial field
7. monumentality	the virtuosic movement feat and the fully extended body
substitute	
1. factory fabrication	energy equality and "found" movement
2. unitary forms, modules	equality of parts, repetition
3. uninterrupted surface	repetition or discrete events
4. nonreferential forms	neutral performance
5. literalness	task or tasklike activity
6. simplicity	singular action, event, or tone
7. human scale	human scale

Steve Paxton: Physical Things

STEVE PAXTON makes dances about ordinary, physical things. Ironically, in their close attention to pedestrian activities and the bodies of everyday people, the dances have at times served extraordinary functions; they have assaulted theatrical conventions, commented on the history of dance and questioned its aims, examined social hierarchies and political acts. In his early dances, Paxton used formal structures and depersonalized methods of teaching the choreography to build frameworks for commonplace steps, especially the act of walking itself. He used prosaic objects made gigantic or texturally altered to emphasize the importance of the ordinary. In the mid-1970s, he was instrumental in organizing and disseminating a new dance form: Contact Improvisation, a democratic duet format incorporating elements of martial arts, social dancing, sports and child's play. In the late '70s, concentrating on teaching, performing, and writing about Contact Improvisation around the country and in Europe, he has also collaborated with musician David Moss, doing solo dance improvisations to Moss' complex percussion accompaniment.

Some audiences and critics have loved Paxton for his revelation of the body as a physical machine, his generous, easygoing yet serious attitude toward his work, and the democratic structure informing the dances. To his advocates, he is a grassroots organizer, a populist finding new social forms through dance, and an analyst of human form, discovering in performance just how the body works, then working it in appropriate ways; or finding out how the theatrical machine works, then changing it, offering alternatives. Paxton himself speaks of his work as deeply involved with conveying information: "We are privileged to pass on the sensitizing information, relaxing information,

Steve Paxton in *Backwater: Twosome*. Photograph © Johan Elbers, 1977.

strengthening information, information of the forces-that-be," he has written in regard to teaching Contact Improvisation.[1]

Those who are critical of Paxton's work argue that it is boring or didactic; that it lacks aesthetic structure, or looks too much like everyday life. Censors have prevented the performance of dances they thought would turn out to be pornographic, or simply not altogether chaste. Paxton's response to censorship has often been to substitute a different performance, one that ends up criticizing scathingly the set of social conventions that condemns nudity and curtails civil liberties while it tolerates war and other serious criminal acts.

Steve Paxton began dancing in high school in Tucson, Arizona. A gymnast, he was offered a scholarship by a girl friend's dance teacher; he accepted, thinking it would improve his tumbling. Soon he was dancing and touring with two proponents of Martha Graham's technique, "one holding forth at the Jewish Community Center, the other [an Episcopal nun] holding forth at the convent out in the desert. That was my background for seeing Cunningham," Paxton reminisces wryly. "Doing religious dances. Morality plays. And Jewish folk dances."[2]

In the summer of 1958, at nineteen, Paxton went to sudy at the academy of modern dance, Connecticut College, where Graham, José Limón, Doris Humphrey, and Merce Cunningham were teaching. It was the first time the modern dance establishment had opened its doors to Cunningham and his company. Paxton was immediately attracted to them. Arriving in New York later, he studied with Cunningham, danced with Limón's company in 1959 in both New York and Connecticut, and worked with other performers: Yvonne Rainer, Robert Rauschenberg, Deborah Hay, Lucinda Childs, Trisha Brown, Simone Forti. He took Robert Dunn's composition course at the Cunningham studio in 1960–1961, and remembers being impressed by Dunn's teaching method. "He taught us ideas almost by neglecting us, by mentioning things but tending to disappear at the same time, leaving with a smile." For Paxton, Dunn's use of musical form was crucial as a key to time, and as a depersonalized scheme for ordering movement material. "When you listen to a piece of music, you listen to intervals, sections and structures. You aren't involved with personality and states of presence."

Paxton recalls other iconoclastic influences: the Living Theater, the Paper Bag Players, James Waring, Jackson MacLow, Diane DiPrima, and others. The Living Theater worked in the same building, at 14th Street and 6th Avenue, where Cunningham had his studio. "As an environment it was very permissive and form oriented. The Living Theater was talking about prison reform and doing plays like *The Connection.* It was where I first saw the peace symbol, where I first saw dope smoked. And I was trying to find concepts that hadn't been dealt with by these people, who we thought had already done everything."

In 1961, he was invited to join Merce Cunningham's company, and he danced in it until 1964, continuing meanwhile to collaborate with colleagues, making his own works, and playing an instrumental role in organizing the Judson Dance Theater in 1962. Paxton traces some of his concerns in his early choreography to his criticisms of work with Cunningham. He felt that one weakness of Cunningham's work — a quality that has been praised by others — was that he refrained from telling the dancers how to perform the movement material, aside from specifying the formal qualities of the movement itself. "You were meant to fill in everything yourself, or else to leave it unfilled — which was what most people did, so that they had a zombie-like appearance at worst."

Another criticism was the hierarchical social structure of the company, which Paxton felt pervaded the performances as well as the work time. The beginnings of modern dance — the work of Isadora Duncan and, later, Rudolf Laban's analysis of movement — had promised freedom and egalitarianism, Paxton thought. Yet everywhere he looked, even in the company considered most radical and democratic, Paxton saw dictatorships and star systems, "the ballet format with a different twist." He was concerned that audiences watching dance performances would leave feeling that their own movement was not worth exploring. And despite Cunningham's innovations in using chance choreographic techniques, and his nonchalance about teaching his dancers stage presence, Paxton still searched for a method of transmitting movement to dancers that would be even less direct and less subjective than personal demonstration.

Proxy (1961), made shortly after Paxton joined the Cunningham company, and conceived while riding in the company's Volkswagen bus on tour, was the child of these preoccupations. A dance in four sections, the movement in the middle two parts was determined by a visual score made from sports photographs and other posture imagery. Each dancer learned the sequences accurately, but according to his or her own individual style, working to imitate each pose exactly and to find efficient transitions between them. In the other sections of the dance, the performers did specific actions: eating a pear, drinking a glass of water, standing on ball bearings in a plastic basin. And they walked.

In retrospect, Paxton realized, the walking was crucial. It opened up a range of nondance movement, a variety of nonhierarchical structures, a performance presence that could be simultaneously relaxed and authoritative. It became the currency of Paxton's populist stance. Walking is something that everyone does, even dancers when they are not "on." Walking is a sympathetic link between performers and spectators, a shared experience that allows for personal idiosyncrasies and individual styles. There is no single correct way of walking. Anyone's method is appropriate for that person. Walking, like eating, drinking, telling stories, smiling, getting dressed and undressed, and even some kinds of patterned dancing, provided a wealth of material for Paxton's investigations over the next nearly two decades.

In *Transit* (1962), Paxton compared three types of movement: classical dance, "marked dance" (movements performed at low energy level), and running in slow motion. *English* (1963) used a walking pace as its rhythm, though its activities included group configurations and pantomimes of routine activities.

But *Satisfyin Lover* (1967) was the apotheosis of walking. It is a dance for a large group of people (from thirty to eighty-four), who walk from stage right to stage left, stopping to stand or sit according to a written score.[3] Jill Johnston, commenting on a 1968 version of the piece, wrote that she was impressed with

> the incredible assortment of bodies, the any old bodies of our any old lives . . . . walking one after the other across the gymnasium in their any old clothes. The fat, the skinny, the medium, the slouched and slumped, the straight and tall, the bowlegged and knock-kneed, the awkward, the elegant, the coarse, the delicate, the pregnant, the virginal, the you name it, by implication every postural possibility in the postural spectrum, that's you and me in all our ordinary everyday who cares postural splendor.[4]

In 1970, Paxton planned to do a version of *Satisfyin Lover* with forty-two naked red-haired performers for a concert date at New York University, but at the last minute school authorities ruled out nudity, even though Paxton had notified them of his intentions from the start. It was too late to cancel the concert, so Paxton performed *Intravenous Lecture* instead. As he talked to the audience about past experiences with sponsors and censorship, a doctor friend walked onstage and inserted an intravenous hookup in Paxton's arm. Clear liquid (a saline solution) seeped into Paxton's veins and blood sometimes backed up in the plastic tubing, but he ignored the whole matter, continuing to speak calmly about performance. His performance made clear his conviction that censorship is more violent, more obscene than either the nudity would have been, or the medical attack actually was.

State (1968) is another walking piece for a large group, in which the forty-two performers walk to the center of the area and stand in a random, scattered grouping. For two three-minute intervals they simply stand. During two fifteen-second blackouts they can "move, adjust or scratch."[5] Then they exit. In *Smiling* (1969), two performers smile for five minutes. They have the option to sit or stand, but they may not relate too strongly with the audience ("that becomes too aggressive," Paxton notes).[6]

The ordinary use of commonplace objects and the body, begun in *Proxy*, was one strategy Paxon used to question theatrical habits and expectations. One important theatrical convention that pedestrian activity assaults is the transformation of time and rhythm. In classical Western theater, conversations are packed more tightly than they are in real life; performers can go through whole lifetimes, or generations, within a few hours. Time on stage is the artificial, manipulated time scheme of an extraordinary world. In most classical ballet and in much of modern dance, even those movements based on walking and other everyday actions are patterned into uncommon rhythms. Cunningham shocked the dance world by incorporating actions like brushing teeth or riding a bicycle into his pieces. Yet those doings were always deeply embedded in a rhythmic, abstract movement design. That was partly why they were shocking. The notion that a simple activity — untransformed rhythmically — could have its own aesthetic significance was a concern Paxton shared with Rainer, Hay, Childs, and other choreographers. It related, as well, to performance and visual concerns of artists like Robert Morris and Robert Rauschenberg: that the simple fact of a theatrical setting, or a gallery setting, could transform ordinary time or ordinary materials into a work of art. Morris, writing about *Proxy*, felt that Paxton was remarkable for his unique use of time: he reduced the incidence of action, and distributed it in an uneventful, even way.[7]

In many of the early works, Paxton used commonplace objects to emphasize the concreteness of the body as it manipulated those objects. Yet he often delighted in using unusual items, too: everyday things made fantastic not by means of a theatrical frame, but because texture, materials or size had been radically altered; animals; and parts of an environment not usually attended to. In *Flat* (1964), Paxton took off his shoes, jacket, shirt, and pants and hung them on three hooks taped to his body. In *Jag ville görna telefonera* (1964), there were three chickens, a full-sized overstuffed chair made of cake and yellow frosting, and clothes with zippers in the seams so that they could be taken apart and put back together in new ways. Rabbits appeared in *title lost tokyo* (1964), another chicken (carried in a suitcase) in *Somebody Else* (1967), and a dog in *Some Notes on Performance* (1967). Paxton describes the duet with the dog as a " 'gland' game of subtle changes in stance, aggressive to wary. Some romping."[8] *Afternoon* (1963) took place in the glades of a New Jersey forest, where some of the trees were costumed identically to the dancers. *The Deposits* (1965) was performed on the grounds of a country club in Monticello, New York.

A whole series of works incorporating the use of huge, transparent, plastic inflatable tunnels began with *Music for Word Words* (1963). The inflatable in that piece was a twelve-foot-square room, which Paxton deflated with a vacuum cleaner until it became his costume. The confusion of textures — skin and plastic — of scale — massive and human size — and of function — room and costume — is an early example of Paxton's juggling of features of culture and nature. This stratagem (also used in the animal pieces, the environmental pieces, *Section of a New Unfinished Work* [1965] — where Paxton was disguised as a woman and also carried a speaker on his head so that music seemed to emanate from his body — and many other dances) functions in art as it did in the counterculture of the 1960s: to criticize rigid establishment traditions and to strip away institutionalized structure in favor of what anthropologist Victor Turner calls raw communitas, a "potentially free and experimental region of culture," a situation in opposition to social structure where spontaneity, social cohesion, and equality are stressed.[9] Turner notes that in the stripping process, a situation of instruction often arises, and that the process is replete with symbols which correlate explicitly to human and nonhuman biological processes.[10] The 100-foot plastic tunnel in *The Deposits* and the huge S-shaped tunnel in *Physical Things* (part of Nine Evenings: Theater and Engineering at the 69th Regiment Armory in 1966) — embellished with domes, towers, tubes and cubes, and furnished with real sod and fake trees — were analogous to human intestines, adding another type of confusion to the stripping, leveling process — that of interior and exterior.

Several of Paxton's works have used biological symbols in an explicitly medical code of images. Hospital imagery appeared not only in *Intravenous*

Lecture, but also in *Salt Lake City Deaths* (1968), which used taped autopsy, accident, and recovery reports to determine the performer's actions — which were either standing beside a table with a sheet on it (symbolizing recovery), lying on top of the sheet (sick), or under the sheet (dead). Paxton is also interested in the ways pornographic films represent the body, and in comparing pornographic acts with other kinds of movement. In *Somebody Else* the medical and sexual imagery mixed: a woman was dressed in a nurse's uniform (carrying a chicken in a suitcase), and a bed placed vertically served as a screen for a pornographic film. In *Beautiful Lecture* (1968), a film of the Bolshoi's *Swan Lake* was projected simultaneously with a blue movie, and Paxton danced in the space between the two images, making small gestures and mouthing a taped lecture on sex and ballet. (At its first performance, at the New School, Paxton was forced to substitute another film for the pornography, and chose a documentary on Biafra, again insisting on the obscenity of war. He refers to that performance as the expurgated version of the piece, and calls it *Untitled Lecture.*)

Jill Johnston wrote:

> What interested him to explore here was a certain energy common to sex and ballet, as he sees it. The key sentence perhaps in the lecture is: "I speculate that some of the qualities which have made ballet, in spite of its practitioners, the second oldest professional physical tradition, is an early infusion of psychologically basic modes of energy use which I find similar to the ecstasy of stretching such as is experienced during certain types of orgasms . . . a positive and energized stretch."[11]

At the end of the lecture, Paxton asked "Why are we in the West so hung up on orgasm?" a question Johnston associated to the re-emergence in the '60s of anticlimactic art — chance procedures, ready-mades, diffused and defocused aesthetics.

The use of the Biafra film was one expression of Paxton's use of political documents — a way, along with showing body states or objects often regarded as unattractive, or even repulsive — or connecting theater to the "outside" world, of linking various types of activities in startling relationships, in order to force the audience to question radically their assumptions about their activities. *Section of a New Unfinished Work* (1965) had used a section of the Army–McCarthy hearings for a sound track. In 1971, Paxton worked with

Wintersoldier, an organization of Vietnam veterans against the war, to make a piece called *Collaboration with Wintersoldier.* The group's film about Vietnam was projected while two performers, suspended upside-down by special overalls, watched it. In *Air* (1973), the metaphor of politics as obscenity was made explicit. The films from *Beautiful Lecture* appeared, along with two TV sets: one screen showed a live telecast of Nixon's "no whitewash at the White House" speech, and the other showed a videotape collage of the Pacific Ocean, Nixon's 1952 Checkers speech, and dancing legs.

Paxton views theater as a powerful machine, that gathers the energy of all the spectators and funnels it concentratedly to the performer. He is curious about what sorts of communications can take place within the theater—among performers, between performers and spectators, and among the spectators themselves. His use of scores to motivate movements provided new ways for the choreographer/director to communicate with the performers. *The Atlantic* (1967) simply presented storytelling as the basic communicative paradigm for theater, in much the same way that the walking pieces reduced dancing to its simplest, most fundamental form. Two pieces made for the audience—*Walkin' There* (1967, later retitled *Audience Performance #1*) and *Audience Performance #2* (1968)—set up loose frameworks in which the audience was to figure out how to collaborate.

Paxton's own works always provided a formal order for events, even if the content of the events seemed casual. But collaborations with others often involved improvisations and other random activities. In 1970, Paxton was one of the founders of the Grand Union (see Grand Union chapter). And starting in the '70s, his own work became more concerned with loosening structures and using improvisation in group, duet, and solo forms.

The duet form began to evolve when Paxton was at Oberlin College during the Grand Union's residency in 1972. He worked there with a group of eight other men on some Grand Union material; eventually, the work centered around exploring the parameters of the basic duet form: what happens when the partners give weight, lift, carry, wrestle each other, give in to the floor and gravity, all in a way that breaks out of typical male habits of aggression or fear of tenderness? The physical investigation took place at a time when men's groups around the country were forming to investigate male roles, as a sympathetic response to the feminist movement. But the dance material, contemporary with this cultural concern, was not inextricably bound to it. Paxton further elaborated the same material in *Benn Mutual,* a collaboration with Nita

Little at Bennington College the same year. And, later in 1972, students from Bennington, Oberlin, and Rochester joined Paxton in New York to give a concert, which formally spawned Contact Improvisation. Since then the work has spread to reach hundreds of participants in dozens of cities in the U.S., Canada, and England.

The movement material used in Contact Improvisation is not exactly commonplace, though specific moments often look familiar. It is movement that originates in a variety of duet situations, ranging from handshakes to making love to brawling to martial arts to social dancing to meditation. There are lifts and falls, evolving organically out of a continuous process of finding and losing balance. There is a give and take of weight, but also of social roles: passivity and activeness, demand and response. Paxton explains that the goal of each participant is to find the "easiest pathways available to their mutually moving masses." The details of the configurations are left up to the dancers, who improvise — although they keep in mind "the ideal of active, reflexive, harmonic, spontaneous, mutual forms." Touch and balance are the two key senses for working within the Contact system. The dancers transmit information to each other about their situation through touch; each partner remains aware of gravity through contact with the floor; and the dancers "touch themselves, internally," by maintaining concentration throughout the body. Balance in this system, unlike most dance techniques, is always relative to the supporting part of the body — whether it is the foot, shoulder, back, or head.[12]

The only rule is that contact should not be made with the hands. Otherwise, a minimal technical program trains one to develop the muscles to facilitate stretching, centering, taking weight, and increasing joint action. The training also aids consciousness of certain principles: sensing time, orienting oneself to space and to one's partner, discovering attitude, expanding peripheral vision. It takes about a week of working three hours a day to learn the basic methods. After that, practicing the form leads to further knowledge. Much of the time spent learning the basics is devoted to relaxation and gentle warm-ups. When the body is relaxed, surprises and emergencies can be met with calm strength. "You don't want to get somebody's adrenalin pumping before there's a need for it," Paxton points out.

> You want the heart to be strong and active, you want the muscles to be well-stretched and prepared, you want the person to be used to taking weight. The

> adrenalin should come from some organic cause, and then it should have a calm on top of it, so that the kick of adrenalin — what you feel when you almost fall — can be enjoyed, and calmly watched. It changes your perception of time, and it's one of the most enjoyable sensations in the whole Contact mode. It happens to me when I'm standing perfectly still and just being aware of the slight fall of the body. There's a real feeling of danger in standing still, if you pay attention to it.

Besides relaxing and stretching the muscles, in class one learns certain movements that become familiar and useful: Aikido rolls, like somersaults but done across a diagonal axis of the body; "bouncing," or pressing the top of someone else's head, then slowly releasing the pressure until she or he feels a floating sensation; giving rides by supporting someone's weight through one's bones and gently rocking. Many Contactors study anatomical and alignment researches, especially release work by Mary Fulkerson and the writings of Mabel Todd (*The Thinking Body* and other works) and Lulu Sweigard. Many also study philosophy and psychological researches they feel contribute to their understanding of the Contact experience.

A concert may begin with all the performers doing a "stand" — a warm-up done while standing for relaxation, sensing gravity, and becoming aware of one's breathing, peripheral vision, and balance. Then, two dancers may gravitate toward each other, or one person may approach a desired partner to begin a duet, while the rest of the group sits to observe. Another couple may enter the ring when the energy of the first duet wanes, or the evening may proceed as a round robin — A & B, B & C, C & D, etc. At times two duets go on at once, or intermingle. At times the duet may be between one person and the wall or floor. The duration of each duet is as functional as the clothing the dancers wear: it lasts as long as the dancers feel comfortable with it, and they wear sweat pants, T-shirts, leotards, sweaters, or whatever feels comfortable while providing some friction.

Contact Improvisation can be a dramatic, spectacular series of events to watch. Yet the presentation in concert format — i.e., in front of an audience — changes very little from Contact done in workshop situations. *You Come, We'll Show You What We Do,* the title of some Contact performances in New York in 1975, indicates the casual, demonstrationlike tone of the evening. *Free Lance Dance* was the title of concerts in 1978. I've seen Contact concerts on the Washington Monument Mall, in the back room of a bookstore in

Milwaukee, in concert spaces, and in art galleries, lasting for less than an hour and for six hours. "We're focused on the phenomenon, rather than on the presentation," Paxton explains. Nevertheless, he points out, the audience is important, because the attention of a group of people focused on a single point generates power. "And the performer gets to use that power." For the audience, Contact Improvisation is sometimes exhausting to watch, sometimes exhilarating, sometimes boring or frightening. But the material is not edited or presented with the audience's pleasure or entertainment in mind, and so the concert may go on for several hours if the dancers find themselves tapping rich kinetic impulses. There may also be lags when exploration, however important to the performer, is not visually arresting. It is sometimes frightening to see a small person hoisting a huge person, or to witness a precarious lift or a fast slide to the floor — and all this done without the protection of floor mats. But Contactors reassure one that a wooden floor is fairly soft, and that there are tactics they learn that ease the falls. The floor is not seen as an adversary but an ally. Some Contact concerts are scheduled to last for many hours, with the audience coming and going at their leisure. Looking for a long stretch of time, one learns to notice individual styles and attitudes. One may feel confronted with too much information but one's body responds even when the visual field is clogged. If one arrives with expectations of virtuosic movement, of beautifully polished dancing, of receiving pleasure passively, one will probably be disappointed. If one likes to see "any old bodies" moving, one may find a great deal that delights: risk, discovery, wild abandon, tenderness.

And yet, although almost anyone can learn the rudiments of Contact Improvisation, some performers do seem "better" than others. The excitement and pleasure for the spectator seem to come from interactions where responsibility is passed to and fro between partners, where the action changes direction — sometimes vertical, sometimes horizontal, shifting from working close to the floor to high in the air — and where weight displaces weight in unexpected places. It is often more interesting to watch performers who take risks, but take them with care. It is less engaging to watch people who are cautious, rather than careful, or who act predominantly passive, or who only give and take weight aggressively. The dancer finding his or her "edge," the limit just this side of danger, but still seeming to move easily, often gives equal pleasure to himself or herself, and the partner, and the observer, through personal incidents, accessible and meaningful. The form itself almost seems to embody metaphors for abstract social relations, bringing the spectator's moral sense into play along with the bodies.

For the Contactors, the form is a part of daily life, a way of using the body and becoming constantly aware of the body that permeates all activity and that is fed by other jobs, arts, sports, readings, social concerns. "Learning again and again/Dance has its place in my life/As eating shitting sleeping and waking/craving balance/and ease/swinging to and fro," Danny Lepkoff wrote in an issue of *Contact Newsletter.*[13] "Inevitably we are talking about our lives when speaking or writing about Contact," wrote Alan Potash.[14] As it spreads, Contact has become a collective, democratic group project, involving workshops, intensive summer sessions, and conferences, and with local, informal groups practicing regularly. A journal, *Contact Quarterly*—which began as an informal newsletter to keep dancers who were committed to teaching, learning, and practicing the form in touch with each other — has evolved into a magazine that prints graphics, poetry, articles on related work, and book reviews as well as reports on workshops, tours, and performances; theoretical articles; suggestions for teaching; administrative news; reprints of reviews; and names and addresses of key improvisers in various cities. Like the food co-op movement that flourished in the same decade, and motivated by the same populist spirit, Contact Improvisation sets up a network for distribution (of dance, rather than vegetables) outside the big business of the dance world.

The preoccupation with the floor and gravity in Contact recalls concerns of the early modern dancers, notably Martha Graham and Doris Humphrey. Contactor Lisa Nelson points out that another pioneer of modern dance, Tamiris, used an exercise called "body contact" to train her dancers.[15] And, as I've noted, fragments of the vocabulary seem to come from a variety of social, sport and aesthetic forms. But the Contact phenomenon is innovative in several respects. The early modern dancers ultimately used falls, gravity, and even improvisation within strictly choreographed designs. Chance, the personal choices of the dancers, the performer's attention to inner action, and the necessity for accommodating to one's partner's decisions were elements that rarely arose in the actual performance.

Although portions of Contact have roots in nonaesthetic activity, and despite the fact that often the aim for the participants is self-awareness and personal pleasure, still, for the observer, Contact performances remain within the boundaries of art. The movement is aesthetically distanced twice: first, by removing it from its original context (social, sexual, athletic, reflex, etc.); second, by presenting it as a theatrical event, no matter how casual. Ultimately Contact Improvisation is a special event with its own distinct features — like sports, like social dancing, like embracing, but not actually any of these; more like the kind of playing we call art, than like the playing we call games.

Although Paxton was the initiator of the form and remains one of its most active practitioners, clearly it no longer belongs only to him. The nature of Contact — its quality of constant change — implies that within the form there is room for elaboration, invention, perhaps even some codification. As more and more dancers and nondancers become Contactors and extend the system's limits according to their own ideas, experiences, and desires, one question has begun to face participants: how much can the form change and still be defined as Contact Improvisation?

Dividing his time between traveling to teach and perform, living on a communal Vermont farm, performing with the Grand Union (until it disbanded in 1976), and occasionally collaborating with other choreographers (he performed his interpretation of "Rinse Variations" in Trisha Brown's *Line Up* in 1977), Paxton also continues to work on solo dancing. *Dancing* is the straightforward title he has used since 1973 for his solo improvisation form in which body sensations are manipulated, through movement, to alter time perception. In dances he calls *With David Moss* (1974 and ongoing) and *Backwater: Twosome* (1977 and ongoing), Paxton performs the material from *Dancing* to improvised percussion by David Moss.

When one sees Paxton performing solo improvisation, even if one does not know the history of his concerns and imagery, the results of those concerns can be observed in his movement style. The performance often begins in a friendly, casual manner. Performing at St. Mark's Church in New York City, Paxton will walk into the stage area, nodding and smiling and greeting friends in the audience. Dressed in sweat pants and a T-shirt, he begins to warm up, walking and flexing joints softly, as Moss takes his place in a houselike construction built of bells, chimes, drums, bottles, gongs, and other percussion objects. The musician and dancer play what Paxton calls a "gland game," just as he did with the dog in *Some Notes on Performance.* One will begin a riff. The other will tune in and respond. Each makes changes, staying in touch with the other's rhythm, dynamics, even posture. When either the dance or the music has run its course, the two performers stop for a few moments, then begin another riff.

There is a curious mixture of tension and relaxation in Paxton's body when he dances. At times one sees analogues to Cunningham shapes, but more fluid, loosened: nimble, intricate footwork executed with floppy ankles and feet; circular shapes made with lax, rather than held, arms. Paxton advances slowly, continuously, his entire body threading along a single sinuous line. Then suddenly he stops with a caught, charged energy. He uses the weight of his head or bent leg to jerk his entire body around a vertical axis with sudden violence, the active lever moving with controlled force, while the rest of the body yields to follow. Then again he assumes a solid stance — that of a classical Apollo, with the weight slung into one hip; or that of a crucifixion, with the arms out to the sides, elbows jutting, and the head awkwardly abutting the shoulder at an angle. Images of sports arise as Paxton makes feinting gestures with his arms, or transmits the gestures to other body parts. At times he looks ready to swing a bat, or pitch or dribble a ball. And medical imagery appears, as he hobbles along, dragging a leg behind him like dead weight, or cradles an elbow while he dips and turns.

There is a quiet, surprising pleasure in watching Paxton experiment with relations between body parts, and with images of body states like strength and illness. He sticks out his buttocks and arches his back, or lifts a flexed arm and leg together. One sees combinations and body attitudes that are unusual for dancing, sometimes even for any activity in our culture. Yet they look satisfying, organic, not like copied images of unusual postures, but like movements and positions arrived at naturally in the course of an uncensored, intelligent flow of energy and weight through the skeletal and muscular systems. One sometimes recognizes the shapes as images from other contexts: sports, medicine, ballet, drunkenness, modern dance, sculpture, painting, nature. But the imagery is fleeting. What remains is a continuing sense of the body's potential to invent and discover, to recover equilibrium after losing control, to regain vigor despite pain and disorder. Paxton's dancing tells us that, for all its problems, dangers, inconsistencies, and clumsiness, the human mechanism is also a grand and elegant machine. He reminds us that the body's grace is rooted in its extraordinarily varied repertoire of capabilities.

Steve Paxton, Satisfyin Lover[16]

GROUP A

1. walk 2/5. 10 second stop. exit.
2. cue 10 steps.
   walk across.
3. cue 20 steps.
   walk across.
4. cue #1 pauses.
   walk across.
5. cue #1 pauses.
   walk 1/5. stop 20 seconds. exit.

6,7,8. cue 5 steps.
enter together. #6 falling gradually behind (at exit be 15 steps behind). 7 & 8 walk across.

GROUP B

9. walk across.
10. cue 20 steps.
    walk to 4/5. pause 1 minute. exit.
11. cue #10 passes halfway.
    walk to ½. stop 5 seconds. exit.
12. cue #10 passes halfway.
    walk to 2/3. stop 20 seconds. exit.

13. cue #10 pauses.
walk to chair 3. sit 30 seconds. exit.

GROUP C

14. walk across.

15. cue 15 steps.
walk to 5 feet of exit. stop 30 seconds. exit.

16. cue 10 steps.
walk across.

17. cue 3 steps.
walk across passing #16. exit.

18. cue 10 steps.
walk across.

19. cue 5 steps.
walk 1/3. stop 15 seconds. walk to chair 1. sit 30 seconds. exit.

20. cue #19 stops.
walk across.

GROUP D

21. walk across.

22. cue 20 steps.
walk to ½. pause 5 seconds. walk 4/5. pause 15 seconds. exit.

23. cue #22 stops.
walk across.

24, 25, 26, 27. cue #23 passes 3/5.
walk across casually changing relative positions.

28, 29. cue 20 steps.
walk across together.

GROUP E

30. walk across.

31. cue 15 steps.
walk to 1/5. stop and face audience. 45 seconds. exit.

32. cue 10 steps.
walk to chair 3, sit for 15 seconds. walk to 4/5. stop 20 seconds. exit.

33. cue #32 sits.
walk across.

34. cue 20 steps.
walk across.

35. cue 10 steps.
walk to 3/5. stop 15 seconds. return to chair 1. sit until final person (timekeeper) passes. exit.

36. cue 5 steps.
walk to ½. stop 15 seconds. walk to 2/3. stop 15 seconds. exit.

37. cue #36 stops.
walk to ⅛. stop 20 seconds. exit.

GROUP F

38. walk across.

39. cue #38 passes 4/5.
walk across.

40. cue 15 steps.
walk to ⅞. stop 5 seconds. exit.

41. cue #40 stops.
walk across.

42. cue 15 steps.
walk across.

Notes to Director of *Satisfyin Lover*

Intervals between groups is to be determined in each performance space according to your judgment. (I begin with thirty-second intervals.) A timekeeper cues the first person in each group, and is the last person to start across the stage. The last person in each group keeps the group card during rehearsals and is responsible for notifying the director of absences, for instructing the other members, et cetera.

At no time in the piece should the performance space remain empty for long, and the pause between groups should not be noticeable as such.

Costuming is casual clothes with some exceptions as is convenient for the performers.

The walking occurs in an imaginary track ten feet wide, the length of which is considered performance space. The track goes from entrance to exit, all performers entering on one side and exiting on the other.

In about the center of the space a little in front of the track, three chairs are very casually arranged, oriented to face front, several feet apart. Performers leave the track to sit, return to it to continue walking, do not pass in front of chairs they will not sit on.

This dance was made for forty people in a space 200 feet long. The number of people can vary from thirty to eighty-four, and the space can be as little as sixty-five feet or horizon to horizon for stationary audience.

Note to Performers of *Satisfyin Lover*

The pace is an easy walk, but not slow. Performance manner is serene and collected.

This dance is about walking, standing, and sitting. Try to keep these elements clear and pure.

The gaze is to be directed forward relative to the body, but should not be especially fixed. The mind should be at rest.

Cues for the first person in each group come from the timer. Subsequently cue from the person ahead of you, unless otherwise directed in the score.

Trisha Brown: Gravity and Levity

TRISHA BROWN had a normal outdoors childhood in Aberdeen, Washington, including tree climbing and football playing. Her dance teacher, Marion Hageage, "organized my bony knees and adolescent mind through tap, ballet and acrobatics which developed into jazz routines in high school assemblies."[1] She went on to study modern dance at Mills College and at the Connecticut College summer sessions, where she worked with José Limón, Louis Horst, and Merce Cunningham.

After graduating from Mills, she was hired to set up a dance department at Reed College in 1958. "I stayed there two years, but exhausted conventional teaching methods after the first few months and then became involved with improvisational teaching."[2] She began at that time to develop her own dance vocabulary.

During the summer of 1960, Brown took a summer workshop with Ann Halprin, the West Coast dancer and teacher who at that time was interested in problems raised by improvisation and tasks. At Halprin's studio in San Francisco, Brown worked with Simone Forti, Yvonne Rainer, La Monte Young, Terry Riley, Robert Morris, and others. Recalling a study Brown did that summer, Forti remembers:

> She was holding a broom in her hand. She thrust it out straight ahead, without letting go of the handle. And she thrust it out with such force that the momentum carried her whole body through the air. I still have the image of that broom and Trisha right out in space, traveling in a straight line three feet off the ground.[3]

Trisha Brown in *Water Motor*. Photograph © Babette Mangolte, 1978.

Arriving in New York the following fall, Brown worked on improvisation problems with Forti and Dick Levine, using simple organization structures that provided a common ground for exploration. One of the structures was called Violent Contact. Its rules included the possibilities of blocking another dancer, running at full force, or dashing away from another dancer's intended collision.

Besides feeding Brown's interest in the ways in which improvisation forces quick decisions and solutions, proliferating original actions without editing constraints, Violent Contact raised issues basic to group improvisation: how can formal aspects of improvisation take social connotations into account?

Another structure, invented by Forti, involved pointing arbitrarily to part of the room and reading the object or area as score:

> If you got a window, you could say the dance should be in four sections, and no one section has more weight than any other section, and the floor of the room should be divided into four parts. When we had agreed on as many details as we needed, we'd improvise, using our individual movement vocabularies.

At the same time, Brown started taking Robert Dunn's composition class at the Cunningham studio. Brown especially valued Dunn's methods of analyzing the student works: his emphasis on the invention of forms, and his use of nonevaluative criticism. "This procedure illuminated the interworkings of the dances and minimized value judgments of the choreographer, which for me meant permission, permission to go ahead and do what I wanted to do or had to do — to try out an idea of borderline acceptability."[4]

Brown's early choreography applied structures to improvisation. In *Trillium* (1962), the first dance she performed at the Judson, the rules were that "I could stand, sit or lie, and ended up levitating. In this dance I did not notify myself of my intentions in advance of the performance." *Lightfall* (1963) was a duet for herself and Steve Paxton based on material — especially perchings and stillnesses — from the Violent Contact explorations. *Part of a Target,* first performed in 1963, set up an elemental situation: Brown struck a ballet fourth position, said "Oh no!" and fell as slowly as possible to the side. *Part of a Target* later became one section in *Target* (1964), a duet which used difficult, vigorous dance phrases in addition to the fall. The phrases were cued extemporaneously by questions asked by the performers — such as "What time is it?" and "Where are we?" These created abrupt shifts from one section to another.

Rulegame 5 (1964) set up very strict constraints within which movement and language appropriate to the prescribed goals were improvised. Five performers proceeded along a path marked by seven parallel rows of tape, with instructions to change level from highest to lowest (on their stomachs) at the end of the course. The performers had to adjust their levels and placements along the tracks in relation to other performers, by talking to each other and making necessary adjustments mutually.

In 1966, Brown performed *A String*. The piece was exactly that, a string of three dances, *Motor* (1965), *Homemade* (1965), and *Inside* (1966). *Motor*, originally done in a parking lot in Ann Arbor, Michigan, for the Once Again Festival, was a duet for Brown on a skateboard (which provided the time structure) and an unrehearsed driver in a Volkswagen (whose headlights provided the lighting). At the Judson performance of *A String*, the Volkswagen was replaced by a motor scooter. Jill Johnston wrote of it: "Pursued by light and motor, starting and stopping . . . the obvious metaphor in a dream-like situation of flight and pursuit, of imminent pleasure and/or danger."[5] *Homemade* was a series of movements taken from real movement — casting a fishing line, measuring a box, telephoning — made minuscule and thereby unrecognizable. In *A String*, Brown strapped a movie projector on her back and, while performing *Homemade*, cast images of herself performing the dance without a movie projector on her back around the performing area, metaphorically setting herself in flight. (In the last performance, a second performer followed with a movie screen to catch the image as the actions of the dance cast the picture all over the room.) *Inside* used the interior of Brown's loft studio as a score. She read the hardware, fixtures, woodwork, and various objects stored around the edges as instructions for movement. "Outside organizational methods force new patterns of construction; I remember being surprised when my right foot would be activated by a valve sticking out of the wall. I would not have selected the distribution of movement across my body on my own." The dance was set and performed at the Judson with the audience seated in a rectangle, recreating the walls of the studio. Brown moved around the periphery of the performance space directly in front of their knees, looking them straight in the eye:

> Up until that time dancers in dance companies were doing rigorous technical steps and one of the mannerisms was to glaze over the eyes and kick up a storm in there behind your eyes. Many people used that device to hide from their audience; we all knew about it and talked about it. So I decided to con-

front my audience straight ahead. As I traveled right along the edge of their knees in this dance, I looked at each person. It wasn't dramatic or confrontational, just the way you look when you're riding on a bus and notice everything.

Yellowbelly (1969) was an improvisation that used another kind of confrontation with the audience to determine the outcome of the piece. Brown asked the audience to heckle her by calling out "yellowbelly":

> The audience was too sweet so I stopped them and asked them to be really nasty. They did. I tried to do whatever came to my mind in response to the name-calling. When I stopped to bow (after what I considered a respectable amount of time), they screamed "yellowbelly" at me, so I continued until somehow we both stopped.[6]

Yellowbelly is a confrontation not only between performer and audience, but also between the performer and her fears, and between the audience and its expectations and inhibitions. The real subject of the dance is those issues: will the dancer forget, through fear or anger, plans for movement? Will the audience agree to participate in the progress of the dance by expressing a reaction in advance, one, perhaps, which does not actually correspond with its own feelings toward the event? In *Yellowbelly,* the ordinary predicament a dancer faces — anxiety that the dance will be forgotten — is systematically intensified.

In 1968, Brown began to construct dances that came to be known as Equipment Pieces.[7] These dances use various external support systems — ropes, pulleys, tracks, cables, mountain-climbing gear, a giant pegboard — in order to pit the illusion of natural movement against the forces of weight and gravity through changes in the setting and direction. For example, a dancer walking down the side of a building or along a wall, or traveling a spiral path down the trunk of a tree, must change the way he or she is actually walking in order to create the illusion of a natural, gravity-governed upright carriage. The result is a remarkable alteration of perspective. Watching dancers traverse the walls of the Whitney Museum, in *Walking on the Wall* (1971), one rarely has the sensation that the performers are executing supernatural feats, à la Batman. (The dance is documented in a short film now in the New York Public Library archives.) Instead, one has the distinct sensation that one is on a tall building, watching people walking back and forth on the sidewalk below. When they turn a corner on the walls, suddenly one feels as though one were positioned sideways, sticking one's head out of a window, perhaps, and seeing a sideways image of an upright person below.

The first of the Equipment Pieces, which profoundly questioned processes of perception, was *Planes,* performed six times between 1968 and 1971. In it three dancers travel across a giant, pegboardlike wall construction. They move slowly and continuously, using the holes for foot- and hand-holds, turning around and upside-down, climbing across and up and down the surface, and occasionally resting in a suspended position. Aerial footage, projected on the wall, completes the illusion of constant free falling motion. A duet for vacuum cleaner and voice, by Simone Forti, accompanies the dance.

In the dance called *Clothes Pipe, The Floor of the Forest, and Other Miracles, Dance for a Dirty Room, Everybody's Grandmother's Bed, the Costume, Adam Says Checkered Sea* (1969), old clothes are threaded through a rope grid suspended at eye level, and two dancers dress and undress their way through it, working mainly above the grid but sometimes resting below it, suspended in the clothes as if in hammocks. The audience is forced to change levels and points of view. *Rummage Sale and the Floor of the Forest* (1971) set the same basic situation above a genuine rummage sale in order to make the audience choose between two separate events. The transformation of an utterly mundane, almost unconscious set of movements — dressing and undressing —into an extremely difficult, cumbersome feat is both comic and illuminating. The mechanics of the everyday action are emphasized, almost dissected. The body's relationship to clothing is altered since both hang from the grid: tights, for instance, are no longer tight but enormous tunnels in which legs dangle. The clothing dictates the position of the person, instead of the reverse, pulling arms and legs into extraordinary positions. The body looks awkward, imprisoned by its normally passive clothing, and suddenly the person is the victim of soft, harmless objects that she usually controls and manipulates without a thought.

The Equipment Pieces raise questions about both phenomenology and the use of theater space. "I always feel sorry for the parts of the stage that aren't being used. I have in the past felt sorry for the ceilings and walls. It's perfectly good space, why doesn't anyone use it?" Brown has wondered.[8]

Leaning Duets (1969), performed on the ground and, in its initial version, without any equipment, sets five couples leaning at arm's length, walking, falling, and helping each other up while maintaining foot contact. In 1971, the objective — maintaining balance as a single unit while both partners are off-balance — was made even more difficult as the angle between the two was increased by means of ropes threaded through two pieces of pipe. Then Brown devised another piece of equipment — boards that fit behind the dancers' backs, connected by ropes — that supports the weight and disperses the stress on the spine and back muscles. In the leaning duets, the dancers developed a specific language to provide, as Brown phrases it, an "audible analysis of their weight-state and imminent needs." Such expressions as "Give me some!" and "Take!" and "Too much!" — fast signals for immediate adjustments of different sorts — are used to maintain equilibrium in the duet, but in a different context would have an entirely different meaning.

In all the Equipment Pieces, the choreographic decisions — time, place, order of movements, kinds of movements, the nature of the sound (for example, dialogue) — are strictly governed by the choice of equipment. The movement and language are generated in terms of the most economical use of the equipment. It is hard to imagine anyone choosing or inventing those particular movements or that language outside of the chosen equipment situation.

By 1971, Brown had come to feel that she had plumbed the possibilities of control imposed by equipment and began making dances based on mathematical systems of accumulation. The deep structures of the dances are disclosed as the piece unfolds. *Accumulation* (1971), done standing in one spot, starts with a movement — the rotation of the right fist with the thumb extended — that is repeated seven or eight times. The next movement, a gesture with the left thumb, is added, and the two are repeated in sequence several times. As the piece progresses, succinct gestures — a twist of the pelvis, a bend of the knee, a turn of the head, a step back, a lift of the leg — are strung onto the end of the accumulation, and sometimes sandwiched into earlier sections of the progression. Originally, *Accumulation* was four and a half minutes long and performed to the Grateful Dead's "Uncle John's Band." The second version (1972) was fifty-five minutes long, done in silence. Once Brown felt that she had mastered the problem of keeping the movement clear in the face of relentless repetition, she complicated the problem, as she is apt to do. In 1973, she began to tell stories about performing the dance as she was performing it and, by 1978, was splicing two stories together extemporaneously while keeping the movement going at a calm, even pace.

Primary Accumulation (1972), done lying on the floor, is a string of thirty movements accumulated as follows: 1; 1,2; 1,2,3; 1,2,3,4; et cetera. The movements are low-key: raise the forearm, raise the whole arm, brush hair back at the temple, turn the head to the side, lift the knee, lift the hip, bring the leg across the body, and so on. The string of gestures is repeated in a smooth, rhythmic, hypnotic flow.

Talking about the accumulation while demonstrating it to me, Brown explained:

> My choice to be on the floor had to do with not wanting to have to deal with the fact that the legs are generally in the role of having to support the upper half of the body. They really don't have the freedom that the upper half of the body has. If I'm lying down, I've freed my legs and they can function like all the rest of the parts.
>
> I went through a period of feeling extremely vulnerable. This position conjured up quite a few feelings which had to be dealt with right from the beginning: feeling infantile, sexual, helpless, lazy. But I got over them and once I got over them I felt fine about doing the piece. I designed it for right straight above my head and I felt that the audience should definitely be on the ceiling.
>
> Each choice of movement has to be comfortable, because it is repeated. That's why the leg doesn't really go straight up to the ceiling, which is what you might hope. It just has to be natural, comfortable, and simple.
>
> I started working on this piece in October 1972 and I got about twenty movements accumulated by the time I did a concert December 1. And then I continued to work on it by going to the studio and using it somewhat like a warm-up exercise, accumulating to as far as I had gone the last time, in a very relaxed manner with no goal in mind. Just accumulating movements. And then the next concert was on March 27, so I stopped at that point. Whatever I had accumulated between October and March 27 was the piece.
>
> I had a heady moment where I sat up for a while — which of course introduced all sorts of possibilities. And then I realized that I was taking the easy way out, and I got back down.
>
> The eighth movement I chose because I have a friend [Suzushi Hanayagi] who's a Japanese classical dancer who does things like that. Her hands are perfect, well-trained. And my right hand has a broken finger on it. And so I had to teach my company to hold the middle finger on their right hand as if broken. That kind of eccentricity I allow.

The twenty-ninth and thirtieth gestures of the accumulation rotate the dancer 45 degrees each. The entire thirty-movement sequence is repeated four times after the accumulation is completed, so that then the complete sequence is seen from four angles and the dancer rotates 360 degrees, returning to her starting point at the end. *Primary Accumulation* has been performed as a solo, a group piece, and — as *Group Primary Accumulation* — a group piece that is interrupted by two movers who carry the dancers around, stack them on top of one another, prop them against walls or on benches, and otherwise alter their positions. Meanwhile, the strict flow of movement continues in perfect unison; the sequence is somehow inexorable, even though it is totally altered because of the new relationships between body parts and the floor. Images of helplessness arise. The precision of the structure fades when two dancers are set opposite each other and the dance comes to resemble a mirror exercise; then they turn away from each other and the original structure returns with striking clarity as the unison continues back to back. *Group Primary Accumulation* has been performed on park benches, on the grass, on the plaza of the McGraw-Hill building in New York, in art galleries and lofts, and on rafts floating apart on Loring Lagoon in Minneapolis.

Split Solo (1974) is a version of *Primary Accumulation* in which the movements planned for the right side of the body are executed by one dancer, and the movements for the left side by another.

The Accumulation Pieces, like the serial variations of visual artists Sol LeWitt and Mel Bochner, are physical descriptions of ideas.[9] The beauty of the dances lies in Brown's attention to the gestures: not only clarity in the face of the distortion inherent when a conceptual system is materialized, but also the delicacy of timing. The freshness of the gesture is continually renewed, its contextual meaning within the logic of the ordering system secured. These are not dances composed of magnificent, fantastic, terrific movement, but they *are* quietly fantastic dances. They are cool, obsessive, intelligent investigations of attention and perception, systematically presenting the human body as both subject and object of research. One cannot help but compare some of Brown's specific concerns in *Primary Accumulation* to those of the floor-bound sculpture of Carl Andre.[10] Both, in their respective art forms, operate initially out of a rejection of the tyranny of verticality. Both then dispense with smooth, logical connections or polish, presenting matter-of-fact arrangements of rather ordinary materials in discrete units, held together by mental systems which focus attention on the properties rather than the presentation of the units.

There is a certain sensuality in the various Accumulation Pieces, an erotic suggestion that comes more from the insistent rhythm of the sequence and the methodical articulation of the body than from any specific symbolic or literal reference. In both *Accumulation* and *Primary Accumulation,* some of the gestures, as Brown remarked of the latter dance, do evoke feelings of sexuality, vulnerability, laziness, and so on, both in the dancer and in the viewer. But these meanings dissipate in the extended performance of the whole dance. What Lucy Lippard calls "sensuous abstraction" in certain works of visual art contributes to the erogenous quality of the dance more than any specific sexual gesture. Lippard compares detached, anticlimactic immediacy of sensuousness with Hindu temple sculpture, where "obsessive but precisely constructed pattern is fused with an ineffable sense of volume, physicality, substance . . . Momentary excitement is omitted . . . The rhythms of erotic experience can be slowed to a near standstill and convey all the more effectively a languorous sensuality."[11] I am not arguing that eroticism is the primary meaning of the Accumulation Pieces. On the contrary, their voluptuousness is a by-product, only one of the many associations that the works — primarily concerned with the building processes, materials, and perceptions of dance — may suggest.

The tension between the mathematical or formal precision of a movement idea and its physical distortion has been Brown's concern in several other dances. In *Theme and Variation* (1972) one dancer performs a string of movements, then repeats it over and over as best she can despite attempts by a second performer to interrupt her. The result is a set of variations on the original phrase. They are not generated by the personal, aesthetic choices of the choreographer; rather, the variations are forced warpings of the theme caused by responses to external obstacles. Similarly, in *Discs* (1973), a dancer attempts to walk naturally across a room while three other dancers pitch cardboard discs under her feet. In *Drift* (1974), an elegant illusion of distortion is deliberately created, as a phalanx of five dancers, lined up shoulder-to-shoulder, advances down a long room toward the audience. By moving their feet a fraction of an inch to the right with each step, they seem to be moving straight ahead; yet they end up (from the spectator's point of view) far to the left of their original starting point.

In *Roof Piece* (1971), a group of dancers stationed on the roofs of buildings spanning a twelve-block area in lower Manhattan relay large, clear, simple movements downtown for fifteen minutes, then uptown for fifteen minutes. Brown's objective here was to transmit the semaphorelike gestures from dancer to dancer as accurately as possible, working to minimize inevitable errors in the reading of details and timing of movement. The problem is similar to that of *Figure 8* (1974) but adds the issue of transmission. Using a familiar technique for sending movement — copying, as in dance classes and rehearsals — while extending the distances between sender and receiver enormously, Brown tests an information system at its limits.

With *Locus* (1975), Brown's movement style changed from the simple, building-block textures of the Accumulation Pieces to complex, quirky actions that appear almost to resemble emotionally expressive gestures. The genesis of these movements lay not in expression but in the solving of two problems. First, Brown set up a mathematical and linguistic system: she posited an imaginary, elongated cube fifty-four inches wide and deep, and long enough to stand in. Each of twenty-seven points on the cube corresponded to a letter in the alphabet; Brown generated a four-part score by translating a written autobiographical statement into numbers, then into points on the cube. Twenty-seven marked the center of the cube and was the space between words in the text.

The second problem, then, was to find ways to "move through, touch, look at, jump over, or do something about each point in the series, either one point at a time or clustered."[12] Often, for instance when several points had to be touched at once, compound aerial movements using the body's total weight were required. After the cube and the phrases had been established, twenty possible imaginary cubes were available to the dancers, who choose in performance which cube, which side of the cube, and which phrase to use as a starting point. The result is a dance that (like *Group Primary Accumulation*) resembles a stationary object but revolves in and moves through space.

The concept of the "line up" has characterized both format and method in Brown's work. Her major concern has always been to find the schemes and structures that organize movement, rather than the invention of movement per se. Yet those structures — ranging from "structured improvisation" to the demands and limitations of the architecture of downtown Manhattan, from equipment that lets her dancers walk on walls and down trees to mathematical progressions and verbal instructions, constitute exigencies that generate not only functional gestures, but movements one can scarcely describe or imagine.

Line Up, choreographed in 1976 and 1977, is a paradigm, but also a history, of Brown's choreographic process. Four previous dances and variations on two other pieces appear explicitly within the work. The program notes explained that the body of dancing through which the older dances are interspersed "was made by the Company through improvisation, recall, then memorization of the material derived from the instruction, 'line up.' The continuous forming and reforming of lines causes the dance to hover between order and disorder."[13] Embedded in *Line Up* are parts of *Structured Pieces I–IV* (1973–76) and other dances: *Sticks, Mistitled* (*5″ Clacker*), *Spanish Dance,* and *Figure 8;* also a variation on *Locus* and a new version of *Solo Olos* (1976).

In *Sticks,* five women lie on their backs on the floor, forming a line head-to-toe and, using verbal communication where necessary, line up long sticks over and parallel to their bodies. Keeping all the sticks in contact end to end in as precise and straight a line as possible, they get out from under them, step over them while switching the hand that holds the stick, and get back under from the other side. There are no unnecessary motions; the dance is over when the prone position is reached by all. The action in *Sticks* is not so different from the actions plumbers and construction workers go through every day. But here a pleasing, humorous tension is evoked not only by the constant wavering, breaking, and resolution of the line of sticks (in contrast to the dancers' bodies, since they each perform the task as individuals and only line up at the beginning and end); but also by the presentation of the solemn, pedestrian task in an aesthetic framework.

In *Mistitled* (*5″ Clacker*), the dancers line up as if to start a race. A tape plays the sound of a wooden stick hitting a glass every five seconds. Between sound cues, the dancers take one step, then return to the start before the clack; two steps, return to start, et cetera, until they can no longer get back to start in five seconds. Racing against time, rather than each other, they try to find the loopholes in the system, by diminishing the size of the steps on the way out and running back as fast as possible. The impossibility of the desperate attempts to beat time, the change from calm walking to frantic haste, and the sudden recognition by the spectator that the action is subject to the discipline of the time segments marked off by the sound all create a successful visual gag.

In *Spanish Dance,* the five women form a line across the room, equidistant from one another. Bob Dylan's rendition of Gordon Lightfoot's "Early Morning Rain" is played. The last woman in the line raises her arms and arches her back like a Spanish dancer. She takes tiny, shuffling steps forward, swinging her hips in time to the music. When she gently collides with the next dancer, *she* raises her arms, and the two keep moving forward until they pick up the next dancer. Finally all the performers are packed together, they reach the wall, and the song ends.

Brown's humor works on several levels here. First there is the strange incongruity between the rough style of the song and the grand, flamboyant, formulaic postures; then there is the way the dancers, with their tiny steps, loose hip swings, deadpan expressions, and baggy pants, seem quite unconscious in their parody of Spanish dancing; and then there is the odd lapse in decorum as the dancers' bodies crush and rub together while they earnestly continue the dance, their faces neutral. And finally, the lighting provokes another image, a pun: as they approach the wall, the dancers cast a shadow of a single body with ten arms, a figure reminiscent of the Indian god Shiva, the dancing destroyer.

Figure 8 sets the dancers in single file facing the audience. With eyes closed, to the sound of a metronome, they perform simple repetitious arm movements — lowering and raising bent arms to touch the top of the head — according to an eight-count measure. In *Figure 8,* one arm is marking a descending time sequence of 8,7,6,5,4,3,2,1, and the other arm performs the opposite, an ascending sequence from one to eight. The result is time crossing. The individual dancer's arms thus appear to be sometimes raised symmetrically, sometimes in counterpoint, but each dancer makes exactly the same movements as the others. The regularity of the rhythm and the repetition create a hypnotic fascination for the spectator. This is edged with a pleasurable suspense, because each dancer's sense of timing and the tiny variations which result contrast with the utter precision of the material and tend to push the movement slightly in and out of synchronization.

In between these pieces (and the variations on *Locus* and *Solo Olos* which come later in *Line Up*), the company forms lines and disintegrates them in all possible ways and positions: sitting, standing, crouching, moving. They line up with each other and they line up their own bodies. They sweep along the periphery of the room, outlining it in semicircles drawn with a windshield-wiper action, but constantly recombining their lines at the edges and corners of the room to compensate for the differences in the space each one must cover. They try to form columns shoulder-to-shoulder but someone is always the odd person out. They line their limbs up against the floor or a wall. They improvise as a group, trying to line up and crystallize the material in order to repeat and memorize it.

There are bits of material recalling Brown's Accumulation Pieces, as well as improvisation in every state of disclosure to the audience — from completely hidden to completely revealed. In *Line Up*, Brown makes movement puns and strange juxtapositions, often reversing meanings once they have been established. Her detached commentaries and surprising timing contribute to the dry humor of the piece, as do the constant subversions of the spectator's expectations in terms of movement or performance behavior.

In *Line Up*, we see a catalogue of the three types of movement that her choreographic grammar has produced: unaltered pedestrian actions, such as walking, leaning, running, and falling; "pure" movement of the joints and limbs, which Brown has described as "not functional or pantomimic. Mechanical actions like bending, straightening or rotating would qualify as pure movement providing the context was neutral."[14] The third type of movement includes gestures that have personal meaning to Brown — perhaps referring to an image or a memory — but would have no specific meaning to the audience and thus remain inscrutable symbols because of their context.

With her workmanlike attitude toward her material — in terms of timing, arrangement of parts, and demeanor — Brown carefully investigates formal comparison and contrast, as well as the expectations and contradictions of performance behavior. *Line Up* examines tensions between order and disorder, control and error, pattern and irregularity, intention and expectation, statement and variation, clarity and distortion.

To create the "Rinse Variations" on *Locus*, for *Line Up* (so called because they "would be watered down in the end")[15] Brown gave written instructions on how to do each movement — omitting any reference to the structure or the title of the dance — to three dancers, Wendy Perron, Steve Paxton, and Terry O'Reilly. The three had never performed *Locus* and did not know its system. They learned the movements on their own and in *Line Up* danced them with Elizabeth Garren, a performer from the original version. The result was an odd, provocative distortion of the material.

Solo Olos was initially choreographed as a single phrase to be performed as a palindrome. In *Line Up* the piece was expanded into three phrases, performed by four dancers (originally, Brown, Garren, Perron, and Judith Ragir), according to extemporaneous instructions by a fifth performer (Mona Sulzman). The two new phrases branch off from and reconnect with the main phrase at specific points. The steps and gestures themselves have moved more into the realm of hieroglyphs: a little hop with the foot scraping along the floor; touching the toe and then snapping the fingers; a certain wag of the head and hands. In performance, the audience is challenged and tantalized by the task of deciphering the instructions in order to discover the underlying structure of the piece. The caller cries out the names of the dancers and their instructions: either "Reverse," Branch," or "Spill." At first it isn't clear whom the instructions affect, or how. But as the dance progresses we start to piece the clues together. The dancers begin and end and re-begin unison movement, repeat actions in retrograde, suddenly change their quality of movement. Two dancers get the same instruction and then one gets a new instruction, providing contrasting information. The result is a complex satisfaction, a combination of the pleasure of watching the dancing with its natural but often interrupted phrasing, and the double gratification both of learning the deep structure of the piece as the dance progresses and feeling a mutual sense of accomplishment with the dancers as they make their shifts from one operation to another.

Skymap (1969) is an attempt to make a dance on the ceiling by verbal instructions to the audience to project words up to its surface. *Pamplona Stones* (1974) compares the functions of words, objects, and human bodies in the dance. In a short adventure involving two women (Brown and Sylvia Whitman), two chairs, two rocks, a mattress, a sheet, and dance phrases, Brown tests certain signals. "Stop!" she calls as Whitman drops a rock. Or, "This is my turn," she says, at first seeming to refer to *turn* in the sense of succession, but then demonstrating a turn (twist) of the torso. With *Splang* (1978), Brown continues to investigate the way words find meaning in embodiment, continuing as well her concern with methods of transmission of movement and the resulting degrees of distortion. Extending the concept of the "Rinse Variations" from *Locus,* Brown gave three dancers in her company (Garren, Perron, and Sulzman) a set of instructions, ranging from the purely descriptive ("Step forward R") to the qualitative ("Hit the floor hard") to the imagistic ("Pass through a sexy woman position") to the impossible ("Be invisible"). This time, however, there was no original to distort. The varying solutions of the dancers to the score constituted the raw material of the piece, which Brown then edited into set time segments that could be taken apart and reshuffled. Three separate translations of Brown's ideas into movement manifest themselves on stage, punctuated by stillnesses and sudden shifts into vigorous action. The gap between words and their realization is made concrete.

In the early works, when tasks or equipment structures delimited the movements in Brown's dances, she casually used available performers: friends, colleagues, students, trained and untrained dancers. They became trained in Brown's own techniques of mastering gravity and solving other physical problems simply by working with her. As the dances grew more demanding technically, as they dealt more and more with pure movement, Brown's need for trained dancers increased. Since 1974 she has worked intensively with Judith Ragir (until 1977), Elizabeth Garren, Mona Sulzman, and, from 1975 to 1978, Wendy Perron.

As I write this, Brown's most recent work is a solo, *Water Motor* (1978). In a sense it recalls some of her earliest concerns; I am reminded of *Trillium,* where the possibilities were to stand, sit, or lie, and Brown ended up levitating. *Water Motor* is a miniature dance, so short — two and a half minutes — that it ends all too quickly. Yet it is complete, exhilarating, concisely packed. A syncopated listing of gestures and positions, it evokes images like the prow of a boat slicing the water, diving, falling; but it also presents the pure movement of joint and limb action, at times in seemingly impossible combinations. Energy is suddenly dropped, then resumed. Often, Brown's body looks as if it is gleefully going in two directions at once. *Water Motor* is a dance that pries open Brown's logical systems to make room for exquisite disorder.

Trisha Brown, Skymap[16]

The words that I am speaking are coming up through a small hole in the floor of the auditorium and following each other one by one around the room, eventually tracing out a map of the United States, including Aberdeen, Chicago, Oakland, and San Antonio. Those words having difficulty keeping up with the others are being helped by invisible gnomes. Those words who refuse to participate will be forced to write "I AM SORRY" in capital letters over and over again on the side panels. Those words representing animals have been asked to fashion their movements after the gait of the animal mentioned. So if you hear "horse," know that H-O-R-S-E-S are trotting out to take their places as border, valley, and capital.

Skymaps are not new. Astronomy has been around for years and years. So relax. If a letter or two or whole word (God forbid) should fall in your vicinity, please function as a gnome assistant and toss it back up. Already the lakes are beginning to form. I didn't realize that L-A-K-E-S, when they got together, could turn blue. I do know and must warn you that clichés, especially "sorry about that," have been known to nest in the pockets of people in the area. If this happens to you, try shouting "fumigator" in an original way. Stutters and uh's unavoidably used by the speaker have been asked to take the position of dotted lines representing unfinished highways and dirt roads. People unable to control coughing or sneezing should be chastised by those people in the audience who care about state lines. All audience members who are unable to visualize the map overhead will get lost on the way home.

Now I have to give you some words, so that you can carry out the project of making a map. Don't get lost in the content. Stick to your task and be kind to the Midwest.

Ourfatherwhoartinheavenhallowedbethynamethykingdomcomethywillbe doneonearthasitisinheavengiveusthisdayourdailybreadandforgivveusour debtsasweforgiveourdebtorsandleadusnotintotemptationbutdeliverusfrom evilforthineisthekingdomthepowerandthegloryforever. I'm sorry to do that to you, but — we have a lot of mountains to place. From time to time I will pause, so you can hear the words working. Snoqualmie Pass . . . Don't forget Alabama . . . Yellowstone . . . Willamette River . . . Skyline Boulevard . . . Boise . . . Tahoe . . . Wyoming . . . Devil's Hopyard . . . Mount Rushmore . . . Black Lick . . . West Virginia . . . Bismarck . . . Texarkana . . . Eunice, New Mexico . . . Pleasington . . . Salina . . . Centralia . . . Delaware . . . Hutchinson . . .

I'd like to get into something now that's a little sticky. Do you remember saying prayers? Saying them so often you couldn't remember what they meant to save your soul? "Our Father Who Art in Heaven" always confused me. I had an uncle Art. I mean for a flash I thought Art was Our Father Who Lived in Heaven. It means that God lives up in heaven it does not mean that my uncle Art did anything up there and it doesn't mean that God makes art in heaven. "Give us this bread" — my mother always bought an extralong loaf of white bread called Wonderbread. "Surely goodness and her sister mercy mild" — no matter how good I was all day I always failed because I couldn't remain alert while I said my prayers to know that I was saying my prayers right. And then "Amen" at the end. I mean — for a little girl to say "Ah men" — uh — I know this is very weighty stuff, but — I told you about the mountains.

Now that I'm into it I might as well tell you about Reverend Shangler. Shangler should go directly to Philadelphia because I understand that's where he lives now. He turned me on to religion in the beginning. I must have been — two. A great guy, skinny and glasses and they ran him out of town. They said he visited the lame instead of the halt or something like that and out he went. I shouldn't be talking about all this because it was a small town and very gossipy and I used his real name and for all I know he's in the audience. Maybe he's all around us. Fort Oglethorp . . . Connellsville . . . Wishkaw, Quinault, Quilliute River, Adirondacks . . . Alaska . . . Woonsocket, Buffalo, Hazelhurst, Willacoochee, Vaughan, Jetmore, Oh Lord, save the day and all the people using it . . . Wolf . . . Frostproof, Florida . . . Wetumpka, Back Bay, Molokai . . . I . . . am . . . sorry . . . Flagstaff, Oklahoma, Brooklyn, Port Arthur, L.A., Erie, Kodak, Seattle, Green River, Bivalve, Washington, D.C.

The beaches are good. One way I considered training the words was to have them pile up on the Pacific Coast and then spread them like peanut butter across the continent. But the words function better as individuals, going along one after another. Then of course we could have added raspberry jam for highlights like the mountains and rivers.

Patriiicia! Goooooordon! Louiiiiiisa! Diiiiiiner!

South Carolina, Oklahoma City, Fort Lauderdale, Hartford, Amazonia, Wheeling, Hinckley, Monterey, Kalamazoo, Smith-Corona, Saturday night, Sarasota Springs, Vista View, spring chicken, answering service, Golden City, prairie dog, Sea Girt, Sitka.

B as in Boise. You begin to notice the individual personalities of the letters as they move out to do their work. B's all right, a little slow-witted. Actually, I'm quite fond of B, it's on all my mother's silver. I find it hard to believe that O is fifty years old. Z I believe but O. Z is not in Boise anyway. I is not clear to me. I can't really put my finger on who I is. S is pregnant. S and W got married. They have a nice house out on the Island. Windows, curtains, cockroaches. E is not blond. E is a good, solid, ordinary working letter.

Lake Awosting, Oyehut, West Point, Phoebe, Monrovia, Plain Dealing, New Braunfels, Orange, Mount Desert Ferry, Muleshoe, Yakima, Noxen, Eldoro. Call weather bureau, botanic gardens, order meat, get photos, tax, Rome meeting, get forsythia, Debbie rehearsal, Shawn. Dinner Steve and Susan, summer flowers, Debbie here, film. Deb and David's, bring slides, set up wall, Alex's opening, get money. View eight millimeter, chicken noodle, tuna fish. Deb ten to eleven, Ann Burton. Four Walter Gutman, one whole chicken. Four pounds chopped meat, nine to eleven Newark State. Animal hospital. Dentist. Nine to one Trish, Adam to Ann's, nine to one Trish, eleven Deb, Martha and Bill. Bob's opening, call animal doctor, Peter Poole, wildflowers, Justin here, call Don Boice, white paper, staplegun. Number 202 tape. Ten Deb here, one Christopher and Jason, 4:30 Julia, seven Joan, Judy, Keith's concert, get two bartenders, order ice, clean Cinematheque.

I had quite a hassle with their union. Words are not supposed to get up off their page. But since this project is of a patriotic nature, permission was granted. Deserts are easy, so why don't we stick a few cities out in the desert, to speed things up. And while we're taking liberties, let's make a rolling hill in the shape of a big chair. Let's make it a very soft chair. There should be a super-soft chair hill.

Red Desert, Hobgood, Benson Junction, Zortman, Wynona Oklahoma,

Lame Deer, Oakely, Dawsonville, New Hampshire, Dover, Jolly, Berkeley, Yakatat, Lydia, DeQueen, Lava Field, Julesburg, Sierra Blanca, Birdsboro Pennsylvania, Manchester, Rumford, Biddleford, Carbondale, Lynchburg, Raleigh, Bemidgi, Enders Reservoir, Red Hills, Eureka, Parsnip Park.

SOS, garbage liners, paper towels, dishwash soap, Borax, suntan lotion, cigarettes, beans tomatoes brownrice mushrooms greens fruit milk bread juice cheese and frozen vegetables.

Those spiderwebby things spreading out from Chicago are railroads. Took a lot of rehearsal.

That should be enough material now. There's really nothing to be done. Except for those of you who are not finished, go ahead and finish up. And the rest of you can sit back and enjoy it.

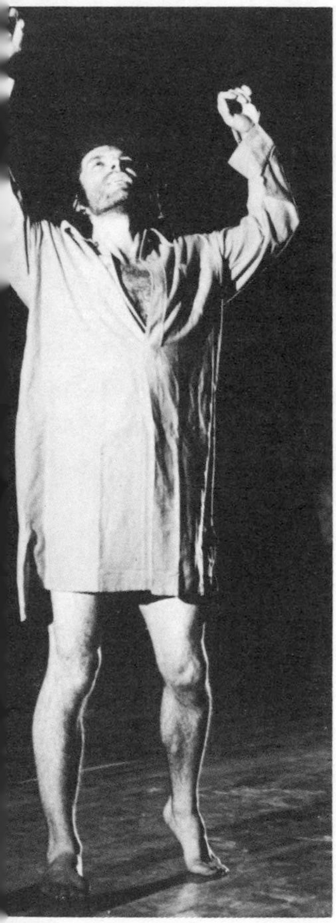
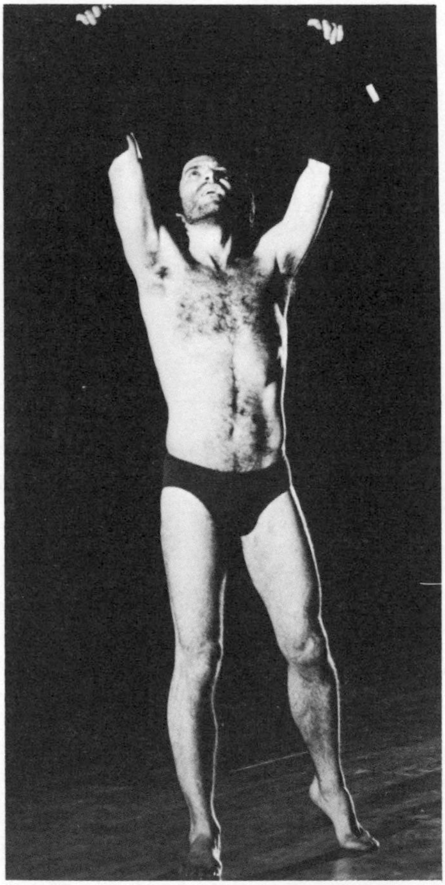
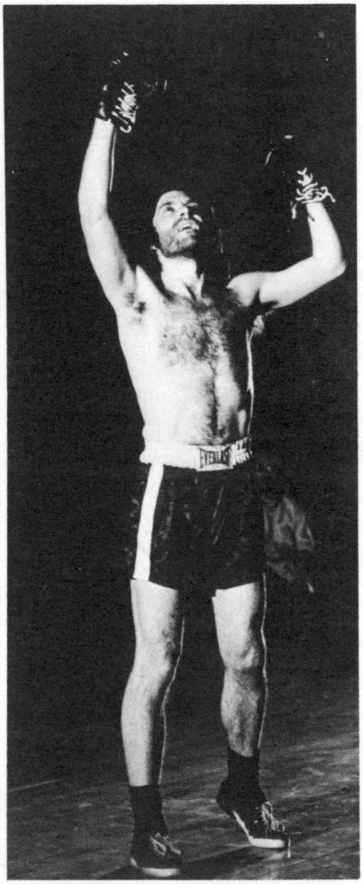

David Gordon: The Ambiguities

David Gordon's work over the past eighteen years has been concerned with finding structures for framing the individual, fleeting act. In one sense, he views choreography as self-defense: since the ideology of modern dance has always promoted tolerance for individual performance styles and body structures, it can be forced to make room for those dancers whose bodies and styles fit into no one's vision but their own. They survive artistically by becoming choreographers. But this kind of self-defensive thinking has also put Gordon on the offensive. Inventing new systems for ordering movement — changing the rules — means criticizing and discarding academic formulae. As a student, Gordon always managed to find the holes in the teaching. But he will criticize the new as well as the old. In the heyday of the Judson Church, his trenchant *Random Breakfast* (1963) parodied his peers' new methods of making dances. And his most recent dance, *Not Necessarily Recognizable Objectives* (1978), comments ironically on its own content and construction.

Refining his offensive/defensive strategies slowly, finding highly systematic constructions with which to frame the most elusive or undistinguished movements, concentrating on minute details of simple actions, and using repetition as a key device, Gordon has evolved a choreographic practice that works analytically. Like a cubist painter, he accumulates and organizes multiple views of a single phenomenon into one composition — a method that despite apparent distortion often reflects more accurately the complex psychological processes of visual perception. As Cézanne and his followers made near and far objects equal in the picture plane, so Gordon effectively erases

David Gordon in *The Matter.* Photographs © Babette Mangolte, 1972.

hierarchies between classes of movement. Transitions between one kind of gesture or step and another become as important as the step itself. Or transitions disappear entirely. Habitual or functional gestures appear side-by-side with abstract movements. But an inclination of the head or the lifting of a chair may be given even more weight than a jump. The process of isolating and focusing on particular movements tends to stress their formal qualities, though Gordon's dances also bristle with humor, irony, and social comment.

In the debate on theatricality among post-modern choreographers, Gordon espouses spectacle. But he uses spectacular moments and glamorous touches cunningly, often intensifying them until a gap between the movement relationships and their theatrical overlay throws the movement into high relief. Or, until ultimately the ambiguity of what is "real" and what is dramatic, or scripted, floats tantalizingly to the surface of the dance.

Gordon was born and grew up in Manhattan. He earned a degree in fine arts from Brooklyn College, where he performed with the school dance club. In 1956, while still in college, he began dancing in James Waring's company. From Waring, he learned to value wit and style, to consider any movement as something that might be included in a dance, to study the work of Merce Cunningham, Merle Marsicano, Katherine Litz, and others who were outside of what was then mainstream modern dance. He studied composition with Waring, choreographing his first publicly performed duet with Valda Setterfield[1] for a program of work by Waring's students given at the Living Theater in 1960.

While studying with Cunningham on a scholarship at Connecticut College in the summer of 1960, Gordon decided to take Martha Graham's technique class and Louis Horst's composition class as well. "I had no knowledge of this work that everybody else had revolted against," Gordon remembers.[2] He wanted to find out what Waring, Cunningham, Marsicano, Litz, Aileen Passloff and others had left behind.

He found Graham "extraordinary" but after the first week, she turned the class over to another teacher who was disappointing. Gordon's interest in Graham technique ended. In Horst's class, Gordon immediately found the chinks when he tried to fit his own content into the preclassic forms Horst assigned. "I did an ABA number in which the A part was jumping around and shaking a lot and the B part had to do with leg lifts and the A part was a return to shaking again." Gordon admits he was looking for trouble when he told the teacher that the name of the dance was *The Spastic Cheerleader.* But he believes that his attempt to solve the next assignment, a duet in ABA form, was earnest. He asked Setterfield to be his partner. She would do the A section, Gordon would come in and together they would perform B, and then he would do her A movement at the end. Horst objected to the dance as soon as Setterfield began it, saying that it wasn't a duet at all. "He didn't let us continue and he wouldn't see it and after that he wouldn't call my name . . . So that ended *that* kind of knowledge-gathering."

Gordon's next duet for himself and Setterfield, on the Waring program in 1960, was *Mama Goes Where Papa Goes.* Setterfield recalls that at the time, Gordon was interested in awkwardness and in disturbing fluidity of movement.[3] Gordon remembers his motivation much more specifically: "Valda was so lyrical-looking and competent." The piece opened with Gordon standing on stage, his arms full of rubber balls. He opened his arms, dropped all the balls, and when they had stopped bouncing and rolling away, he walked off. Setterfield had a solo that was a series of jumps, one followed immediately by the next, involving different body parts, without any transitions or preparations. At another point in the dance, Setterfield limped on crutches to center stage while Gordon followed her; he pulled away the crutches, and she walked.

Nascent in *Mama Goes Where Papa Goes* are a number of themes that were to continue as concerns in Gordon's work. One is the ironic tribute to the myths cherished and disseminated by Hollywood. Another is the reversal of the notion that dancing is movement made to look easy; in the jump sequence, dancing was awkwardness and blatantly difficult maneuvering. A third theme, embodied in the opening sequence, is that the handling of objects and the duration of an action can dictate timing, a rejection of musical or dramatic sources for rhythm that has occupied the work of other post-modern choreographers as well.

Continuing to study sporadically with Cunningham, and by now married to Setterfield, Gordon discovered that refining technique interested him far less than making dances. He took composition with Cunningham, and then in the class taught by Robert Dunn, which later exploded into the Judson Dance Theater. But having learned chance techniques already from Waring, Gordon found himself as uncomfortable with what he perceived as a rigid approach to chance in the Dunn class as he had been with Horst's preclassic forms. He continued to look for ways to beat the system. When Dunn allowed the option of using Satie music in various ways, Gordon chose to ignore the music entirely. He made *Mannequin Dance* and *Helen's Dance* (both 1962) partly, he claims, to irritate the teacher.[4] But despite his discomfort with Dunn's dogmatic approach, he recalls that class as "an extraordinary meeting of explosive material with its catalyst . . . the contact with each other, many of us for the first time, was as instrumental as the classes in producing that explosion."[5]

Mannequin Dance was originally conceived as material to be repeated ten times in one evening, surrounded by clothed or nude department store mannequins which would be moved around and have their costumes changed in between the solos. Another continuing concern — repetition — emerges, though Gordon never did perform the piece more than once in an evening.

Gordon's fascination with show biz reached an apotheosis in *Random Breakfast* (1963), in which all sorts of performance styles and conventions are presented and pulled apart, from Spanish dancing to Milton Berle's imitations of Carmen Miranda, from striptease to happenings to the Judson Church dances to Judy Garland.[6] In several dances before and after *Random Breakfast* he has used flamboyant costumes, stagy demeanor, lavish music, or Hollywood cliché imagery: he sings "Second Hand Rose" and "Get Married Shirley" in *Mannequin Dance;* in *The Matter* (1972), the performers imitate the frozen glamour of fashion models, striking bathing beauty poses, and later in the same piece the group performs low-key movement material accompanied by a recording of the wedding march from *Lohengrin.* Gordon's *Chair* (1974) opens with a sixteen-piano rendition of "The Stars and Stripes Forever." In some versions of *Sleepwalking* (1971), the dancers put on coats and hats that suggested gangster or spy costumes. And in *Not Necessarily Recognizable Objectives* (*NNRO*), Gordon is compared to Nijinsky in the spoken text.

But his use of glamorous signals is paradoxical. Glamour excites a whole set of romantic cultural connotations: luxury, power, mystery, instant success, sexual display and desirability, vanity, artifice, and nostalgia. Partly these signals function as sincere tributes to movies, performers, and music Gordon admires. But also, embedded in the context of a Gordon dance, the glamorous qualities clash violently with other elements: casual activity; everyday or sloppy clothing; repetition approaching tedium; the acknowledgment that dancing is work and the demystification of the choreographic process; and, especially, the presentation of individuals as unique beings, with highly idiosyncratic bodies. The notion of glamour proposes a standardized ideal of physical beauty, one that must be emulated and that will provide a key to the total transformation of one's life. But Gordon's dances ultimately emphasize the differences between bodies, celebrating the qualities of awkwardness and confusion, as well as grace, elegance, and authority. The stark contrast between the spectacular and the mundane in the dances has several functions. It raises the common features to the status of acceptable theatrical material, by lending them the fanfare normally spent on extraordinary elements. But also, it raises fundamental questions about theatricality by distancing spectacle from movement. During the performance we are forced to consider how movements become theatrical. How is the peculiar aura of glamour manufactured? Does the glossy exterior of spectacle hide, alter, or enhance serious content? Can a performance ever escape its own historical moment — the fact that it has inherited a legacy from the institution of theater, whether it follows or breaks from that tradition, and the fact that the audience brings to a performance certain shared expectations about theatrical dancing? By referring directly to theatricality in his unconventionally theatrical works, Gordon situates his dances firmly. They are not entertainments, but artworks that analyze and criticize entertainment. They show the power and mystique entertainment can create, the art it can popularly present. Invoking symbols of nostalgia, Gordon shows that his work is the product of a historical process, yet very much of the present.

In 1966, Gordon gave up on choreography after his solo *Walks and Digressions* was badly received. He describes the piece as "a sequence of events, non-related, with bridges . . . I remember very clearly as the material came out thinking what the fuck am I doing, this is really grotesque, I'm walking around holding my crotch and pulling my pants down and spitting. These are really ugly things. And I thought all right, I'll keep it, I'll see what happens. And when it came time to perform it I was exceedingly uncomfortable . . . and so I set the lights so you could barely see it." The audience booed and walked out across the stage as Gordon performed. Robert Morris, reviewing the dance for the *Village Voice,* was harsh: "Certainly the work was not shocking (the underwear was so very clean) nor did it manage any incisive humor. When a work is presented that suggests that it might have aimed at such results but fails to bring off either, the performer is stranded in his own vacuum of self-indulgence." And Clive Barnes called the entire concert (which included works by Steve Paxton and others) "nothing but the exercise of puerile egocentric minds in the futile quest of shocking the already unshockable . . . pitiful, adolescent caterwauling."[7]

Gordon had felt like an outsider in the Judson Church situation from the beginning. At this point he was dancing with Yvonne Rainer as well as making his own work, and he questioned his own methods seriously. He was not prepared for a strong negative reaction to his work, and he stopped choreographing until 1971.

By that time he was partly fortified by his work with Rainer and with the incipient Grand Union. Rainer asked him to teach her students during her trip to India, and the classes, affording a leisurely situation in which to work with a large group of dancers and nondancers, impelled him further. The piece that emerged was *Sleepwalking.*

The basic movement theme of *Sleepwalking* is acceleration. The dance is a cluster of identical solos — a sequence that moves from strolling to walking to running to racing, between two walls. Finally the performers lean against one of the walls as if asleep, leave to put on hats and coats, return to the wall and fall, writhing violently, as if shot. Because walking is such a simple activity, the differences between various styles of walking among the group come clear long before the movement changes, giving the spectators time to examine them carefully. Turns, a twist of the torso, the switch from walking to running, are all magnified enormously because the background is so consistent. But as the walking metamorphoses rapidly into running and then racing, we make another set of comparisons. We notice how effort and muscular deployment change as speed modifies the action. Since each performer chooses randomly when to change pace, at times the dance is a rich field of walking, running, turning, and bolting. The shoot-out imagery at the end provides an overlay of meaning, a possible (though not necessary) motivation for the speedup. And the accompanying sounds — sexual moans, sighs, and shrieks that intensify as the movement quickens — provide another possible, conflicting significance.

The Matter, another large group piece, made with twenty-five performers during a Grand Union residency at Oberlin College and performed by forty in Manhattan, uses the opposite operation for clarifying movement details.[8] Here halting, freezing, and interruption of movement prevail. Performers strike poses; at one point, involved in manipulations of objects like a stool, a box, a piece of wood, or their own pockets, they halt at random as the action progresses. Throughout the piece they suddenly freeze, or take positions and revise them. Setterfield's nude solo in *The Matter,* a series of held poses taken from Eadweard Muybridge's *The Human Figure in Motion,* exemplifies Gordon's shared concern with the photographer: to capture accurately the mercurial attitudes of the body by arresting it constantly in flux. The comparison between nude and clothed bodies, and among people in underwear, sleepwear, and street clothes, underscores the differences between readings of a single pose.

In *Chair, Alternatives 1 through 5* (1974), Gordon uses persistent repetition to point out two types of distinctions. The dance begins with an empty stage and a sixteen-piano recording of "The Stars and Stripes Forever." Next, two conflicting, fictional accounts "explain" how the piece was made. Then Gordon and Setterfield repeat four times an eight-minute sequence of evenly flowing action, with a folding chair — sitting on it, kneeling on it, lying on it, falling off it, folding it, pulling it over the body, leaning in it, stepping on, over, or through it, et cetera. But each repetition of the double solo is a slight variation. First the sequence is stated by the two simultaneously. The second time, each performer stops the flow at various points to repeat a fragment over and over. The third time, Setterfield reverses directions, so that instead of a double image of the same dance, we see one image and its symmetrically inverted reflection. And the fourth time, the two sing the Sousa march while executing the actions slightly faster. The dance ends as the two finish the fourth sequence and stand during the finale of "The Stars and Stripes Forever," this time played by a military band.

During the first statement of the chair material, one notices the distinctive ways Gordon's solid, muscular male body and Setterfield's thin, angular yet sinuous female body accommodate the physical facts of the chair and, reciprocally, are emphasized by it. (There is one action Gordon performs but Setterfield does not: lying across the back of the chair on the pelvis. It simply was painful for Setterfield, though it was not for Gordon.) The functional actions with the chair act like markers to point out the workings of the joints, muscles and bones; during the part of the phrase where the chair is lightly dragged over the body as the dancers lie on the floor, the chair literally traces a profile of each body. The differences, rather than similarities, are stressed since the movements are rarely synchronized exactly and tend to slip into rhythmic canon. Though the individual actions are simple, the sequence itself is complex. It is slippery, hard to remember, since the various actions have many elements in common and they flow by without transitions. Their diversity is glossed by a fluent, uninflected rhythm which slows down and accelerates but rarely pauses. The pace of the movement also changes the action from task to dance.

But the second time the sequence is repeated, reiteration functions within the phrase to clarify individual actions, rather than to emphasize physical differences. Each performer can decide where and how long to get stuck, so the repetition changes from one performance to the next, and it throws the entire canon out of order. The repetition also creates a tension between simplifying the movement — it becomes familiar to the spectator both because it repeats what we saw in the first alternative and because it magnifies certain details — and complicating the movement. The repetition evokes images that lend meaning to the abstract activity. For instance, when she touches her head to the floor repeatedly, Setterfield appears to be bowing submissively. Sexual imagery is suggested when the chair is rubbed back and forth over the body, or when the movement of the pelvis from side to side is rhythmically repeated while hunching over the seat of the chair. At other times, though, the action suggests child's play: sitting backward on the chair with one leg through the back, it is walked around in circles. Or the action resembles a child's tantrum: the chair is placed emphatically on the floor over and over until it turns into obstinate banging. Getting up from the floor converts into situp and pushup regimens; stepping forward and back over and over again seems to signal indecision; rearranging hands and feet or shifting weight repeatedly while sitting implies nervousness, or even autistically ritual behavior. When Gordon's head is stuck through the back of the chair and he almost lifts it off a number of times, we suddenly see him as a powerless prisoner. The second chair alternative shows us the power of our tendency to create contextual meaning for movement.

During the third repetition of the phrase the movements, now clarified and familiar, are done in their original form, but we see them in mirror image. Again our attention is called to the formal details of the actions and the way the pattern changes when we see it from a different angle. Gordon's execution of the movements in their original direction serves as a glancing board against which Setterfield's reversals stand out saliently. The fourth alternative, when the performers sing as they manipulate the chair, again imparts psychological meaning to the phrase. We see it as a difficult task requiring effort; we hear them losing their breath or going out of tune at troublesome points. This time, the rhythm of the phrase seems altered, dictated by the rhythm of the song. The action begins to look perfunctory in a way that the previous three versions had not; though it may be because the phrase is performed faster, it seems to be because the singing predominates over the action. The contrast between the significance of the action when juxtaposed to music or repeated methodically and its relative neutrality in different contexts makes any interpretation ambiguous.

The duet *Wordsworth and the motor + Times Four* (1977) carries this ambiguity further. A series of arm and leg gestures, again performed several times in overlapping rhythmic canon, reads differently when the performers (a) describe what they are doing ("turn, jump, straight arm, circle arm, walk, walk, walk"); (b) assign functional meaning to the gestures ("hi, put it there, where did I put it, who's he, go away"); (c) give soliloquies from Shakespeare while moving, the gestures seemingly turning into conventions of stage oratory. The spectators' visual screens are wiped clean with an interlude, *Times Four* (1975), a chain of semaphoric actions performed in precise, side-by-side unison, with each gesture or step repeated in four opposite directions. Then the Wordsworth sequence is done again, accompanied by the sound of a motor, as a wall, which blocks each dancer from the view of half the audience, is built between the two dancers. One remembers the text one heard on tape before the dancing began — from David Pye's *The Nature of Design* — and one starts making logical connections.

In order to understand how Gordon's repetitions and ingenious variations operate, one has to visualize his movement style. He says of himself that he is not a technically trained dancer, and that he is lazy. "My leg never went up very high, and turning still makes me vomit."[9] Yet movement looks easy and authoritative on him. Whether working with dancers or nondancers, he uses movements that look more like *behavior* than choreography — the sorts of movements people make routinely, unconsciously, and therefore often decisively. Legs rarely go straight in the air; even a high kick is done with a bent knee. Torsos yield, arms relax. In every Gordon dance I've seen, the movements are specific and deliberate, yet performed with a casual demeanor that nearly belies their careful design. Thus Gordon's repetitions are often shocking. We don't expect to see two people, or a whole group of people, duplicating movements that look spontaneous and idiosyncratic. Nor do we expect dancers to remember so precisely a long string of movements that are nearly indistinguishable. And we are surprised that material so similar to unconscious behavior can be varied so distinctly, and in so many ways.

If all behavior is performance, as sociologist Erving Goffman argues,[10] how can we distinguish between performances that are spontaneous/rehearsed, scripted/improvised, accurate/flawed, controlled/out of control, fact/fiction?

Not Necessarily Recognizable Objectives solves the dilemma by emphasizing the contradictions. The distinction between polar opposites becomes less intriguing than the tensions and ambiguities. In *NNRO,* occurrences at rehearsals — arguments, laughter, mistakes — were incorporated into the (verbal and kinetic) script; also, the structure allows for spontaneous action and talk at specific times. The spectator is never allowed to feel certain about what is planned and what is new. And since the planned events often look very much like the sort of disruptions that might mar a performance, every action carries ambivalence and tension. The dancers stumble, but when they stumble in unison, you realize it's planned. But one dancer falls during the stumbling; when Gordon glances at him, then continues across the floor, you wonder again if it's "for real." The performers stop to have an argument — is it genuine? They express confusion verbally as well as in movement, but at the same time they provide clues that all the confusion is scrupulously choreographed. They scratch their arms, smooth their hair, rest their hands on their hips, stop to complain, hold their noses, mutter to themselves, ask to go back to the beginning, consult with each other. And all this behavior forms around a movement combination that is repeated many times, and varied. They run, but in slow motion. (The running occurs at points throughout, with different pairs and with the whole group. Once again, you compare body types, as first Gordon and Setterfield run together, then Setterfield and Stephanie Woodard — whose heights are in the same uneven proportions as Gordon's and Setterfield's had been.) They look in one direction and move the opposite way. Clear positions crystallize momentarily during transit. *NNRO* is a ballet of crossed signals. And the spectators participate in the ambiguities, reading the crossed signals first one way, then another.

The performance begins with a tape of Agnes Moorehead, from *Sorry, Wrong Number,* asking the operator to dial again the wrong number she's just reached. Then a voice recites a passage from Erving Goffman's *The Presentation of Self in Everyday Life* that outlines all the little mistakes that can botch a performance. Gordon and Setterfield enter, run in a circle, then along diagonal lines. Then they stand facing the wall. A script is taped to the wall. You can see that dialogue is written on the script, but as they talk it's hard to tell what they're reading and what they interpolate. They tell each other what comes next. But when they quote ostensibly correct lines, the quotation marks are lost in the telling, and the statements curl back on themselves enigmatically. "So I never say 'what' like it's a question . . ." the dialogue begins. "You have to say you have to say now it's you," Setterfield insists. "You have to say now it's you," Gordon says obediently. "*Now* it's you," she responds. They argue about whether they've turned at the right time, and whether they ought to start the dialogue again from the beginning, and soon they actually do start again from the beginning, but this time switching roles. When the dialogue is repeated exactly, down to the laughs and about-faces and hugs and pauses, we realize that the entire scene was scripted.

Next comes a movement sequence, concentrated and silent, in which the two revolve constantly, their arms wrapping and unwrapping each other's shoulders, slowly and deliberately, as they adjust their bodies to fit snugly together. Their taped voices appear, to start another circular discussion, this one about arguing. Predictably, it turns into an argument about their inability to argue constructively. Woodard enters and she and Setterfield start the slow run around the circle; as Woodard's body enters the running circle, becoming Setterfield to Setterfield's Gordon, her voice slips into the verbal circle on the tape. Later, the same movement circles and diagonals are done by the whole group of dancers.

During the piece, the performers casually join and leave activity; Martha Roth stops to wonder aloud whether the movement, continuing inexorably without her, would look better as a duet than as a trio, and she ruefully concludes that no one will even miss her. Gordon and Setterfield join the two, and suddenly Roth is left out of a quartet. But when she repeats the punch line of her earnest speech again, and when the other four stop to determine whether they've picked her up at the right spot, it's obvious that the whole interruption has been rehearsed.

The three women press together gently to repeat the arm wrapping sequence Gordon and Setterfield had done. They turn around and around, and add lying down and getting up in unison, so that now you see knees descending, now an arm resting across a back, now buttocks rising in the air, now shoulders coming forward. Romantic music from *Swan Lake* and *La Fille Mal Gardée* suddenly fills the room; abruptly the women, balanced delicately in a row, look like wilting ballerinas about to bourrée primly across the floor. But they lie down again, piling slowly on top of one another, then cradling like spoons across the floor.

The other four dancers stand in a cluster to watch Gordon do "his new solo." They become a corps de ballet that functions now as dance critics, now as groupies, joined by the stage manager, assistant stage manager, and coordinator. They all comment on Gordon's performance and on the structure of the dance: an erratic distribution of seemingly arbitrary, offhand gestures — stifling a yawn, folding the arms, looking down, moving the chin — mixed with preparations, transitions, repetitions, and stillnesses. He strikes an exquisite, pliant pose — the head held back, both arms lifted limply in front of his face. He lunges, turns, and quickly changes directions several times. He points his finger against the tip of his nose and swivels his feet. The corps discusses every action minutely. They misunderstand each other. They note his character and depth ("Oh, I didn't know his work was like that," one exclaims), and they worry that his appearance of indecision will be misread ("What if someone thinks he doesn't know what he's doing?"). A taped voice has earlier explained that these comments are supposed to undercut the vanity inherent in the solo; but "Don't be fooled for a minute," the voice warns. And yet, the solo as egocentric manipulation by the choreographer *is* undercut when the group replicates it exactly, and in its slowest, most concentrated version it is transferred to Setterfield as a grand finale. Singing by the Alabama Sacred Harp Convention gives the dance grandeur as the group performs it; when Setterfield, who has started later than the others, is left alone on stage, Joan Baez's voice appears. One recognizes the song she's singing — "Amazing Grace" — and the term seems apt for describing Setterfield's rendition of the by-now-familiar solo. Yet Baez teases, never singing the chorus; her voice is cut off after a transitional riff. The spectator's imagination is left to fill in the blank. Yes, amazing grace.

Gordon's dances, persistently changing meaning, construct circles of perception that are suggestive but elusive. When Gordon uses words, despite the way they change according to context, they are specific in a way that movement refuses to be. Yet the most appropriate description of Gordon's stratagem is a literary one, in spite of his kinetic medium. He is a supreme ironist, subverting impressions as fast as he projects them.

David Gordon, Response[11]

"... he accumulates and organizes multiple views of a single phenomenon into one composition ..." (page 97). A terrific description of what I think I'm doing.

"Gordon admits he was looking for trouble ..." (page 98). I *was* looking for trouble. I still am. I thought that one of the things about making art was looking for trouble. I teach now sometimes. I always look for the student who is looking for trouble.

"They are not entertainments, but artworks that analyze and criticize entertainment" (page 101). I like this sentence. And I like it about my work. I would, however, change "criticize" to "comment on." I have no desire to criticize but I talk a lot and I can't help talking about digested information. It is part of a process through which I discover whether or not anyone sees what I see. I want to discover that they do indeed see what I see. Somebody recently said to me "... but you've chosen to walk alone ..." Bullshit. I never knew I was going to be alone. I thought we were all in the same boat. It was and continues to be shocking to discover myself, by myself, at sea.

Writing about someone's life, in relationship to their work, leaves out the days, the weeks when nothing was happening, or when nothing good was happening. Or the times when one doubted. Or the times when one doubted everyone else. The lows seem not to have existed and the great highs seem somehow flatter than they were. Example: "Inventing new systems for ordering movement — changing the rules — means criticizing and discarding academic formulas." Actually, "inventing new systems for ordering movement . . ." means yippee and some terrific Chinese food if you happen to know at the time that you have indeed invented a new system which most likely you don't even know until someone writes about it. Or tells you.

And what about the dancing? What about how amazing it is to be hurtling along and stopping still and making some personal order out of all the movement information you have gathered and continue to gather and continue. And performing? And all of the implications of being a "performer." And how to make money. And being young, and getting older. And how all things change your relationship, day to day, every day, to your work, the work which is all these things and more.

I'm trying to say that what reads as a matter of fact plan achieved with intelligence and foresight is often a network of chance or fate and foolishness and paranoia and alternating aggressiveness and passivity and envy and naivety and good humor and some smarts and time and more time.

Deborah Hay: The Cosmic Dance

DEBORAH HAY'S choreography during the 1960s and '70s has evolved from theatrical to social to almost sacred dancing. In her early dances, she stressed the raw physicality of pure movement, contrasting natural, pedestrian locomotion like running, walking, or ordinary jumping with abstract dance-technical steps. Later, her reductionism led to simple, natural movements and the most basic steps. Perhaps her most radical act was to blur subject and object; in some early dances, the roles of performer and prop were switched and in the later Circle Dances and *The Grand Dance,* distinctions between participant and observer are erased. Hay's compositional methods and her materials articulate a consistent underlying concern: what is the nature of experience, perception, and attention in dance? As she intensified physical and mental sensitivity to the dancing experience, the role of spectator grew irrelevant. As she stripped away movements and structures to find the essential qualities of dance, Hay's view of the art intersected with a vision of a life integrating a continuous, refined consciousness of changes, motion, and rhythm with all other aspects of daily living. In such a scheme, the outside observer is superfluous. *Life* is dance and to experience it fully one must not stand outside it.

Because Hay believes that at times people need guidance to discover their innate capacities to enjoy dancing, and because she feels drawn to communicate to others her own joy in and knowledge of movement, she created a group of Circle Dances that, because they are technically and psychologically comfortable, are accessible to anyone. They are based on easy, familiar movements, yet they provide physical and social experiences that transcend mun-

Deborah Hay, *Solo Performance.* Photograph © Ellen Wallenstein, 1979.

dane events. The Circle Dances are rooted in Hay's belief that "breath is movement and movement is dance and anyone can dance."[1] Each of the ten dances, about an hour long, is a hybrid of meditation, folk dance, ritual, Tai Chi Chuan, and American social dancing. The dancing draws not only on the breath cycle of the individual, but also on the power of the group and the rhythmic impulse of popular music, to provide reservoirs of energy. Moments of strenuous activity exceeding normal stamina are powered by this energy, which is restored by moments of quiet, inward-directed centering. Hay's instructions for the dances provide a simple structure. The basic directions informing each movement section are read by a leader during the dance. The structure, alternating between inner and outer sensing, slow and fast movements, surges of power and times of quiescence, is shaped like a tide, generating a whole that is harmonious, balanced, and refined, despite its enormous range and freedom.

The Circle Dances and later, *The Grand Dance,* were inspired in part by Hay's experiences with Tai Chi Chuan, a sequence of movements and postures developed over centuries in China, according to the tenets of Taoism. In order to understand how the Circle Dances operate, it is useful to look at Taoist values and methods. But before analyzing Tai Chi, I want to talk about Hay's earlier choreography and the way her prior concerns contributed to the development of the Circle Dances and *The Grand Dance.*

Born in Brooklyn in 1941, Hay learned to dance as a small child, beginning with lessons from her mother, and continuing with classes at the Henry Street Playhouse from Bill Frank and others. Later, she studied with Mia Slavenska, James Waring, and Merce Cunningham. During a summer at Connecticut College, she performed with José Limón's company. At this time, her desire to dance was insatiable. She remembers that after training and rehearsing in the studio all day, she still had the stamina and enthusiasm to go out dancing socially until late at night. Hay danced in James Waring's company, and joined Merce Cunningham's company for his world tour in 1964. She had taken the Robert Dunn composition class in 1961, and performed and choreographed primarily at the Judson Church in the early '60s, as well as at Judson-related events like Surplus Dance Theater, First New York Theater Rally, and Nine Evenings: Theater and Engineering.

Like many of her Judson colleagues, Hay reconsidered the experience of time during performance. Contesting the aesthetic of ballet and modern dance, which proposed an abstract, artificial meter based on either the rhythm of the accompanying music or the demands of stylized actions, Hay, Paxton, Rainer, and others substituted a system of duration founded on the actual. Their sources for measuring time included the everyday movements of tasks and games, repetition, reduction of movement, contrasts between filmed and live movement, disjunction between sound and action, and the handling of objects. Annette Michelson, writing about the sculptural work of Robert Morris, compares his achievement — the substitution of real space for "virtual" space — to the innovations of the post-modern choreographers, who installed "within the dance situation a real or operational time, redefining it as situation within which an action *may take the time it takes to perform that action.* Neither self-contained, nor engendered by pre-determined rhythmic or rhetorical patterns, it was not 'synthetic.' "[2] Time became real, concrete, non-mimetic, resulting in "an ascesis of a profoundly philosophic character . . . systematic focussing upon the ways of organising and apprehending the movement of bodies in space. A central focus for modern epistemological inquiry."[3] By redirecting attention in real time, the dances heightened the spectator's consciousness of attention and perception.

Thus the vitality of Hay's early dances, like *City Dance* (1963) — with its hurried, complex dispersions — and *All Day Dance* (1963) — with its childlike, energetic jumps, slides, and somersaults contrasting with dancey turns and kicks — was no more or less accurate or appropriate, in terms of timing, than the pared down, monotonous pace of *No. 3* (1966), in which three helpers toppled and dragged three stacks of bricks while Hay ran evenly in circles. Yvonne Rainer commented that in such a work, it almost seemed as if the ordinary attributes and energy of the dancer had been transferred to the inanimate objects. Rainer approved of such subversion, for it made the objects into dancers and the dancer an object, shifting the focus away from the performer's virtuosity, and eclipsing the "glamour, apotheosis, or accentuated vagaries of the prima donna, prima ballerina, and prima starrinarosa."[4] The neutrality of the dancer's role was a refreshing antidote to the emphasis on virtuosity and psychological expression that had strangled most modern dance for the previous two decades.

The important issue was that movement, rather than the mover, was paramount. So the action of the bricks, impersonal and inexpressive, was as important as, if not more important than, a woman moving or the helpers pulling on the string that operated the bricks. Correlated to this value was the idea that untrained performers manipulating objects could be as interesting to watch as skilled dance technicians. They might even be more interesting, for they would introduce unconventional movements, in dance terms, that would not usually be seen on stage. Who could say whether the actions of Alex Hay and Robert Rauschenberg, as they poured water in buckets, tangled their legs in strips of cloth, played with a rubber hose, and inked their hands and faces in *Serious Duet* (1966), would be enhanced by a dancer's posture? The anonymous power of a gray flat being manipulated by two assistants as Deborah Hay posed against it and moved near it in *Rise* (1966) proposed a negation of the dance aesthetic in which the "partnering" of the flat gains significance. It becomes nothing less than an act of erasing the entire code of classical dancing: the emphasis on personality, the flashy costumes, the dramatic phrasing disappear. Just so, in *All Day Dance for Two* (1964), the seamless quality of academic dance, in which the movements fit neatly together, was undermined by generating the dance with taped instructions. But Hay humorously subverted this process further by having two tapes play conflicting sets of instructions simultaneously, so that the dancers had to run and scratch something, and run, turn, and lie at someone's feet, all at the same time. The genesis of a movement or a movement relationship, Hay and her colleagues insisted by example, can be an integral part of the act of seeing.

The paring down of the timing, dynamics, activity, structure, and color in Hay's dances made some argue that they were monotonous, boring, or even a hoax.[5] But others argued that with her resolute reductionism, Hay cleansed the screen of vision, so that attention and awareness of that attention became compelling problems for the viewer. Seeing so much undifferentiated material forces the spectator to work to find diversity. Paradoxically, the simplification of temporal or spatial structure, of colors or textures, often makes viewing more difficult, and more rewarding. When Hay's sweat suit blended in perfectly with the gray of the flat in *Rise,* her dance became harder to distinguish from the "dance" of the decor. When she and Steve Paxton danced in chartreuse clothing against a grassy golf course in *Hill* (1965), the same challenge to perception confronted the audience. The entire view, having been equalized, provided a neutral ground for the low-relief emergence of the dance itself, of its essential features. In *Hill,* Hay exploited the natural and unnatural elements in the landscape: she and Paxton wrestled each other to the ground; he drove off in a golf car; she stacked up bricks and ran down the hill.

The found materials, task operations, raw movements, austere formats, and acknowledgment of the dance-making process in performance all evoked a sense of immediacy, concreteness, and direct perception that was not only appropriate to the cultural climate of the '60s, but also to a particular moment in dance history. Modern dance was weighted with drama, expressed through phrasing (i.e., a hierarchy of movements and moments), ornamentation, characterization, and variation.

One way to eliminate drama in dance is to reduce phrasing to a monotone, making climaxes impossible. Another is to limit personal decisions by the choreographer, by creating arbitrary structures of time, space, or movement, or by introducing elements that exert external control over the dancers. The instructions in *All Day Dance for Two* provided such agents, as did the more concealed instructions of *All Day Dance,* in which six dancers listened for prearranged signals to change their movement, coded by certain sounds in an unknown musical accompaniment — changing radio programs. In *Solo* (1966) — made with the help of an engineer from Bell Telephone Laboratories for Nine Evenings: Theater and Engineering — a group of sixteen performers, all executing the same slight movements, glided through the armory on small pedestals operated by seated performers through remote control.

Hay's concert at the Anderson Theater in 1968, including *Group I* (1967), *Group II,* and *Ten* (both 1968), was a signal event. Jill Johnston, reviewing the concert in the *Village Voice,* remarked that the three dances "leave me searching for superlatives. I'm tempted with platitudes like 'breakthrough' and 'come a long way.' "[6] By now Hay was articulating her concerns with the commonplace in highly schematic formal systems of comparison and contrast. She was using, by preference, "very 'comfortable' bodies, regardless of whether they are performers or not";[7] bodies that could adapt to situations as they arose. In the two *Groups,* the ordinary qualities of the performers was underscored by their wearing street clothes. In *Ten* all the dancers dressed in white. The movements in all three dances consisted almost entirely of casual steps, ordered into strict geometric configurations in the *Groups,* and into follow-the-leader poses in *Ten.*

Each *Group* began with a film. In *Group I,* the black-and-white picture showed about twenty people taking tiny steps in and out of a corner. In *Group II,* the color image depicted a group of the same size, out-of-doors, moving in and out of the frame in a double column, and forming circles, diagonals, and other patterns. *Group I* had five "movers" dressed in black and white (business suits for the men, dresses and high heels for the women) walking on and off stage, forming and reforming lines, and making very simple gestures. Eight "musicians," led by an unseen conductor, intermittently shifted ten-foot white poles from upright to upright, clattering them against each other with each turn. In *Group II,* the same five movers wore bright clothing and made more complex movements and floor patterns while the musicians manipulated brightly painted metal poles.

Ten, which divided the two *Groups,* used the same basic materials: musicians, movers, poles. But this time the musicians were a rock group, The Third Eye. And the number of movers had doubled. Two poles, instead of serving as musical instruments, provided a visual design and a marker for the activity. The dancers, divided into three groups (five men, three women, a man and a woman), played a version of follow-the-leader, assuming poses in relationship to the horizontal bar that crossed the entire stage in front of the rock band, and the vertical pole that crossed the horizontal line on one side. The dancers, in their cool, blasé demeanor, contrasted with the "hot" music and actions of the band. In between poses, the ten performers milled about, creating a texture of occasional order and clarity in a field of chaos.

Over the following years, Hay continued her investigations with highly organized structures supporting the casual, colloquial, infinitely variegated movements of people dressed in ordinary clothes. In some of the dances the confusion between performers and audience was heightened by the fact that the performers were visually indistinguishable from the spectators, and their activities — until the drill-like formations of the dancers were discerned — were also nearly identical. In *Half-Time* (1969), at the Whitney Museum, the performers were all women dressed as if for an art gallery opening. *26 Variations on 8 Activities for 13 People and Beginning and Ending* (performed as part of Yvonne Rainer's *Rose Fractions* at the Billy Rose Theater in 1969) was simply that: thirteen young women in street clothes, running forward or backward, walking up and down ramps, posing, and jumping. The same year, *20 Permutations of 2 Sets of 3 Equal Parts in a Linear Pattern* deployed three men and three women on a V-shaped shallow ramp. In 1970, on a program by three choreographers whose assignment was to use twenty minutes, an arbitrary length, for their dances, Hay designed *20-Minute Piece,* for thirty dancers, in three sections that decreased in time and ended with the dancers dispersing into the audience.

Hay's use of large groups is particularly striking. During the late '60s, other choreographers had also used large groups of untrained performers —

Yvonne Rainer in *Untitled Work for 40 People* and *Rose Fractions,* Steve Paxton in *Satisfyin Lover* and *State,* for instance. The defocusing of attention from any single performer could be achieved easily in a throng. The democratic intention, the quality of sheer crowdedness, the task of choreographing masses of people correlates to similar social concerns of the period: the search for community in the American counterculture; the organization of individuals into cooperative living, working, and buying situations; the mobilization of individuals and political forces by the New Left, not only into political groups but, physically, into marches and demonstrations.

Hay's time limit in *20-Minute Piece* was also significant in terms of comment on the modern dance aesthetic. It acknowledged openly the packaging of dance concerts into a predictable format: three pieces, each about twenty minutes long, separated by intermissions. The post-modern choreographers had challenged that consumer package with concerts that presented several dances simultaneously, or three-minute, or several-hour dances. To call a dance *20-Minute Piece* and to make the implicit, conventional limitation the subject of the work, was to call attention to and criticize a marketplace value of modern dance.

As she worked on the low-contrast group works, Hay began to give free classes at her Soho loft, in order to collect dancers to test her choreographic ideas. But "over a two-year span these ideas became less and less important to me. What was happening to us all, individually and as a group (we were a pretty steady twenty-five) moving together, was much more exciting." While practicing Tai Chi Chuan, Hay often experienced a sensation she had only occasionally known during dance classes and performances, the feeling that "I transcended my body and no longer felt responsible for my own movement." In Tai Chi, "I began to let go of all I had learned, and to trust a new thing called flow, or myself, or the universe."[8]

Tai Chi Chuan originated about a thousand years ago (its exact date of origin is unknown) as a nonviolent martial art form among Taoist monks in China. Now it is practiced primarily as a solo form of kinetic meditation. It is a living embodiment of Taoist philosophy, stressing the ever-changing process of nature, the circularity of the life-force, and the ultimate unity of apparent dualities in balance. A key concept is *wu-wei* ("not doing" "letting go") — yielding to the flow of nature in order to enter its pure, intrinsic harmony, and to discover effortless effort, the genuine source of power. Water, seemingly weak and soft, but able to defeat the strong and hard, is a favorite example of *wu-wei* and a central image of Taoism and Tai Chi. In Tai Chi Chuan, the alternation of the breath cycle, and the putatively circular pathway of the breath through the body, are the models for circular movements and rhythmic interplays of qualities of movement, symbolizing and enacting in miniature the flux of eternal motion in the cosmos generated from the "still point" of *wu-wei.* Every movement comes out of its opposite.

Taoism is a philosophy of paradoxes, and in Tai Chi Chuan the principal paradox is the attainment of great freedom through the discipline of the form. The process, not the product; the passage, not the path; the motion, not the positions; these are the values that enable a person to live in harmony with the universe, to enter into its rhythms instead of standing outside, observing analytically.

The attainment of nonbeing, or ultimate reality, is firmly grounded (as it is in Zen Buddhism, a descendant of Taoism) in daily life. "In carrying water and chopping wood — therein lies the wonderful Tao."[9] Stressing simplicity, unity, natural living, and yet respect for the individuality of people and things, Taoism was in part a reaction to the repressive, highly codified, artificial, and hierarchical society of Confucianism. The parallels between the Taoist criticism of Confucianism and the counterculture's attacks on American bourgeois society in the 1960s are obvious.[10]

Hay, in accordance not only with the appreciation of the commonplace equally valued by minimalist artist colleagues and Tai Chi practitioners, but also with her own conviction that one need not be specially trained in either dance or Tai Chi techniques to enjoy movement, wanted to combine the flowing, flexible discipline of Tai Chi with the familiarity of vernacular dancing steps, in order to share with as many as possible, in ordinary life, the pleasures she found in practicing Tai Chi. Her choreography moved from formal designs to nondancers executing arrangements of pedestrian movements, to no performing, to "practically no choreography."[11] Hay moved to Vermont in 1971 and continued to work on her dances, traveling to colleges to teach them, rooting them more and more in breath imagery, and finding them becoming slower and slower. She performed them to popular music and noted that — as if the movement had its own will, endowed by the group — "each movement slowed down 'til we were doing one movement per song. My choreography was following a similar pattern until the only direction was to form a circle and see what happened."[12]

Out of these experiences, Hay evolved a set of ten circle dances. Instructions for doing the dances are written down in Hay's book, *Moving Through the Universe in Bare Feet: Ten Circle Dances for Everybody.* It is a cookbook for making the dances, including a general explanation of how to do the movements, pointers on how to conduct the dances, a list of records recommended for each dance, and specific directions for each dance, both in words and in drawings by Donna Jean Rogers.

The precise timing of each dance is determined by the three sides of popular records chosen to accompany the dance. Each cut on a record corresponds to one movement instruction. If the cut is seven minutes long, the movement lasts or is repeated for seven minutes; if two minutes, the movement lasts for two minutes. Many of the movements are directly circular (running in a circle, or letting the arms swing in a circle, for example) or are based on circular imagery (holding a ball in the hands, for instance). The participants form a circle to do the dance, creating an unbroken flow of energy within the group. The group practice diverges from Tai Chi, which is a solitary form; even in its martial form it pits no more than two in combat. As in Tai Chi, the stomach is always relaxed, the joints always soft (slightly bent) and open, the weight low. Every movement comes from the breath and the movements are calm and sustained (even when vigorous). Again the circle dances break from Tai Chi Chuan in the range of their dynamics. But by substituting alternating dynamics for the slow motion of Tai Chi, Hay makes the fluctuations of yin and yang even more pronounced. The movements are done sitting, standing, or moving together in place or in the circle.

There are three different arrangements of movements: one movement realized one time (for instance, taking the whole song to move the head gradually from facing forward to facing the left shoulder); one movement repeated slowly on one's own time (based on one's breathing rhythm); one movement done in time to the song's rhythm (e.g., bouncing, jumping, step-hop, or step-step-step-hop).

"Bring fresh oxygen to your body with each breath," Hay urges in the instructions. "Feel the blood carrying it everywhere; through your toes, under your arms, around your scalp, under your fingernails and in the palms of your hands. Sensitize the surface of your body to the particles of air surrounding, and gently bombarding you."[13]

The environment for the dances should be comfortable and relaxing: enough room to move around in, but not so much room that the group feels lost in it; a good, clean floor; soft lighting; the music loud enough to hear but not too harsh. The dances are made to be done, not observed. Their significance comes from the experience of embodying them, of grasping physically their deep design, rather than from watching their surface pattern unfold.

The dances are brilliantly structured to foster a process of growing awareness. Each one starts off slowly and gently, with slight movements, often evoked and anchored by a highly specific cerebral image: the instructions say to "think of a line down the center of your body from the top of your head along your face and neck, your chest, stomach, genitals, dividing you in half. Slowly open out from this center, all of you falling gently away from it, like turning inside out." Or, to imagine "two large weightless silver balls touching your palms. Lift them and maintain contact with them, like helium inflated balloons." These actions are done with the eyes closed. The concreteness and detail of the imagery focuses concentration narrowly and strongly, moving attention slowly through different parts of the body and creating a flow of sensations and relaxations that is deep, almost hypnotic. The pulse of the music guides this current.

Then gradually the focus expands to include awareness of other people. The instructions guide one to make contact by standing together holding hands and to "feel the circle, feel its energy"; or to walk in rhythm with the others around the circle "naturally, flowing"; or to very slowly sway with the others in the circle. (By the tenth dance, the contact with others occurs much earlier than in the previous dances.) During this stage, contact is made not only by touching, but by meeting each other's gazes, copying each other's rhythms, "essences," and motions. Yet during this stage there are also times when the contact is broken and one returns to self-involved movement. The communication at this point is tentative, experimental.

Next the sensing moves beyond the group and its interrelations to the space and the movements of the consolidated group in the space. The music now seems to follow, rather than lead; the fused energy of the group incites each person to keep on moving long after the first wind is lost. You are instructed in run in the circle; or to "step hop traveling in circle, do your own thing, move into circle if circle too contained"; or to bounce in place, "jumping when you feel like it." It is difficult to convey by the instructions how large and powerful and rhythmic these movements become.

Finally, the energy subsides through intervals of slow, spun-out breathing. The arms hang and swing effortlessly in small circles, pulling the relaxed torso "forward and earthward." One concentrates again on one's breath, on the infinitesimal movements of the spine as one breathes "spine to vertical position vertebra by vertebra, lengthening, fresh oxygen lifting you to standing." Or as one stands, holding hands, sensing changes in the body and the breathing, one senses the cohesiveness of the group, created by the recent experiences of mutual exertion.

The dances make one feel good: relaxed, strong, charged with continuously renewed energy. But they mean much more than simply feeling good. The circle symbolizes many things in many cultures: zero, the starting point; infinity; the sun; the cosmos; the microcosmos; the sky; the path of the stars; creation; the intellect (the shape of the head); time; perpetual rebirth. The circle is perfect, without beginning, end, or variations. It is indivisible. Some metaphoric meanings of the circle are embodied in Hay's circle dances. Others seem appropriate as metaphors to describe emotional experiences during the dance. The mental, intellectual images lead the body into a meditative state where one senses the cosmos as a circular unity. Concentrating on a mental picture, one's mind seems to operate in cycles, as fantasies and thoughts slip in and out. Concentrating on doing one recurring movement, suddenly one is lifted into timeless easy flow, a plateau of weightlessness, a connection with something outside one's body — something invoked by the group but larger than it; some sense of unity and order. And then, just as suddenly, the intuitive flash is over. Holding hands, breathing together with friends and strangers, an odd fusion occurs for a moment — a felt understanding of interplay. Traveling in a circle, faster and faster, sweating, hands slipping, the room is lost because it spins around too quickly; one feels anchored at the center of the spinning room, where the largest reality is the immediacy of the moment, the people next to one, the power of the group.

The repetition or the slowness mesmerizes and relaxes the body, producing an oceanic exuberance, transforming experiences of time and perception. The shared process of increased awareness, of deepening consciousness, knits the group together. It is not simply heightened sensitivity to one's own body state, but an earned knowledge of the group's process: together we learn this particular group's rhythms, relationships, needs, resources — by making adjustments, communicating through nonverbal signals desires to slow down, speed up, lead, follow, and urges to jump higher, run faster, rock slower, and so on. That knowledge is mutually discovered during each dance and it broadens and matures during the set of ten dances, over the course of time.

In the instructions for Dance #10, Hay quotes from Stephen's (a counterculture communalist) *Monday Night Class:*

> Well, look in the Sufi trip for instance, a lot of the transmission of magic, or baraka or vital energy or life force is done through dance. And the way it's done is the dance don't have to be fancy, all you gotta do is get several people together, stand there together, and go through the same motion at the same time. The dance neither has to be pretty nor graceful nor anything else all it's gotta be done in, is unison. See? And if you do something at the same time as somebody a few times, you pick up their vibes a little bit. Your field meshes with theirs because you're both varying at the same kind of time . . . And that's how you transmit magic in the Sufi Tradition.[14]

She quotes from religious theoreticians as well. And, as we have seen, the dances borrow heavily from Taoist principles. But, although the dances have mystical overtones, they have been translated into the vernacular of the American counterculture, to function more as folk dances with social meaning than as religious rituals or ecstatic techniques. Hay has substituted for the esoteric gestures of Tai Chi steps that are familiar to young Americans, or that are so simple they could easily become familiar. She has provided a musical system that is equally commonplace (unlike Tai Chi, which is practiced in silence). And, most importantly for the social function, she has changed the form from a solo to a group activity. Like folk dances, the circle dances are not "performed" for an audience, but "done" un-self-consciously (aside from the basic self-consciousness one feels in any group situation) for the sake of the participants — both individually and as a group. And, as in social dancing, there is no one correct way to do the dances, despite the precise structures. Within the forms there is room for a wide variety of personal choices.

Some would argue that although the eradication of the role of audience pushes the circle dances away from the realm of art, they are not really folk dances either. They are not traditional. They are not anonymously or un-self-consciously choreographed. They belong to no particular national or religious group. Yet as anthropologist Joann Wheeler Kealiinohomoku argues, these features do not disqualify an item from the category of folk dance. She defines folk dance as

> a vernacular dance form performed either in its first [surviving] or second [revived] existence as part of the little tradition within the great tradition of a

given society. It is understood that dance is an affective mode of expression which requires both time and space. It employs motor behavior in redundant patterns which are closely linked to the definitive features of musicality.[15]

With this definition in mind, Kealiinohomoku points out that as long as a dance reflects vernacular expression and functions viably, "it has its own intrinsic authenticity, even though it may be the product of change and innovation, or even direct creation."[16]

With her circle dances, Deborah Hay closes the circle of dance tradition, returning to folk dancing, the source of theatrical dance, at a time when those who are trying to instill vitality into our theater look to ritual and folk traditions for models. In the 1970s, we everywhere express the need for deep, integrative physical experiences; watching dancing often seems much less significant than doing it. Hay urges us to

> Bring the dances with you to the lab and the A & P.
> Bring 'em on the bus, into the garden, and upstairs.
> Take them out walking and take them to bed.
>
> Trust yourself. Use the images to take you as far out
>   and as far in as you will go.
> Trust yourself, your breath, to feel everything there is.[17]

After making the circle dances, and during several years of traveling around the country to lead them, in between trips living and farming in Vermont (until her move to Austin, Texas, in 1976), Hay's interest in the meditative, heightened consciousness of the body continues in terms not only of the dancing, which she practices privately for hours every day, but also in terms of eating, bathing, even touching at "a cellular level of awareness."[18] In 1976, she decided to present her first solo dance concert. Since then she has performed a series of solos, in New York and other cities, especially at Studio D in Austin and throughout the Northwest, bringing her questions about dance performance frankly into the performance itself. The result is a highly personal, almost confessional view of dance and art: she brings food to share with the audience, talks to them and into a tape recorder about her thoughts and ambitions (or lack of them) at the present moment, before the concert, in the past. She sprinkles spices in the air, lays out her favorite objects on the floor. Her approach to the dancing is devotional, totemistic. She puts on a record with a strong soul or rock beat, begins by deep breathing, gradually letting the breath carry her into vigorous bursts of jumping or, more concentratedly, delicate tremblings in the outstretched fingers. As in the circle dances, the movements correspond roughly to the cuts on the record; when the record is over, Hay resumes her monologue, or asks for questions from the spectators.

At one of the solo concerts, she explained her goals:

> We see people who are experiencing the moment and we know what it is when we are seeing it. I hope that these dances will evolve to a place where I can suspend the moment for myself and for you the whole time we are together. So the dance is my being here in this space, totally, and preparation for this performance is my entire life and nothing more, or less.[19]

She speaks of feeling her body moving toward a state of health and preparing itself for emptiness, of becoming intensely conscious, through her identification of herself as her breath.

> i dance for love
> i dance for awareness
> i dance for the moment
> i dance to see
> i dance like a deer
> i dance to feel the ground
> i dance to be free
> i dance to grow
> i dance to disappear
> i dance for life
> i am dancing breath[20]

A further development in the solos has been to abandon talking.

With her solo dances in the late '70s, Hay has pushed dancing even further: from the social realm into a private one. The spectators, receiving communication about changing body states, are onlookers, not participants, in ritualized meditation. Hay's explicit intention is to "[leave] her body as much as possible and at moments completely so that I can act as a vehicle for the dance."[21] She has renounced her role as a choreographer, implying an egoless state in which the dance becomes a revelation. There is a delicate balance between a profound experience with slight but concentrated movements that the viewer can enjoy empathetically and aesthetically and moments that remain cryptic, locked in Hay's private experience.

In 1977, Hay began a new work that continues her investigations of consciousness and sensations in group movement. *The Grand Dance,* a work in progress, created, as the Circle Dances were, by a learning and sharing process of experimentation with groups of participants, is a three-hour meditation. It is based on cosmic imagery but, unlike the Circle Dances, permits much more privacy, with intermittent physical contact between the dancers and with more personal choice in terms of timing. The introduction to *The Grand Dance* lasts about forty minutes. It is a meditation composed of seven images of surrender: the giving up of focalization, form, "I am," personal experience, light, will, and stature. This is accomplished by the repetition of special movements. After the introduction, the dancers manipulate fields of energy together by actions called Stepping on the Earth, Turning in Place as a Celestial Being, Star Walk, The Dance of Celestial Being, and Rock Dance. Hay points out in her instructions to the score of *The Grand Dance* that unless the dance is done with total focus and commitment, it seems like very slight activity. Yet when the group sustains a common focus, "a galactic order in balance and harmony" is created and nourished.[22] In a sense, Hay has placed dance at the boundary of the physical; *The Grand Dance* is an act of consciousness.

Deborah Hay, Excerpts from *The Grand Dance*

There is only one way to do The Grand Dance and that is completely. The focus is consciousness; without it there is very little to experience. It is like the bowing we just did. You are either bowing or you are not bowing. There is no halfway. Harness your attention, your energy, so that you do not wander. You will, so don't be hard on yourself for leaving. This is the nature of the work of The Grand Dance — coming back to our common focus. "Returning is the motion of the Tao; going far means returning," Lao Tzu.

I will lead you through the first meditation several times, verbally and physically. I will enter in and out of our dance verbally, until we are all familiar with the material. So, try and make room for me without being too distracted from the dance.

The Introduction to The Grand Dance is divided into seven images of surrender, performed in sequence by everyone.

surrender of: focalization
form
"I am"
personal experience
light
will
stature

(The Introduction lasts about forty minutes.)

We begin by holding hands in a circle and each of us leaves to begin the first meditation when we are ready. When everyone has left the circle and is performing the first movement, anyone can start the second. Gradually, everyone moves into the second image of surrender and we do it until everyone is doing this together and then someone, anyone, may move into the third . . . etc., until all seven movement meditations are completed.

We are now ready to begin the first movement of The Grand Dance: surrender of focalization.

Stand anywhere in the space facing any direction. Your feet are relaxed and parallel to one another on the floor. Knees and stomach are relaxed and open. Your spine is long and wide. The distance between your hips feels like a half moon. A band of light from one hip to the other . . . full, light, and curved. Feel a string pulling you up very gently from the top of your head as your spine releases earthwards. Your ears and eyes are opened and receptive. Now open your eyes to perceive 360 degrees. What is happening to your eyeballs is symbolic of what is occurring throughout your body. In this moment, the body opens up to the space we are in; to the light, to the present, to each other and beyond. Surrender how you see, your focalization, in order to perceive everything. Include your peripheral vision as strongly as you normally do your frontal vision. The top of your head is open and your face is exposed, like a flower. Your heart opens. The back of your body is alive and receptive. Every cell is opened, vulnerable, trusting, exposed. Now close your eyelids slowly, the dance happening in every moment that your eyelids pass through space. This is a bow. Experience this bow throughout your body. You are giving away your light, selflessly. (This happens in a slow count of three, without counting but recognizing this approximate duration.) The eyes return to open, the dance continuing to unfold. Now your body leaves the place you are in. You leave the place you now occupy and take up to three steps to another place. Feel yourself leave the place you are in. Approach a new space. Every cell approaching. All that is happening is approaching. You then experience entering a new space, and stand. Standing is a state of consciousness that is emptiness. All you are is standing. Now, once again, open every cell in your body . . . your eyes, your ears, your whole consciousness opened 360 degrees to the space you are now in. Again a 360-degree acknowledgment of here and now. The top of your head, your ears, heart, and eyes surrender their patterns to pure acknowledgment. Every cell opening like a morning flower. Acknowledgment. Then, lower your eyelids, slowly bowing, letting your light out into the world. Open your eyelids, the dance continuing. Leave the space you are in. Every cell leaving. Three steps. All approaching. Enter. Stand. All you are is standing. Continue until you or someone else begins, surrender of form.

• • •

Introduction then,

We have gathered at The Place of Origin. In our own time we begin Stepping on the Earth. The bottoms of our feet are relaxed and receptive to all the healing and regenerative energies coming through the earth. The entire body is engaged in the locomotive, step by step, ongoing act of Stepping on the Earth. The palms are upturned, out to your side, at whatever level they are comfortable. Your entire focus is facing, that is, eye level. There is a perceptible field of energy created by this focus. With each step we experience a clarifying flow of energy up through our feet and out through the top of our heads. We cross and re-cross the performing area Stepping on the Earth and also, whenever you wish, Turning in Place as a Celestial Body. With this movement every cell is uplifted. Every cell moves from facing, in Stepping on the Earth, to focusing upwards. As we turn, are Turning in Place as a Celestial Body, we attune ourselves to the whereabouts of everyone else. We are now part of a galactic order. In balance and harmony with everyone passing through space. The back as well as the front of us experiences our mutual interconnectedness. It is as if we are no longer isolated entities but rather a dynamic network of relationships (a description of atomic physics). Stepping on the Earth with an intermittent Turning in Place as a Celestial Body. As we turn, we merge, we join, we disappear only to return to the nourishment of Stepping on the Earth. We cross and re-cross the performance area as long as the meditation happens, washing the performing area with these two energies and the transformation of the one into the other.

• • •

. . . we gather in a cluster and walk together. The walk is a bow. Walking Is Bowing. We travel through space in a cluster and there is no leader. The cluster is a large family, a flock, all listening bodies. No one decides where we walk, rather, as listeners, we respond. If the call is strong we will naturally all follow. In Walking Is Bowing there is the acknowledgment of our dance together, the grandness of it and simultaneously, its frailty. There is the cellular acknowledgment of our present and ever changing and ever to be acknowledged, hereness.

Lucinda Childs: The Act of Seeing

LUCINDA CHILDS grew up in New York City and began taking dance classes when she was six. But her ambition was to become an actress, not a dancer, and at eleven she started concentrating seriously on dramatic training. She resumed dancing when she was fifteen, studying at the Hanya Holm School. The following summer she went to Colorado to take classes from Tamiris, a choreographer who since the 1930s had developed an unconventional, eclectic style, and who had made dances for musical comedies (including *Annie Get Your Gun* and *Touch and Go*) as well as for the concert stage. Tamiris invited Childs to perform with her; she was terrified, recalls Childs, but "after it was over I wasn't sure I even wanted to be an actress anymore."[1] Determined now to become a dancer, she questioned the value of college, but Tamiris encouraged her to go to Sarah Lawrence, where she majored in dance, studying with Bessie Schönberg, Judith Dunn, and visiting teacher Merce Cunningham.

She came to New York City for classes with Cunningham during vacations ("with all the other Sarah Lawrence girls") and after graduation moved back to Manhattan. For Childs, Cunningham was important because he "elucidated a kind of particularity and clarity in dance that felt distinctly separate from anything I had experienced up to that point."[2] At the Cunningham studio she met Yvonne Rainer, who invited her to participate in the newly formed Judson Dance Theater.

Impressed by the "strength and simplicity" of Rainer's work, Childs joined the Judson group, there to choreograph thirteen works of her own and to appear in the works of many others — including Rainer, Robert Morris, Steve

Studio shot of Lucinda Childs. Photograph © Jack Mitchell, 1977.

Paxton, Aileen Passloff, and James Waring — over the next four years. From 1963 to 1965 she studied with Waring and, in 1964, took Robert Dunn's composition course. At the same time, she took ballet classes.

Most of Childs' early works were solos, based on a method of construction that used objects and monologues as sources for movement. Like Rainer, she tried to find new movements, a new vocabulary that could still be considered dance, by mining the gestural lode of ordinary activities. In borrowing from actions not usually thought of as dance material, Childs has noted, "the movements do not in and of themselves evoke that [everyday] experience, but rather match that experience in the degree of exertion involved in doing them."[3] Such a principle is allied to the project of minimalists in the visual arts who, during the early '60s, criticized abstract expressionism by eliminating painterliness and subjectivity.

Rather than using chance techniques or tasks, Childs devised her own method of evolving movement material by manipulating objects. At first, she mixed that activity with pure dance phrases. Soon she incorporated monologues in the dances and used the movements to refer to the content of the speeches, drifting in and out of the context of what the spectators heard. She did not try to make any coherent illustration of subject matter but, rather, created a scattered context of words, movements, and objects.

Her first dance at the Judson was *Pastime* (1963), which in one section involved the slow manipulation of stretchable cloth with her legs while seated on a long table. Music by Philip Corner ("that sounded as though all the plumbing at the Y was out of order," Louis Horst complained when *Pastime* was performed at the 92 Street YMHA later that year) provided the accompaniment.[4] *Carnation* (1964) was a scrupulous manipulation of various ordinary objects, beginning with hair curlers and sponges, and punctuated with intense facial expressions. Jill Johnston described Childs' action in the solo:

> She puts the curlers between the sponges, places a salad colander on her head, pulls out each curler with a neat swift pull, and places them around her head on the prongs of the colander. That done, she sticks the sponges in her mouth, removes the curlers, the colander, gets up and dumps them with unceremonious relief into a blue plastic bag, into which she injects her foot. The next section involves a head stand, a sheet, and two socks (attached to the sheet) with some difficult maneuvering. Finally, she caps this perfect and meticulous nonsense with a meaningless assault on the blue plastic bag. After careful placement of the bag she runs toward it, jumps on it, stands

> immobilized, glares in frenetic silence until her face starts to cry, and at the final moment of wrinkled distortion returns to deadpan normal and prepares for another attack on the bag.[5]

In *Geranium* (1965), a taped broadcast of the National Football League's championship game between the Baltimore Colts and the Cleveland Browns was the "sounding board" for different images to illustrate or play off. The edited tape included descriptions of the players' movements, a list of the players' names, and interludes of rock-and-roll music. In the first of four sections, Childs sits in overcoat and sunglasses, indicating with a pole the level of excitement of the spectators (audible on the tape). Later, when the commentator describes a fall, Childs, standing padlocked to the free end of a hammock attached to the wall, falls in slow motion, taking two minutes to complete the action. In the final section of the dance, she repeatedly steps in dirt and brushes it forward with her feet until a diagonal line of footsteps appears. The piece referred to different aspects of the experience of a football game but did not use actual football movements per se. Asked at the time if she liked football, Childs said not particularly.[6] But like comic strips and soup cans in visual art, football games at that point provided a new, rich, and impersonal source for Childs' imagery.

In *Museum Piece* (1965), Childs made an enlargement of dots from a section of Seurat's painting *Le Cirque,* laying the dots down on the floor while describing Seurat's principles of using the dots to capture luminosity. Looking into a hand-held mirror, she backs into the area and walks between the dots, speaking of angles, "getting an angle on this material,"[7] and the measurement of the angle between the mirror and the image it reflects. She then demonstrates several times the position of the acrobat figure in the painting, and obliquely refers to her own audience by mentioning the spectators depicted in the painting.

As part of Robert Dunn's composition class in 1964, Childs made an extraordinary piece, *Street Dance.* It extended the definition of dance by marking off an area of a street and — intensifying the perception of the audience almost entirely with words — turning the activity and objects on the street into a performance. The audience was looking out of the windows of the Dunns' loft into the street below. Childs and another performer, stationed in the street, either blended in with the normal activity or pointed out architectural details and objects in windows. A taped, minutely detailed description of the view was synchronized exactly to their actions. The performers acted as markers, not altering the environment, but facilitating the spectator's discovery of it.

Vehicle (1966) was a complex technological experiment done in collaboration with Bell Telephone Laboratories engineers for Nine Evenings: Theater and Engineering. In *Vehicle* three performers interacted with static and moving objects, light and sound sources, and a sonar beam which converted motion into sound. Shortly afterward, Childs left the Judson; the momentum of the original group of the Judson Dance Theater had languished by then, and the choreographers were going their separate ways — to perform on their own, to teach outside New York, to work in other media. Childs created *Untitled Trio* in 1968, and then did not present work for public performance for five years.

When the revised version of *Untitled Trio* was performed at the Whitney Museum in 1973, along with two new group pieces and a solo, it was clear that although the look of Childs' work had changed — for example, she had dispensed with props and words — her basic concerns had not changed. During those five years, Childs had been practicing ballet, teaching, working in the studio, writing about her own work and that of other choreographers, and thinking about problems of cognition and perception.

In *Untitled Trio* and the subsequent dances, Childs' concern with modes of attention, recognition, and point of view focuses directly into the movement material. In her earlier pieces, the movement created additional perspectives on the objects and the texts in the dance. But in the dances of the 1970s it is the very structure of the dance that supplies divergent points of view. Phrases and fields of movement are stated, broken down, and reconstructed. Paradoxically, what seems to be an undeviating reductionist strategy proliferates minute variations on already basic themes. In a given dance, although a single movement phrase appears to be repeated over and over, with close viewing the spectator can see that within the strict limits of the phrase, small insertions are made, changes of direction alter the paths of one or a pair of dancers, the phrase reverses or inverts. The dances last as long as it takes to explore the variables, usually just over ten minutes. The only music is the sound of the dancing: feet pounding or padding rhythmically on the floor, hands slapping against the floor, deep breathing.

Untitled Trio has three sections. In the first, the three performers remain either parallel or perpendicular to each other while distances between them increase, thus tracing a grid pattern on the floor while performing simple movements like walking, lying on their backs, rolling, and lunging in nonstop sequences. The relationships between the phrases constantly group and regroup the dancers into various spatial and movement permutations of two against one or all three in unison; the various elements that the slightly different phrases have in common provide momentary unison movements from which they again diverge. In the second section, a diagonal line is etched across the dancing area as the dancers mark it with another combination of walking, sitting, and lying. The center is demarcated by jumps, and the distance between the starting point and the center is subdivided and further subdivided with jumps and turns. In the final section, curved forms are traced with activities of varying speeds: walking forward, walking backward, and a seated progression shifting weight from feet to buttocks to hands.

In *Calico Mingling* (1973), four dancers have similar, but not identical paths that consist only of circles, semicircles and straight lines. They walk either forward or backward, completing every phrase in six steps; the circle takes two phrases, or twelve steps, to complete. The paths, which are totally mapped out in advance, are repeated four times. The first time, all of the dancers face the same direction. Then they all face the opposite direction. The third time, one pair faces the other pair, and finally, the pairs reverse. The result is a clear pattern of unison, divergence, interweaving, and intersection. Each dancer's strand of movement consists of so many similar elements that within the four main sections there seem to be an infinite number of repetitions. Yet one feels that if one could view the dance from directly overhead, one would be watching a design being engraved onto the floor: the body as stylus.

Congeries on Edges for 20 Obliques (1975) sets five dancers on diagonal paths in groups of two, three, and five. As they cross the room, their method of locomotion expands from simple walking to a walk augmented, one by one, with a hop, a squat turn, a jump, and a cartwheel. In the meantime, the shifting directionals of the movement pattern and the diagonal routes force a clustering of the dancers in the center of the room and uneven regroupings along the periphery. The elaborations are deducted one by one until only the walking is left and the dance ends.

In *Radial Courses* (1976), four large circles are established diagrammatically on the floor as the four dancers walk quickly in three-quarter or half circles, switching directions frequently to pair off in varying combinations. In *Reclining Rondo* (1975) the constantly changing relationships between the dancers as they sit, lean, and lie down, shifting directions separately, generate a set of insistently regular flat triangles and squares.

The dances range in tempo from the liquid *Reclining Rondo* with its soft movements flowing and rubbing almost lazily along the floor, to the exuberant run and crisp directional switches of *Radial Courses.* But each dance sticks to its own unvarying pulse. These are not "well-constructed" phrases with beginnings, middles, and ends. These are simply uninflected modules of time, with no climaxes and only rare accents.

Many contemporary choreographers, beginning with Rainer, have come to appreciate the fugitive quality of movement and gesture. So much detail escapes observation because we have no language to think in a refined way about it. So many physical features of an action are forgotten because there are no concepts with which to categorize and perceive them. Repetition fills this gap, ingraining gestures in the mind through systematic contrast and comparison. By presenting a single, simple set of movements that repeat with only slightly contrasting variation, Childs demands close attention. Some variations are based on the subtle structural reordering of the movements. Others flow from the natural distortions and limited stylistic differences she permits among the dancers as they execute the prescribed steps. Although the jumps, pivots, walks, and hops must be done precisely, the arms, head, and torso of each dancer are free to function in a comfortable, economical way that facilitates performance of the footwork.

Although the movements and shapes are simple, the sequences and routes for each performer are so complex — a three-minute phrase may appear to have many repetitions, but may actually have none at all — that Childs began notating the dances as she made them. The scores also make it possible to teach new dancers their roles. *Transverse Exchanges* (1976), for instance, is an arrangement of five dancers staking out parallel lines with turns and jumps. The spaces between one group, of two, and the other group, of three, alternate as they approach and leave each other. There are eleven-, eight-, and five-count phrases in the dance which add up to 1449 counts —and the dancers are constantly counting, to keep the phrasing absolutely precise.

Childs' reductionist program magnifies and frames the slight shifts, which makes us notice how we recognize movement. "While the dancer is fully cognizant of the particular adjustment she is abiding by, the spectator is not," Childs has written:

> Either he perceives that the same thing is different when it is not, or he perceives the same thing as the same through an awareness of the manner in which it has been removed from its original mode of presentation. In drifting between prediction and speculation, he is dislodged essentially from any single point of view.[8]

The detached presentation and the movement that generates and defines classical, flat geometric forms has elements in common with the works of such minimalist painters as Ellsworth Kelly, Frank Stella, or Brice Marden. A solo like *Cross Words* (1976), compulsively tracing a diagonal corridor with gallops and walks, is analogous to the neutrally hued canvases of Robert Mangold, which emphasize their surfaces with a line that forms a groove in the paint.

Perhaps the most striking thing about Childs' solo work of the past five years is her absolutely compelling performance presence. In works like *Particular Reel* (1973) or *Mix Detail* (1976), the structure of the dance is even more severe than in the group works, since a movement can only occur or vary in terms of time (rather than across a group of dancers). In *Particular Reel,* Childs walks along twenty-one parallel lines, making her way from one corner of the space to the opposite corner, while rotating and reeling her arms in a three-minute phrase which then reverses and finally repeats in its original order. At times she appears to be pulled, at times the puller. Perhaps no other performer could sustain the rapt attention of the audience with such aloofness. *Mix Detail* alternates between images of a feinting boxer and a magician, as Childs circles her arms inward and outward while walking backward and forward on a spiralling, zigzag path.

When Childs appeared in the Robert Wilson and Philip Glass opera, *Einstein on the Beach,* in 1976, it was not only as one of the lead performers, but as a collaborating choreographer. Her *Solo: Character on Three Diagonals,* in Act I, scene i of the five-hour opus, was structurally linked to the numerical obsession of the opera: three visual themes (train, trial, field with spaceship), each appearing three times, linked to three musical motifs. At a distance, the dance looks like a typical Childs solo. She advances and retreats schematically along different diagonal lines barely distinguishable from each other, making high pointing arm gestures in rhythmic counterpoint to the springy pacing. Yet if one sat close enough to see the gestural detail, one realized that, unlike her own solos, the *Einstein* dance expresses a character, many characters. This did not come through dramatic pantomime, nor even through facial expression; the character constantly changes as images evoked by posture and arm gestures flicker across her body, images of sternness, mirth, urgency, inebriation, pedantry. "I was thinking about Einstein's sense of humor, his playfulness."

Childs has also collaborated with Robert Wilson as actress and co-director in his 1977 play, *I Was Sitting on My Patio This Guy Appeared I Thought I Was Hallucinating* . . . The play is a single monologue performed twice, once by Wilson and once by Childs. As each performer adds nuances, giving expressive meaning to the multiple stories in the text, the same words seem to convey entirely different connotations. And, having heard the entire monologue once, the audience itself supplies a more coherent narrative framework the second time it is spoken. In *Einstein,* the challenge for Childs was to "coexist in some mutually desirable fashion . . . I found myself working with a number of images simultaneously, taking the option from time to time to branch off on some private limb here or there but remaining, as far as I was concerned, plausibly connected to the formal structure in general. In *I Was Sitting on My Patio* . . . there are over 100 little stories. There are a zillion transitions which you abide by and push through." Though *I Was Sitting On My Patio* has a dramatic dimension absent from Childs' own work, the repetitive structure functions in a way that corresponds strikingly to her own choreography. And her performances in the play showed her to be a consummate actress.

Although the actual steps that constitute Childs' dances are rarely more complex than everyday movements, the dances could only be performed by trained dancers. In fact, increasingly they require a real technical virtuosity in terms of endurance, precision, clarity, composure, and memory. The dancers in her company change from year to year but since 1973, have always included Judy Padow, a choreographer whose own work since 1968 (after leaving graduate school in physics to become a dancer) has influenced Childs, who has noted her own interest in Padow's exploration of changes of directions.[9]

The three new pieces Childs presented at the Brooklyn Academy of Music in 1977 marked a new stage in her work — a style that is, in relation to the work of the previous four years, prodigiously elaborate. The derangement of a set of moves, always an important facet of the composition, is much more complex. Yet the abiding rhythmic pulse and the persisting geometrical figures, triumphing over tangling paths, regulate the whole and restore an underlying order.

In *Plaza* (1977), a solo, the basic scheme is the constant tracking of a diagonal line. But the floorplan is complex, diminishing systematically, and at the same time changing from a slight zigzag path, with exaggerated arm swings working at odds to pull the body in different directions, to a smooth, direct set of chaîné turns. Occasionally the achievement of the corner is marked by a knot of half-turns in place, the arms shooting out emphatically in high swings, crossings, salutes, gathering motions. At first each new diagonal is traversed either with the brisk walk or with the turns, although not necessarily alternating regularly. The punctuation at the corners, too, follows an irregular pattern: sometimes the corner is simply reached, then left. But after one diagonal is divided in half by switching at the center from the walk to the chaînés, the entire order of the dance then switches directions, and the irregular pattern of walks, turns, and corner embellishments plays out in exact retrograde. This intricate symmetry is apparent only after several viewings of the dance, although when one sees it for the first time one is conscious of a systematic logic — inscrutable perhaps, but rigorous — that governs the bewildering array of variables.

Interior Drama (1977) arranges five dancers, all facing the same direction, in a V formation. The spectators, seated at both ends of the space, see either the point of the V, with the dancers facing them, or the broad base of the configuration and the backs of the performers. As the dance progresses, the performers maintain their facings except when executing quick whirls in the last few minutes of the piece. They move the entire formation with soft, shuffling steps, periodically sweeping one leg back in a large arc as the standing leg dips. At the beginning the V moves as a unit, but as it ranges over space, the two dancers on the inside often move in a separate direction from the other three. The effect is that of a moving yet rigid form with a detachable, slippery center pursuing its own orbit. The meter of the stepping is a complex polyrhythm, based on eight- and twelve-count phrases, that contrasts with the steady, cyclical timing the visual oppositions create. After the relationships between the parts of the figure have been proposed, the dancers add whirling steps to their phrases, complicating the ornamentation by flinging a leg out during some of the turns. But they never break the steady beat. Finally, after the figure once again moves totally in unison for a moment, the dance stops short.

Melody Excerpt (1977) also sets two dancers moving against three, at first with one of the groups stationary. But soon this obvious opposition disintegrates, as do the triangular configurations that form and disappear. All five

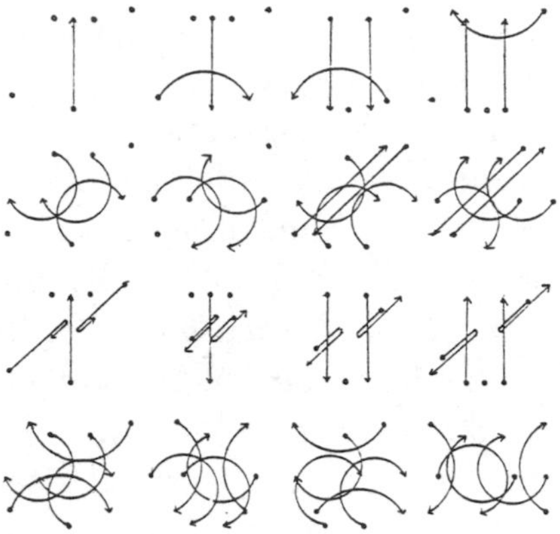

1

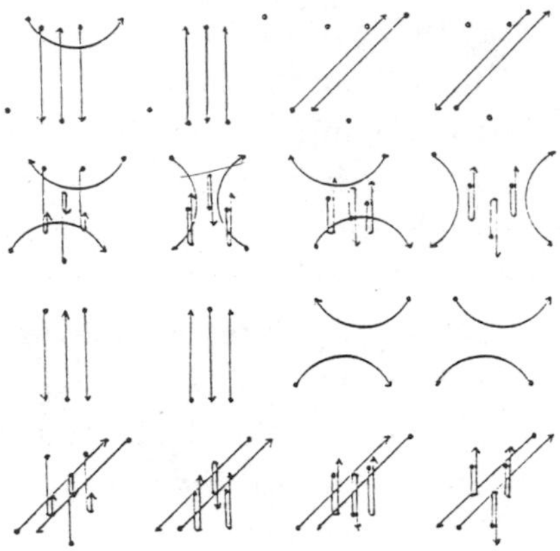

1A

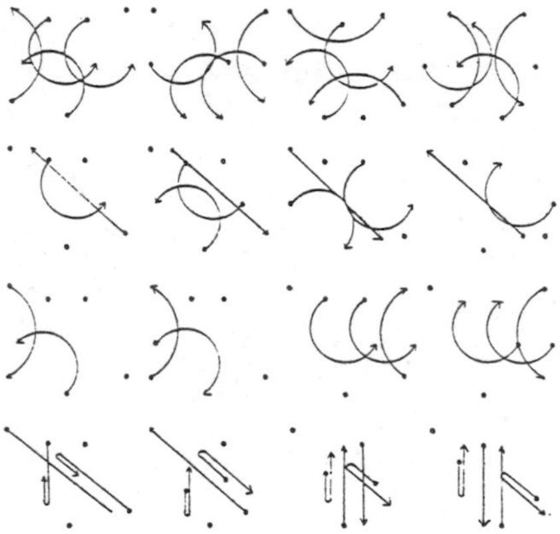

2

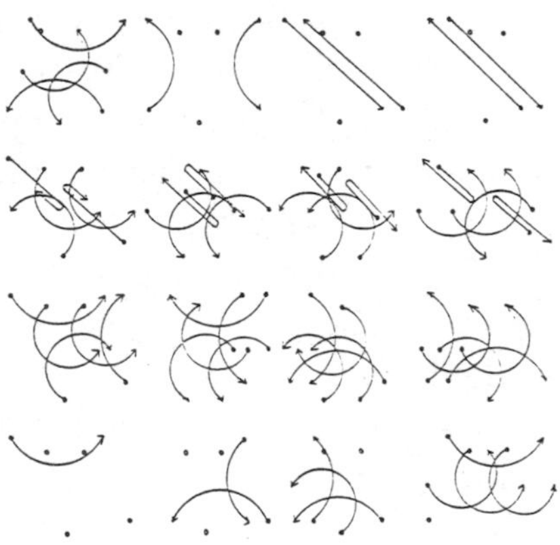

2A

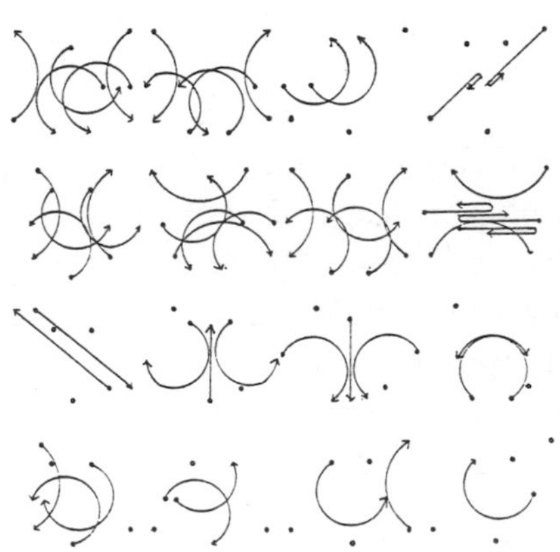

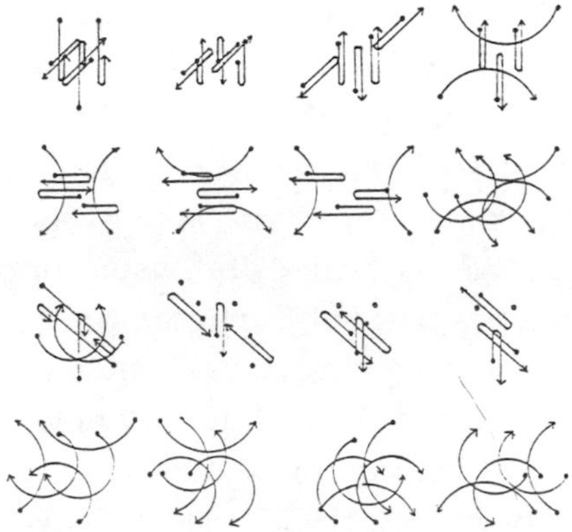

3A

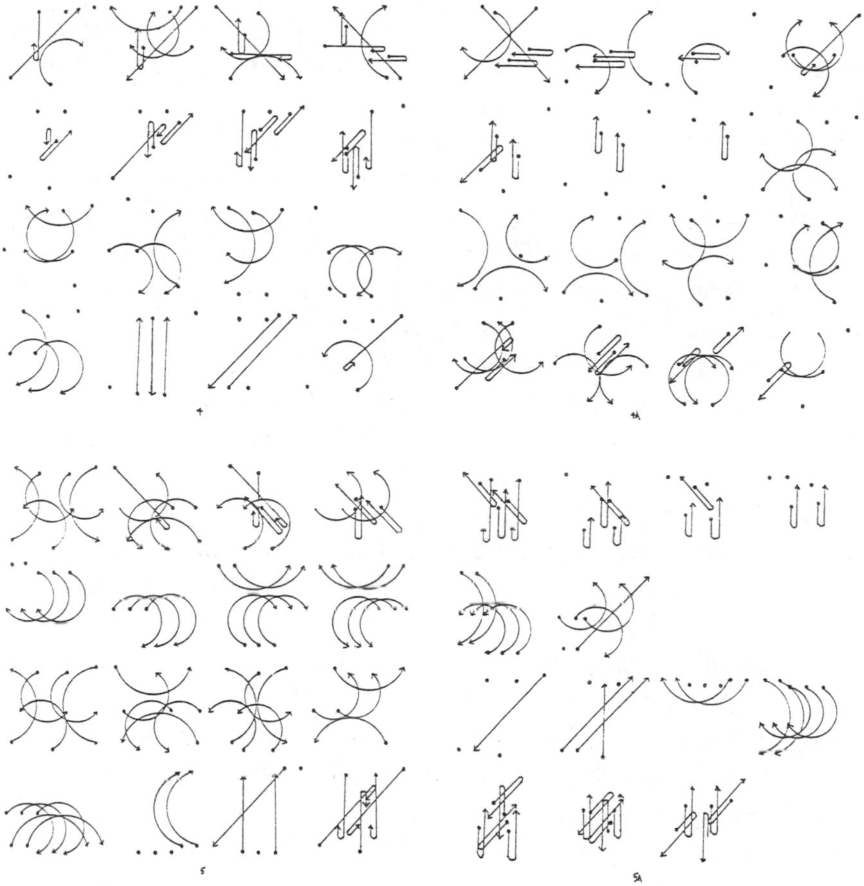

Score: *Melody Excerpt* (Lucinda Childs, 1977)

begin to diverge in seemingly random ways. On closer examination, they prove to be making complex variations on broad curving paths, diagonal lines looping back on themselves, and perpendicular, intersecting channels. The overall consistency, both of the movements and the shapes of the pathways, serves as a coherent fabric on which their utterly disparate routes — sending them now converging on one spot, now rambling over a wide area — traces a spider web of crisscrossing. The syncopated beat of their feet marking out ten-count phrases, with accents on the third, fifth, or seventh beat, supplies a steady pulse, a richly textured anchor for the variety of the visual themes. The formal pleasure of recognizing and sorting out the spatial motifs as well as the rhythmic fragments is profoundly intensified as the dance constantly appears to approach chaos, then to reorganize itself, then to disperse once more.

Katema (1978), a solo, sets up a straight line advancing toward and retreating from the audience. The line, which gradually becomes longer and longer, is marked off with steps surprisingly intricate for Childs: small steps, slide-steps, coupés, turns with one leg open to the side. I think of *Katema* as enormously elaborate, almost baroque with its constant dips, its detailed footwork, its smooth flow of movements continually caught by turns. But no baroque dance was ever performed with such speed.

As I write this chapter, Childs is working on a new dance, a collaboration with composer Philip Glass and sculptor Sol LeWitt in five sections for a proscenium stage. In 1978 she presented one section of the work, with the interim title *Work in Progress with Philip Glass,* the first dance since the 1960s in which Childs has danced to music. In the section performed in 1978, Childs gradually maps out — with simple walking steps, skips, and a slightly more complex step-skip, and later turns — a matrix of two lines that form a cross the size of the entire dance floor. But much of the tracing of this rectilinear form is carried out by traveling in large arcs, as if each leg of the cross were really one quarter of the circumference of a circle, and as if the midpoint of the axis described the point where four circles met. The grid pattern emerges after Childs spends time etching each quadrant in turn, changing her step sequence from arcs to lines as the music theme shifts. The air seems very bright with the loud, rich tones of the electric organ vibrating and the swift arcking patterns danced across the entire field of vision. Using music for the first time in many years, Childs seems carried by it in an odd way, since the sound of her locomotion is obliterated. As usual, Childs has seated her audience at various points of view on the dance. Each quarter of the audience forms a base for two of the legs of the matrix, and the audience as a whole forms a square that the matrix quadrisects in two diagonal lines. As Childs traces out the quadrant closest to the spectator, one is forced to scan the room so widely and so quickly that at the point in the dance, the room seems to spin. The experience of whirling is transferred from dancer to spectator.

The investigations of repetition and point of view continue. Childs' line of inquiry remains steady. Like her earlier dissections of everyday realities, like the low-contrast group works, like her obsessive solos, the collaborative work functions didactically, turning attention to modes of perception. Repetition and shifting contexts make a world of detail come alive, as the act of dancing provokes a conscious act of seeing.

Lucinda Childs, Street Dance[10]

(At Robert Rauschenberg's studio, fall 1965, dialogue on tape.)

To see this dance the observer must stand by the window at the south end of the loft and look across the street toward the south side of Broadway onto the sidewalk extending between 11th and 12th streets.

I am concerned with the area between the Bon Vivant Delicacies Store and Surplus Materials of Norbert and Hausknect. I am not concerned with either of these buildings specifically but I am concerned with the area between.

Old Europe Antiques Incorporated, a black sign with white letters, is framed in gold. The window below the sign displays various objects, presumably European: clocks, chandeliers, candelabras, various antiques labeled with white tags: B 103, Fa VR, another 64, another 20. The remaining tags remain overturned or blank or no information is on them. On the door a small sign informs that the building is license bonded by New York State protected by a Mr. Louis Lewis. L-O-U-I-S L-E-W-I-S. There is a reward for information leading to the arrest and conviction of any person committing burglary or larceny against this concern and to call ALgonquin 4-5952.

Next to the antique store is a stairway concealed by a grating. The stairway is closed on Saturdays by a padlock which attaches to the center of the grating; to the right of the grating is 816 Broadway, a Flea Market. A white sign is numbered 8 1 6 in black. The numbers 8 1 6 are written vertically and surrounded by a fine black ellipse. Four miniature cameras are displayed in the window, one for $15.00, another $10.00. On the left wall in the window two carved wooden owls face each other. The owls are from Spain. A white sign with red lettering beneath the window square explains that the nonautomatic sprinkler is in the basement.

814 Broadway is a Gurbob building — the numbers are in white against the maroon color of the building. A steel ladder extending from underneath the

fire escape to the right intersects with the letters. Next to that Caltype Wholesale Office Machines — a white sign with black lettering. The Y of Caltype extends downward to the line of the black squarish ellipse that surrounds the sign, the round ball at the bottom tip of the Y is cut in half by the bottom line of the ellipse. The sign is repeated below in the window, however in this instance the C of Caltype is surrounded by orange. There are three rows of cardboard boxes to the right in the window. A red arrow extends upward on each one and the word *up* is written to the left of each red arrow in red. To the left of this, typewriters, adding machines, calculators, photocopy, mimeograph, and dictation machines are advertised in gold writing in a vertical column. A square pillar extends in front of the second of three doorways of 814 Broadway. The building is sprinkled at 814 Broadway, with the exception of the cellar and subcellar which is sprinkled at 812 Broadway, also a Gurbob building.

This is a snow street — no parking 8 A.M.–6 P.M. Monday through Friday. There is a broken arch on the roof of the Caltype building and an identical broken arch at the right, but it does not extend as much into the lower fringe embordment of the building.

Street Dance: Score
Minutes/Seconds

:50	Old Europe Antiques	3:42	Gurbob
1:05	Window	3:50	Fire escape
1:25	B 103	3:55	(Action of performers)
1:45	End of tags	4:05	Caltype
1:50	Door license	4:10	Y of Caltype
2:10	Burglary, larceny	4:20	(Action of performers)
2:22	Grating	4:30	Repeated below
2:30	Padlock	4:35	C of Caltype
2:35	Flea Market		cardboard boxes
2:54	8	5:08	Typewriters, etc., written
2:55	1		in a vertical column
2:56	6	5:09	(Action of performers)
3:10	Cameras	5:10	
3:20	Dolls	5:15	
3:22	Face each other	5:25	Aluminum column
3:30		5:50	Snow street
3:35	(Action of performers)	6:00	Arch

Meredith Monk: Homemade Metaphors

MEREDITH MONK'S theater is a place of transmutation and transfiguration. Events occur, but their meanings shift and are wiped away. Time and space become shattered and rearranged. Objects shrink or become luminous and powerful. Inside the magically real universes that Monk creates within the borders of theatrical space, simple and familiar things accumulate into dense, resonant, fabulous images. Individual lives and actions and prosaic objects become symbols for larger systems through the spectator's act of meditation and integration.

Although she is often considered a choreographer in the tradition of the Judson Dance Theater, Monk the visionary and technician is more the child of Artaud than of Cage. An alchemist in the theater, she carefully plans and measures the elements of her spectacles both to present stories — albeit plotless, mysterious tales — and to acknowledge lovingly the theatricality of their presentation. Even though some of her techniques have analogues in early theater forms of both the East and the West, Monk's work is radical — partly because it contravenes the direction of modern theater; partly because it unabashedly exploits the theatricalism of its techniques, whether they be traditional or new. These contradictions lend the work a primitive, enigmatic quality: Monk's performances describe a reality of essences, rather than surfaces. She might declare, along with Artaud,

> We believe in all the threats of the invisible . . . We are totally dedicated to unearthing certain secrets . . . [We seek] to present to the eye certain tableaux, certain indestructible, undeniable images that will speak directly to

Meredith Monk as the Child in *Quarry*. Photograph © Johan Elbers, 1976.

> the mind ... There will not be a single theatrical gesture that will not carry behind it all the fatality of life and the mysterious encounters of dreams.[1]

A fanciful program note from 1969 states that:

> MEREDITH MONK was born in lima Peru/grew up in the West riding horses/is Inca Jewish/lived in a red house A COMMERCIAL: SHE WILL PRESENT A NEW WORK: "TOUR: DEDICATED TO DINOSAURS" ON MARCH 4 IN THE ROTUNDA OF THE SMITHSONIAN INSTITUTION IN WASHINGTON, D.C. Started dancing lessons at the age of three because she could not skip/did Hippy Love Dance at Varney's Roaring 20's Topless Club in California/has brown hair.[2]

As an autobiographical statement, it is the real Monk, even though some of its details may not be accurate — if one refers to rational, external verities. But in its stream-of-consciousness mixture of the most mundane details with unabashedly romantic figments, it is revealing of the texture of her work and life.

Monk *was* born in Peru, where her mother, a singer, was on tour. But she grew up in Connecticut, the descendant of European Jews — including her great-grandfather, who was a cantor, and her grandfather, who founded the Harlem School of Music. Monk learned to sing before she could talk, read music before she knew how to read words. At three she began to dance, first studying eurhythmics (a system of teaching musical rhythm through body movement, invented by Émile Jaques-Dalcroze) and then ballet. As a child she also studied music theory and harmony; at sixteen, she began composing. Monk's first dance performances were with a New York group doing Israeli folk dances.[3]

In college at Sarah Lawrence, Monk majored in performing arts, studying with Judith Dunn and Bessie Schönberg among others. In 1964, she moved to Manhattan where, besides choreographing and dancing her own works, she performed in Happenings, off-Broadway plays, and other dance works. Monk's own work since 1964 can be divided roughly into five categories: early dance works; large works for specific sites; chamber works; collaborations; music recitals. She has also made several films and recordings.

By the time Monk arrived in New York City, the dance world had seen the first stage of a creative rebellion and the choreographic revolutionaries of the first Judson generation were consolidating their discoveries and advances. Monk's work, in a sense, reacted against the aesthetic of that revolution, while taking advantage of an ambiance that fostered formal experiments. Her program did not involve rinsing dance of spectacle and theatricality — as had, for instance, Yvonne Rainer's — but, rather, exploring the very theatricality of expressive performance. *Break* (1964), for example, used the wings and back entrances of the theater to mask parts of the soloist's body, and at one point Monk left the stage to view from the audience the vacuum thus created. Movements in *The Beach* (1965) were tailored for an imaginary persona — the beach lady. Like the Judson pioneers, however, Monk was less concerned with the attention to technical virtuosity that deadened modern dance, and more with generating new movements, if need be, in order to make new statements.

Using stratagems like chance composition, improvisation, games, and tasks enacted during the performance, as well as repetition and fragmentation, Rainer and others sought to isolate movements for their own sake, to be examined and valued as objects in themselves. Rigorously defying illusion, these choreographers often presented openly the process of arrangement. The aim was to call attention to the beauty of ordinary, simple movements and (somewhat) ordinary bodies. Monk, on the other hand, wrenched quotidian movements and objects from the context of the everyday world, transmuting rather than presenting ordinary things by exposing them in new frameworks, forming within the theater a separate world with its own logic and customs. Although she also used repetition and fragmentation, her meanings emerged — more in the tradition of some Happenings and even Graham's expressive dances — not through chance, rarely through improvisation, but through the careful, poetic arrangement of visual and aural imagery, juxtapositions of surfaces, sounds, gestures, and spaces. "The artist's hand isn't something I want to eliminate because that's like giving in to the machine," Monk has stated. And "John Cage would say there's enough structure and I would say there's enough chance."[4]

In *Break*, a typical Monk structure is already evident. Jill Johnston described the piece as "a clear solid solo of expressive gestures and exclamations in the chunky continuity explained by the title. Moves are sudden, images are sustained (slow or still) for a sharp etch and erased by the quick transitions that are like black-outs — empty canvas with spattered incidents."[5]

16 Millimeter Earrings, a solo created in 1966, presented overlapping images of the body as a medical phenomenon and a sensuous medium, through the use of a complex technology. Layers of sound, both live and taped, included Monk singing "Greensleeves," chanting, sounds of a crowd, and a taped description of the orgasm from Wilhelm Reich's *The Function of the Orgasm.* The visual track included the dancer's live actions and several films. One film, of Monk's face, was projected on a large sphere placed over her head; another showed a doll burning and, then, as Monk stood up from a trunk naked, in front of the projection screen, the film changed to images of flames over her body. Earlier, red silk streamers had blown up from the trunk, fake flames. The systematic distortion of the body and its actions — expressing emotions, executing movements — recalls the apparitions and modified forms of the Surrealists.

With *Blueprint* (1967), Monk began to design her pieces for particular, architectural or natural (nontheatrical) sites. At the first performance of *Blueprint,* in Woodstock, New York, the audience moved from place to place to view activities, and at one point sat outside a building to watch events in the windows. In New York City the audience returned a month after the first section was given, to see the second part which included Monk dancing *The Dying Swan.*

Monk moved her audience around the Guggenheim Museum and the island of Manhattan in *Juice* (1969). The first installment, for a chorus of dancers and many separate characters, had three parts. First, the audience, on the ground floor of the Guggenheim, looked to see events including the chorus singing and migrating toward and away from the railings, three women in period costume lined up vertically along the spiral ramp and slowly rotating, four red-dyed people trampling up the ramp in a clump. Second, the audience strolled up the museum's spiral ramp, viewing many tableaux, some scenes with repeated movements, and the current exhibit of Roy Lichtenstein's paintings in the background. All eighty-five performers were wearing red boots. Finally, the audience, having reached the top, saw everyone rush down past them, dancing and playing jew's-harps. A man sawed wood; another man played the violin; a woman with a death mask on her belly, unnaturally tall (her dress concealed another person on whose shoulders she was carried), stalked up the ramp and around the ground floor.

In the second installment of *Juice,* three weeks later at the Minor Latham Playhouse at Barnard College, everything had diminished. At the entrance to the theater, a child sat on a pony or rocking horse — a smaller echo of the woman who rode a horse down Fifth Avenue as the audience waited outside the Guggenheim for the first part. Inside the theater, the four red characters gave information about themselves in recitatives, and performed real-life activities — frying a pork chop, mixing chemicals. The red mountain woman (Monk) whirled and sang in a trance; a log cabin was gradually dismantled to reveal the violinist from part one, in a room replete with wallpaper, books, a quart of milk, and a print of a Lichtenstein painting. A rock opened to reveal objects and the characters performed operations on the objects; the woman with the death mask belly appeared, normal height. Many more elements from the first part were rearranged and shrunk in this presentation.

In the third installment, a week later at Monk's loft in lower Manhattan, the audience wandered through an exhibit of artifacts — costumes and objects — from the previous two installments, and saw a videotape of close-ups of the four red characters as they quietly discussed their roles.

As Deborah Jowitt has suggested, the scale of the piece diminished as the information about the characters increased, yet any resulting sense of growing intimacy was offset by distancing devices.[6] At the museum, the performers were living sculptures that the spectators could hear breathing. At the Minor Latham, the audience was separated from the performance by a proscenium arch. Finally, at Monk's loft, though one could even smell the sweat on the costumes, the performers were made totally remote, once-removed by the video screen. The museum and loft had switched functions by the end of the piece.

Vessel (1971) reversed the progression of size and scope *Juice* had accomplished. A passion play about Joan of Arc, it began with an "overture" at The House, Monk's loft — a slowly shifting tableau of people dressed in black. They made minute gestures, and each took a turn under a light to momentarily transform into an alter ego — one, a king scattering coins, another a woman scooping them up, and so on. Monk played the organ and sang, invoking Joan's voices, and later spoke lines from Shaw's *St. Joan.* A group of straggly pioneers (who had also appeared in *Needle-Brain Lloyd and the Systems Kid* in 1970) filed through; a woman representing a waterfall unrolled her long hair; two soldiers fought with rakes. And more.

From The House, spectators were brought by bus to The Performing Garage at Wooster and Grand streets. Here, on a "hand-made mountain" of scaffolding draped with muslin, Joan, now painted silver, stood trial in a court presided over by paper-crowned king and queen buffoons, and was questioned by two Bishop Cauchons. A traveler journeyed in a circle from birth to death; the House people — now mountain people — performed such tasks as reading, chopping vegetables, and mixing fluids. They communicated in yodels. At one point the only sound in the room was the crisp noise made as everyone tore leaves of lettuce.

Part III, "Existent Lot," took place in a parking lot down the street from The Performing Garage. Not only the scale of the setting, but the cast, colors, and lighting sources magnified as Joan neared her immolation. The eighty performers included pioneers sitting around campfires and dancing with ears of corn; children in court costumes; a kazoo army battling a pennywhistle army with rakes; a Spanish dancer; a Scottish dancer; a motorcycle cavalcade, a VW bus full of "cuckoos" continually emptying itself; and the House people in their living room, transplanted intact. Finally Joan, in a black derby, skittered away into the sparks of a welder's torch at the far end of the lot.

During the late '60s, Monk had collaborated on music for performances with Don Preston (of the Mothers of Invention) and others, and had composed her own music as well. In 1970 she gave a music concert at the Whitney Museum, the first of many different Raw Recitals. These recitals always have a theatrical frame; at the first, Monk satirized a diva, whose appearance became weirder as the music progressed from Bach to Monk. Dressed in a fancy pink dress and red work boots, her hair done up regally, she fragmented the usual singer's gestures, stopped abruptly as an assistant pinned a corsage on her. Gradually her hair fell down. The platform she sat on moved around the concert hall. Monk's music, always as integral to the theater pieces as her sense of theatricality is to the music recitals, has been called reminiscent of Satie, or of Hebrew chants, or of muezzins' calls. It has a simple folk quality, often with a nasal edge; repetitive melodies consisting of circular chains of small phrases are teased out on jew's-harps, kazoos, a wineglass, or a keyboard. Chords are distilled, repeated, explored, and magnified on piano or organ; her own voice makes discoveries and gestures in wordless sound, circling, twisting, traveling. Though her compositions are rather simple in terms of instrumentation, they are primarily vocal works, demanding technical flexibility and a wide range.

As with many of her productions, Monk presented several different versions of the two-part *Education of the Girlchild* both in New York and on tour over a two-year span. Some versions consisted only of the solo (later, second) section. In late 1973, a final version took place at a Soho loft and, with a larger

Drawing for Poster: *Education of the Girlchild* (Meredith Monk, 1972–73)

cast, at the Cathedral Church of St. John the Divine. *Education* is an epic with ambiguous meaning: its strange tribe of women could be goddesses, heroines, ordinary people, or different aspects of one person. The actions of the epic may describe a journey or the landscape of a planet; explain the structure of a family; map a soul. In the first part of the piece, six women dressed in white populate the stage, forming tableaux, traveling, enacting odd rituals. They dig up a colorfully dressed creature, a wide-eyed woman who learns to be one of them, to walk and sing their way. The second section is a solo for Monk: it is a voyage down a white canvas road, down a lifetime; from ancientness to middle-aged womanhood to virgin/saint; from remembering to knowing to wondering, the changes marked by transformations in voice and movement.

Like the later *Quarry* (1976), *Education* seems to retrieve images from the very borders of memory, playing with them and rearranging them as if in reverie or a dream. And, as the film in *Quarry* teaches us to displace scale, the way the women in *Education* play a contemplative game with a miniature Stonehenge suggests interpretation on a vast scale. Rituals of burying and unearthing, of eating, of traveling, tell of a time — either in the primordial experiences of humankind, or in an individual's life cycle — when experience was this structured, this ritualized. The simple, graphic imagery of maturation or coming to consciousness gives *Education* the flavor of a folktale, the traditional method by which the elders in a society subtly pass on to their descendants instructions for mastering life's crises, struggling for self-realization.[7] But because Monk's symbols and stylizations are self-imposed, rather than the product of a historical process within a collective culture, there is a strange visionary edge to the folktale quality — it almost seems to be a metaphor about the making of metaphors.

Quarry begins with a child's complaint, patterned into a chant: "I don't feel well. I don't feel well. I don't feel well. It's my eyes. It's my eyes. It's my eyes. It's my hand, it's my hand, it's my hand. It's my skin, it's my skin, it's my skin." The child is lying in the center of the floor, the audience lined up along the side of the large rectangular performing area, sitting on narrow balconies. (The piece was performed first at La Mama Annex.) In the four corners of the broad space surrounding the child, four households function simultaneously, and the viewer's attention is pulled to the diverse tableaux as each in turn comes alive. A family of young women sits at a dinner table, an actress rehearses her lines in her study, a scholar talks about his research to his wife in their living room. Among these twentieth-century people, whose world is permeated with radio broadcasts, an Old Testament couple sifts grain and reads scrolls in the fourth corner. Later, people from all the different households become dictators. Later still, they become victims — suggesting a complex metaphoric structure in which each transformation reveals another facet of a character.

Juxtaposed against the different possibilities of these individuals are the actions of a chorus of thirty. They appear, and wash away the previous actions by chanting and moving across the space; they rally in support of the mesmerizing dictator; they sing a requiem. The changing scale of the piece — it is the story of a child, widening to a story about a family, a people, a world — is epitomized in a film, shown halfway through the performance. From what at first looks like a pile of tiny pebbles even tinier people emerge, and one realizes with a shock that the stones are enormous. The film seems to be a paradigm for understanding *Quarry:* history can change its scope as well as its shape; the history of a child in certain ways duplicates the history of humankind.

Children perceive and organize the mysterious workings of the world (which includes the mysterious workings of their own bodies and consciousnesses) from their vantage point at the center, according to a personal, highly subjective standard of measure that distends perspective. Adults learn to correct for distortion. Yet the artist chooses consciously to present a private system for interpreting reality. The child's, the psychotic's, and the artist's fantastic distortions often describe more accurately our disorderly, nameless perceptions. In *Quarry,* Monk uses the bulging perspective of a child's feverish projections to tell of a reality too grim — and a hope too irrational — to be conveyed except by symbols. And the suggested event of the Holocaust is distanced twice: once through the artist's frame, the second through the child's.

The title shares the ambiguity of the film and the images and sounds in the piece. As a verb, *quarry* can mean either "to excavate" or "to hunt down," and as a noun it can mean "a place designated for the excavation of building materials," or "the object of a hunt" — implying a trapped animal. If we choose to read *Quarry* as a psychoanalytic model of a child's fears and anxieties, the theater itself serves as a kind of a quarry, a metaphorical couch where the excavation for the purpose of rebuilding the personality is accomplished. (In fact, Freud's favorite metaphor for psychology was archaeology.) But the piece also suggests the hunting down of Jews in Nazi Germany and generalizes to warn of the necessity for victims in any dictatorship. And it also uses the quarry as a metaphor for memory: the Monk music with its strange nostalgic strains, the fragmented images of the family, the predominance of the radio as an icon, the 1940s costumes, all seem to serve as universal augers, boring holes in the surface of the present through which one can magically see and recall fragments of the past. The chorus that washes away the action, the man who destroys by taking photographs or by rubbing away his own chalk marks, seem to embody processes by which history or our own individual memories select and preserve certain events but erase others.

The radio, symbol of an era, is the central image in the opera, both visually and aurally: it is a means to power, a source of information that is both true and distorted. Broadcasting reaches so many people, yet one sees the radio announcer in the sound booth, lonely and isolated. Monk shows us how subtly we can be controlled by sound. Listening to songs and speeches in nonsense language, we realize that verbal content is only part of meaning. We don't understand the dictator's words, but his tone and delivery make perfect sense. The slow organ crescendos induce a Pavlovian response of melodramatic expectancy.

Paris/Venice/Milan/Chacon is a trilogy. Ranging widely in scale and tone but linked structurally, the three pieces are strange and lovely hybrids of mystery novels, silent films, and living travel guidebooks. Here Monk and Ping Chong, Monk's collaborator, a *bricoleur* who also makes imagistic theater pieces independently, act as surrealistic Baedekers.

In *Paris*, an intimate duet, the relationship between the two characters — known only as the Paris couple — is established, as is each one's relationship with the world. They are ageless, poignantly dependent on each other like two fading grandparents, but strong and dark-haired, dressed in work boots and sturdy eastern European clothing. They limn the empty space with a recurrent, circular peregrination and create a landscape inside it with their actions. A pianist intermittently plays a Monk tune: simple chords unraveling into embroideries.

The couple sits in a formal, stiff portrait pose; they stand facing the back wall and weep; stand one at a time at the very edge of the audience to be scrutinized, a flashlight illuminating their faces from below. They hold hands, stroll, hum a folk song. But stranger things than these happen in this Paris of the mind. They dance together: Chong suddenly turns into a scampering monkey; Monk abruptly skitters sideways across the room and falls, again and again. One moment they're possessed; the next, serene.

The world of everyday life, postures, and gestures seems only a curtain masking another corresponding world where everything changes unpredictably. Monk and Chong take us on trips that begin ordinarily enough, but suddenly detour through places where people dance instead of walk, exchange glances rather than talk; where women have mustaches and the air is infused with snatches of music. And then, just as suddenly, things resume their quotidian states.

In *Paris,* the piece is announced by a whimsical human puppet, whose head pops out of a screen. In *Venice/Milan* the beginning is marked by a grand, serious formation of gondoliers chanting and plying invisible oars. The head gondolier remains to provide a frame and metronome for the action through her rhythmic, unchanging activity.

Everything else is a shifting field of mysterious comings and goings, greeting rituals, characters, and objects. The Paris couple, now dressed in velvets and tails, pursue a diagonal, zigzag path. A sinister thread appears: a masked man in black lace. A countess greets guests, turns cartwheels. A turbanned visitor brings curious gifts, and weaves another diagonal dance through the space, a space which constantly expands and diminishes as two moveable screens glide to and fro. As this mystery without a plot unfolds, people begin to collapse, to receive cryptic documents, to be marked by the hand of fate as gossips and liars. One senses an elegant, decaying society with many formal rules, in which the Paris couple constantly blunder and remain outsiders despite droll attempts to behave properly.

In *Chacon* (the name of a tiny town in New Mexico), the scale of the piece ironically expands further; the stage (originally, a gym at Oberlin College) is repeatedly erased by the passage of chanting, dancing farmers; paths are at right angles; a chorus of musicians shaking homemade gourds (of beer cans filled with rice) replaces the trio of silent musicians onstage during *Venice/Milan.* (The piano remains in all three pieces.) A cup disappears and reappears, carrying curses, enchantments, and historical impact. The exotic visitor of *Venice/Milan* (Blondell Cummings) becomes the sorceress in *Chacon;* here the countess (Lee Nagrin) has become the artist/historian who paints a mural depicting the New Mexican landscape while its actions unfold on stage. The Paris couple walks through only at the end. Here the rituals are more elemental: the stress is on water, on birth, death, and rebirth; on planting and waiting and watching for rain.[8]

In this surrealistic travelogue, Monk and Chong treat theatrical space much as Joseph Cornell treated his boxes — as a repository for odd items, scraps of gestures, sounds, and habits. They assemble selected fragments inside a well-crafted frame. This odd juxtaposition of mementos, again like Cornell's boxes, evokes a nostalgic object, one that also serves as an analogue to the notion of the mind as a dusty attic, its memories hidden away in corners. In certain ways, too, the trilogy is like a dream or fantasy about a trip: the same people show up in utterly disparate communities, although often symbolically enacting similar roles; objects seem to take on special meaning as keys to obscure situations; maps of terrain and behavior seem condensed into one format, and yet every image yields several layers of meaning.

One of the most striking contributions Monk has made to post-modern theater is the radical reorganization of space. Her training as a dancer and choreographer must have given her a special sense for deep spatial organization, but just as often she seems to operate with the eye of a painter or film maker. Monk's works since 1967, as I have pointed out, have been primarily concerned with formal explorations of specific places: both nontheatrical sites (churches, gyms, museums, fields, lakes, parking lots) and nonproscenium performing spaces, such as La Mama Annex, various Soho lofts, MoMing in Chicago, and Brooklyn Academy of Music's Leperq Space.

In a revealing interview with Brooks McNamara that appeared in *The Drama Review,* Monk analyzes in detail, among other scenic features, some of her strategies for making principles of spatial organization legible in *Vessel.*[9] If *Vessel* moved the eye like a film over flat imagery, from close-up to wide-screen pan — while changing from black and white to blazing technicolor — then *Juice* emphasized sculptural compositions in space. Here the tableaux in the first part and the objects in the third part could be circumambulated; the function of the museum was disrupted and transferred to the loft; the three ways of using the Guggenheim embodied the notion of in-the-round. In *Juice,* the careful contrasts and comparisons between the three performance stations, and between the kinds of activities taking place in the three installments, were explicated by a diminishing scale. The progression moved from monumental figurative friezes to a small reliquary.

In part of *Blueprint,* at Woodstock, the spectators sat outside a building to view events in windows. Some of the events were live, some filmed, some a combination of a projected film image on identical live action. In another section of *Blueprint,* after two performers left an upstairs gallery space, the audience was instructed to look out the window; in the courtyard below, two effigies were positioned, their backs to the audience, as if to begin again the performance that had just concluded. Throughout, there was a confounding of inside and outside actions — a notion that serves as a kind of groundwork for many of the metaphors in Monk's work. By extension, the borders between private and public, interior and exterior events, the body and the universe, the individual and community are seen as divisions that can dissolve as well.

Several of Monk's performances have involved a switch of the passive role from spectator to performer and of the active role from performer to spectator, requiring the invasion of space by either faction. As in *Juice*, Monk's *Co-op* (1968), *Tour: Dedicated to Dinosaurs, Tour 2: Barbershop* (both 1969), and several later tours had the audience walking around to examine relatively static performance tableaux. During the Avant-Garde Festival at the Billy Rose Theater in 1969, Monk placed performers inside boxes in the lobby during intermissions; the audience could peek inside and watch them change positions. Finally they emerged.

Even stages designed to be used flexibly are given unprecedented uses and shapes. For instance, at The Dance Center in Chicago, a cavernous place with seats that move readily according to the demands of a particular performance, Monk set a version of *Vessel I* on the resident troupe in 1974. She turned the audience to face the entry to the hall — the one seating arrangement that had never been used, or probably even imagined. All the doorways, exit lights, risers, refrigerators, and other normally offstage apparatus came into the composition of the piece. When performed at her own loft, Monk used *Vessel I* to reverse the usual geography of a dancer's loft by putting the performers in the living area and the audience in the dancing area.

A program for *Tour 4: Lounge* (at Alfred University, Alfred, New York, 1969) instructs the audience where to relocate for different parts of the performance:

> Section I. The performance will take place on the stairs, raised area to the rear of the lounge, and the sides of the lounge. The audience may be seated in the middle of the lounge . . . Section III. A twenty minute interval consisting of six simultaneous events distributed in different areas of the lounge. Each event contains changes, progressions, and permutations. There are no climaxes, beginnings and endings. Within each event it is to the advantage of the spectator to move freely from event to event. It is expected that the audience will wish to observe the changes in the various events and to go back and forth among them. Section IV. Performance will take place in the middle of the room. The audience will be at the edges of the room.[10]

The program for *Tour 5: Glass* (Nazareth College, Rochester, New York, 1970) offers a map of the auditorium in the Arts Center, with its thrust stage upstairs, a glass alleyway, and two downstairs auditoriums. The timing and diverse locations of various events are noted clearly.

Why this attention to space and scale? I have described how Monk has arranged journeys for the spectators from one performance station to the next; the way in which she activates zones and niches not usually used for theatrical ends, sometimes not even noticed; the deliberate, rigorous contrasts and comparisons between flat and deep expanses, between enormous and tiny proportions. Generally she initiates the audience before they enter the performing area. All these techniques for heightening the viewer's sense of place, space, and scale serve several purposes. First, they evoke a sense of pilgrimage. The activities in the works often hint at and sometimes even depict voyages and quests. On one level, these travels are actually explorations of a specific geographic entity, whether a theatrical representation of a place on stage — Paris or Venice, for example — or a "real" place — lower Manhattan or the Connecticut College campus — that is explored. On another level, they are also symbolic journeys, exploring inner space, or the landscape of a body; incarnating metaphors for spiritual, artistic, psychological, or even biological development. The audience, participating physically in these journeys by virtue of Monk's insistent critique of space, replicates that progress.

Similarly, time is stretched, warped, sped up, turned backward. The distortion of the space-time continuum undermines both rational everyday experiences and classical theatrical conventions. It gives us grounds to support our suspicions — confirmed in such other realms of experience as dreams, fantasies, drug-induced euphoria, or trance — that space and time are, after all, inconsistent. In this world of superrealism, the essences of things and their relationships materialize; things appear to us visually as our minds and ears know them, rather than precisely as we customarily see them. By rearranging the elements of our perception within an apparently familiar context, Monk reveals the extraordinary, which we sense is latent in the ordinary. Astonishing metamorphoses take place not in the surface of an object (or movement) itself, but as its function or spatial context or timing changes — in much the same way that Lautréamont's "fortuitous meeting" of a sewing machine and an umbrella releases new meanings.

For the unusual, the extraordinary, the fabulous in Monk's work always has its roots in the everyday world. She does not create fireworks through sleight of hand, but, literally, with a welder's torch (*Vessel*). A necromancer mixing strange fluids is, in real life, a chemist. A pile of wondrous fruits is on closer inspection merely a cluster of eggplants. People are dressed in clothing anyone might own, but in combinations people do not usually wear. The mixture of classical and new elements, of familiar objects and actions in strange synthesis is crucial: it provides the surreal edge, and also the grounding without which the audience would founder.

Similarly, the audience's expectation that a performance in a theater will proceed as some kind of narrative with a beginning, middle, and end gives shape and coherence to the chunky imagery, even when there are no normal beginnings, middles, climaxes, or ends. One survives the bewildering explosion of time, space, color, and imagery because one looks for an order with which to structure the fragments. At the same time that Monk teaches us new ways to look at and listen to old things, she provides familiar frameworks as guideposts. A puppet announcing the beginning of *Paris;* the traditional *trois coups* of French theater that announce the beginning of *Education* and *Vessel;* the organ music that sounds as if it came from a radio melodrama that heralds the start of *Quarry;* the queuing up and waiting before each performance: all these reassure the audience that a familiar ritual — the theater performance — is about to begin. But the familiar soon skews into the curious. Theatrical demarcations of territory do not hold. The play does not proceed like a play, but like a movie, or a piece of music, or some other art form.

Monk provides clues for the spectator to show that there are extra-dramatic, yet recognizable, models by which to order the imagery: she has called her works "a live movie" (*Needle-Brain Lloyd and the Systems Kid*); "a theater cantata" (*Juice*); "an opera epic" (*Vessel*); "an opera" (*Education of the Girlchild* and *Quarry*). During *Chacon,* a map is painted on the back wall of the performing area and depicts, in another mode, the same dry prairie that the actions evoke. In *Quarry, Blueprint, 16 Millimeter Earrings,* and other works there are films, and in *Quarry* and *Chacon,* photographers who freeze certain images. In *Small Scroll* (1975), the actors introduce themselves as fairy-tale characters. Many of the staging devices that seem so unusual for the theater, so new, in fact have precedents in these genres. But to use them in live theater is radical. Again and again Monk "cuts" or "fades" or "washes" from one scene to the next; she zooms in to show details, or pans across a broad expanse. She uses flashbacks and flashforwards. Both Monk and members of The House (her company) speak of "editing" during the course of composing a work. In *Juice,*

Monk translated onto bodies and objects, as well as using the customary media (voices and musical instruments), the cantata in its choral schema. Conversely, in musical composition, Monk speaks of the dancing voice.

Monk's pieces proceed through association and accretion, rather than through narrative. They evoke textures and moods by poetic concatenations of images and variations, their multileveled meanings enriched by their very ambiguity. So it is hard to talk about the literal meaning of Monk's theater. It speaks, in a sensuous rather than a literary language, of events and intuitions that usually escape naming or logical description, suggesting that Monk has chosen the only possible form — multiple avenues of sensory approach — to give body to these visions. But generally the pieces seem to tell about a certain kind of world and a certain way of being in the world: peaceful, cooperative, harmonious — despite some difficult ordeals. Often the images revolve around a home or a tightly structured community. Each character has his or her special, emblematic identity. People eat, or cook, or sit together around a table. People labor together, and collectively encounter cosmic events: births, deaths, rites of passage. There is dignity and weight in the smallest glance, in a touch, in the slightest nuance of gesture or sound.

The sense of community, of a cohesive group with magic powers of communication, is evident not only in the moment of presentation, but in the choice of place (e.g., Monk's loft, or a neighborhood parking lot in an artists' community), the offering of food to the audience before the performance, the name of the company, and the way personal material from the lives of people in The House is woven into the performance. Not all of these aspects are fully evident to all the spectators, but their effects permeate the work. This communal sensibility reflected the spirit of the times in the '60s; in the '70s, it has a compensatory function, offering a vision of an integrated, productive, and stable society, one with a unity of purpose and nobility of means, one that is fashioned of materials at hand, and contains wonders and small miracles among the ordeals.

Though she sometimes mines the past for material (St. Joan in *Vessel*, The Holocaust in *Quarry*, a Russian shtetl in *Education*[11]) and uses formal devices to invoke nostalgic imagery, Monk's use of history is not nostalgic, but forward-looking. In her theater, life is intensified, not effaced. Her utopian societies are not traditional: they are not nuclear families, nor clans, but groups of strong individuals — often solely or predominantly women — whose social ties are unclear but whose emotional connections are obvious.

Perhaps they could serve as models for feminist utopias, but they are not offered as political tracts or patent moral tales. They are descriptions of things as they could be.

By recasting the experiences of the past into future legends, by putting together small, familiar things in new ways, by embedding folk materials in new structures, and using folk forms to create new meanings, Monk's performances obliquely suggest possibilities, resources, and tools for refashioning our existence together. In this sense, Monk is not didactic. Her lessons on seeing and hearing may be very strictly taught, but the morals of these lessons are not drawn but, rather, left to the spectator to ruminate on. The ambiguity, the mystery of Monk's meanings are so important to the work that when she is explicit the magic disappears. In much the same way, folk tales, rituals, and even dreamwork teach us indirectly and with many possible readings. The patterned attention to the small details of ordinary lives, the celebration of everyday as well as cosmic actions, the harmony of group rituals, the hinting at large meanings and connections glimpsed suddenly in our lives — all these suffuse Monk's hand-honed tableaux with a sense of solace in community that yet promises change and looks to the future. They are modernist folk tales for city dwellers.

Meredith Monk, Notes on the Voice[12]

1. The voice as a tool for discovering, activating, remembering, uncovering, demonstrating primordial/pre-logical consciousness.

2. The voice as a means of becoming, portraying, embodying, incarnating another spirit.

3. The dancing voice. The voice as flexible as the spine.

4. The voice as a direct line to the emotions. The full spectrum of emotion. Feelings that we have no words for.

5. The landscape.

6. The body of the voice/the voice of the body.

7. The voice as a manifestation of the self, persona or personae.

8. Working with a companion (the accompanying instrument: organ, piano, glass, etc.): repeated patterns or drone creating a carpet, a tapestry of sound for the voice to run on, fly over, slide down, cling to, weave through.

9. The voice as language.

10. History:

Beginning — 1967, duet of voice with Echoplex reverberating unit (*Blueprint*), the free voice as electric impulse.
1968, voice (voices) and violin, jew's-harps (*Juice*), the raw voice (rough, plaintive, primitive, brash), repeated chants; the voice as an indication of character — the red mountain woman, how does she sound?

Continuing — 1970, duet of voice with electric organ (*Raw Recital, Key: An Album of Invisible Theater*), the traveling voice (moving through dreamscapes).

1971, opera epic (*Vessel*), the voice of God (high, transparent piercing), cosmic telegraph: the voice as a supernatural phenomenon — St. Joan's voices, how do they sound?

Now — 1972–73, opera (*Education of the Girlchild*), the voice of the 80-year-old human, the voice of the 800-year-old human, the voice of the 8-year-old human; Celtic, Mayan, Incan, Hebrew, Atlantean, Arabic, Slavic, Tibetan roots; the voice of the oracle, the voice of memory.

1972–73, duet of voice with glass (wineglass filled with water) (*Our Lady of Late*), the naked voice, the female voice in all its aspects; gradations of feeling, nuance, rhythm, quality; each section another voice ("character, persona"), each section a particular musical problem, area of investigation; the full range of the voice (pitch, volume, speed, texture, timbre, breath, placement, strength); the voice as the vehicle for a psychic journey.

Kenneth King: Being Dancing Beings

IT SEEMS THAT Kenneth King sees life as an enormous puzzle, a set of interlocking mysteries that provides endless discovery and systematic contemplation. One of the parts of the puzzle is dancing, an activity that continually presents clues to be tracked down, information to be further analyzed and investigated. As in a set of Russian dolls, inside dancing are more puzzles, with more infinitely interlocking secrets.

King's use of dance is expressive. He combines dancing with mise en scène, film, characters, machines, words (both spoken and written), lighting, and costume, creating a chain of signals and symbols to convey metaphoric meaning. Through dancing, embedded in a total theatrical experience, the human body becomes both a key to knowledge about the body, space, and time, and also reveals itself as yet another term in the riddle. The metaphors King makes are dense, fragmented, offering no clear single meaning. Because he approaches his subjects obliquely — using so many disguises, secret codes, and simultaneous messages in a variety of media, it's often hard to say exactly what the dances are about. Yet when you look at his work as a whole, it seems to be poetically setting forth a statement on the bewildering impossibility of finding a resolution to the quest for certain knowledge.

Like Meredith Monk, King returns dance to symbolism and expressionism, but a kind of expressionism that could only have come about in a post-modern context. A second-generation Judson choreographer (he began giving performances in New York in 1964, while still in college at Antioch), King was always conscious of, even analytical about, principles and techniques gleaned from other choreographers, as well as from film makers, Happening artists,

Kenneth King in *Space City*. Photograph © Lois Greenfield, 1980.

philosophers, visual artists, and cultural theorists. Repetition, the everyday objects used by pop artists, the commonplace movements Yvonne Rainer, Lucinda Childs, and others used as analogues to found objects, the static imgery of the new American cinema, the indeterminate structures of Happenings, a McLuhanesque fascination with technology and computer information theory, a cool, deadpan performance presence, all were used not to undercut expression, as the original Judson group might use them, but to expand it.

In the '60s King saw the objective presence of the post-modern performer as important because objectivity eliminated point of view. It functioned even more effectively when combined with the immediate visual experience of material objects in the dance. But once point of view and stress and emotion were removed, a dance could still have content, King pointed out, since this reductive method itself commented existentially on the human condition. He used Sartre's *Nausea* as an example. As Sartre used "*objects-in-themselves,*" the functional "movement-as-movement," he wrote, "transconnects the performer to and with the environment."[1] For King the new dance, pared down to its essentials, was now ready to operate as an "arena of transacting techniques" where a synthetic form of dance-theater, transcending a set of already shattered boundaries between the arts, was the only means — a mixed means — for rendering ideas and experiences of mid-twentieth-century life.[2]

King's earliest pieces, heavily influenced by the acausal, nonpurposive structures of Happenings, and the banal subject matter of pop art, were static forms with hot content. The *New York Times* dance critic Allen Hughes, who had already lived through the shocks and excesses of Judson, called King's *cup/saucer/two dancers/radio* (1964) "a rather startling work,"[3] perhaps because the two dancers wore underwear, or perhaps because all the elements in the title were considered equally important by King, a principle announced on tape during the dance. In six preset sections, whose order and transitions were determined spontaneously before each performance, King — wearing undershorts and a black tie — and Phoebe Neville — dressed in brassiere, girdle, curlers, and toe shoes — performed repetitive sequences of movements. Neville marched across the floor on pointe, King repeatedly put his hand on his crotch, and both spilled colored solutions from coffee cups all over themselves. It was a vision of suburbia as action painting. Jill Johnston, writing in the *Village Voice,* referred to the characters, with their deadpan gazes, as "middle class mummies," suggesting that the toe shoes symbolized the suburban housewife's secret fantasy identification with ballerinas and movie stars, and that the male character had "a lustful mind and castrated everything else."[4]

Self-portrait: Dedicated to the Memory of John Fitzgerald Kennedy (1965) juxtaposed a collage tape of fragments of speeches by Kennedy, mixed with everyday sounds, to a repetitive series of everyday movements involving an attaché case, an ace bandage, a wristwatch, and a newspaper. Here repetition of an action again reinforced, rather than subverted, the dramatic creation of a character, since the sum of the actions personified the routinized bourgeois working man.

In *Blow-Out* (1966), King made literal his determination to reconnect the performer with the environment. Sitting in a foreshortened chair, in a setting composed of distorted objects that confounded perspective, he was attached to the wall by elastic bands coming out of his gloved fingers. King — dressed in a motorcyclist's outfit, complete with leather jacket, boots, and sunglasses — and Laura Dean — also dressed in black and wearing sunglasses, and handling fake fruit glued to a table — moved at first in slow motion, then at high speed. Marbles spilled from both their mouths. The accompanying tape included excerpts from Descartes' reflections on finding truth through the senses, music by Vivaldi, and a steady-state electronic siren. The Descartes reading provided a clue that *Blow-Out*'s ambiguities might be interpreted as yet another epistemological meditation.

Camouflage (1966), to readings from Alain Robbe-Grillet's *In the Labyrinth*, simulated the novel's static structure. King, costumed in a green helmet, green toe shoes, and green leotard, tights, and gloves, remained in a small area defined by a green rug. He repeatedly walked, fell, bourréed and jumped on pointe, shivered, silently screamed, talked on a blue telephone, and stood on his hands. Snow (white granules) fell from a plastic bag under which he sometimes stood. As critic Jack Anderson pointed out, the repetition and constraint in the piece aptly depicted military drill and fatigue, making *Camouflage* an effective antimilitarist piece that charted a breakdown of logic through the theatrical analogue of fragmented, repeated action.[5]

In *m-o-o-n-b-r-a-i-nwithSuperLecture* (1966), King delivered a polemic on the birth and death of choreography. On tape, his voice talked about the influences of rock-and-roll, film, television, metaphysics, sex, death, and electricity on dancing. Films showed a flower growing out of a dead rat, and a snake crushing and eating another rat. Disguised as a shabby old man in a mask and bald wig, King manipulated props, including stuffed, oversized gloves, a dummy, and a cloth rat that he stuffed with balloons. By the end of the dance, during which he executed only one recognizable dance movement (a grand rond de jambe), he had hung a number of objects on a clothesline, including his own leg. These, Constance Poster has suggested, represented the "*objets trouvés* of the mind, the collected debris of history and personal experience which . . . has to be shovelled out to allow new forms to develop," just as the death of the rat allowed for the growth of the flower in the film.[6]

Audiences were hostile to the films in *m-o-o-n-b-r-a-i-n.* Gregory Battcock, writing about the piece as an example of "expanded cinema" in *Film Culture,* read a political meaning into this reaction.

> One wonders how this same public would react if the rat had been diseased, splotchy, ugly and black, or if the snake were instead, an American Eagle. Or, put in more realistic terms, how does this public react to the killing of a dirty, unshaven, yellow, suspected Viet-Cong by a peace-loving, clean-shaven, butch-cut, white American Marine. It's almost as though the figurative cruelty of Euripides and Sophocles (among others) [has] gone unnoticed . . .
>
> King's protest is directed not only against "dance" but equally against our current sleep-walker's state . . .[7]

King "explained" his position on dance and everything else in the witty *SuperLecture:*

> Dancing was about Moving until moving got in the Way. The Abstract Expressionist expressed Everything. Now there is nothing left to express: not even Alienation and Meaning-in-Life . . .
>
> That's why THE MOST PERFECTLY IMAGINABLE DANCE would take place in some sealed-off, empty, white-walled room with Nothing in it . . . I think the Best Dance, though, would have no movement because the movement would get in the way of its being Original. I Mean movement was Invented a long Time ago already. I mean Moving is everywhere. Movement is Larger-than-Life. Television, you know. Movement Connects everything Up. Seeing, feeling, hearing, tasting, thinking etc. are Forms of Movement . . . Sex is about Moving and Electricity . . . Our skin is one schizophrenic medium in which the Moving Under the skin is Connected-Up to the Other Moving Over the skin . . .

> Cause if Kant had put on toe shoes we would have had to take off our watches . . .[8]

For King, one way of expressing the feeling that human experience is fragmented has been by using disguises. He literalizes in performance the feeling that life consists of contrasting layers of experience and shifting personae within the self, by appearing as first one alter ego, then another, then another. At times he has even denied, outside the theater, that these characters were played by himself.[9] These various personae include Sergei Alexandrovitch, the young Russian dancer who didn't perform at the New School on a program of avant-garde dancing there in 1967, but who did show up to dance in *A Show* at the Judson Church in 1968, and who wrote a long letter to *Ballet Review* about American dancing.[10] King also plays Pablo (a persona created for *Print-Out*), who delivered the letter to the producer of the New School program to say Sergei couldn't perform that night; Zora A. Zash, an entrepreneur of uncertain gender and the director of Global Art Shows International, who discovered Sergei and has produced several of Kenneth King's dance concerts; Pontease Tyak, the gray-bearded, Slavic-accented custodian for the Transhimalayan Society for Interplanetary Research; Mater Harry, a transvestite spy in *The Ultimate Exposé* (1975); Patrick Duncan (Isadora Duncan's son who drowned as a child); Friedrich Nietzsche; and other, sometimes unnamed, characters. The idea of alter ego threading through King's work corresponds, in his own analysis, to mystical notions of the double, to Nietzsche's concept of the "shadow," and Sartre's ideas of the "other." King thinks of his theatrical alter egos as archetypes, means for crystallizing and then integrating partial aspects of human totalities. These "semblances of character" are suggested in the writings of Jung and Plato.[11]

Print-Out (1967–68), subtitled "(CELE ((CERE))-BRATIONS: PROBElems & SOULutions for the dyEYEing: KING), and performed at Judson Gallery, offered another solution for mind/body, language/gesture splits. Other than a theatrical entrance by King swathed in a black hood, carrying a bucket from which he took a rubber snake and lizard and draped them over his shoulders, the performance contained no movement. It was designed for a small space that permitted little action. King sat while a text was projected on a screen and his voice on tape read the text. The subtitle gives some idea of what the writing in *Print-Out* is like: a series of linguistic adventures, in which King constantly explodes words and phrases, making nonsense, double senses, and triple senses out of every phonetic unit. In many texts accompanying or constituting his performances since then, he has continued to crack words open to insert extra sounds, stuttering purposefully to create new meanings, wringing extra words out of words — demonstrating that language itself is yet another secret code encapsulating layers of hidden meanings. King's writings have included what he calls "mappings for a meta-grammar" (*Metagexis,* 1972), "mappings for a meta-theology" (*The Great Void,* 1972), "mappings for a meta-machine" (*The Telaxic Synapsulator,* 1974), and "mappings for a meta-poesis" (*The Dansing Jewel,* 1971). The writings show a futurist's fascination with the technological jargon of the postindustrial age, but also an ingenious and whimsical humor based on punning and tongue-twisting, meditating on the conditions and mysteries of "being being bodies," among other things.[12]

In 1967, King claims in his cryptic, prophetic style,

> I started whirling freely and as fast as possible too. I would tie a clerical white *rope* around torso and over shoulders, then imagine a circle surrounding my body, extending and axially flipping over itself as it travels through SPACE . . . After the "rope" is tied around the body, a long, sustained whirling dance generates a high pitch of intensity causing a formidable change in consciousness. During the automatic firing of psychically-relayed impulses — telesomatically and parakinetically it became possible to "step out of time"! — DANCING MADE ME TELEPATHIC![13]

Dancing also put him in touch with Joseph D. Devadese (a pun on *devadasi,* a Hindu temple dancer), a member of the Inner Seercret Service, who revealed to King the information on the CIA-FBI scandal (i.e., a prediction of Watergate) in 1971. "SEE the first Programmed Dancer who telepathically intercepted the greatest scandal of the century," the flyer for that concert read. Two years later, after the Watergate scandal, King performed a revised *INADMISSLEABLE EVIDENTDANCE.* Disguised as Pontease Tyak, he read from Nietzsche, then as King he danced while his own voice on tape told of more government coverups: the secret use of Mesmex, a new energy/fuel resource, and the Master Control Panel, a computer that unifies all presently known and not-yet-invented technology and communications media, and which could do away with dualisms, like political parties, if the government were to open access to it. Through a montage of technological, philosophical, and political information, as well as dancing and disguising, King set up a dense web of associations, emphasizing McLuhan's notion that communications systems and electronics are extensions of man's nervous system.

The body, as this and so many other King dances tell us, is yet another medium for relaying information, through images and gestures. Yet King uses language along with moving bodies to make his prophecies, revelations, and celebrations, in all seriousness and at the same time with humor, for as long as dualisms are still part of our experience, King will evidently settle for no single information system. Though it is impossible to find exact or literal correspondences, within his montages there are hints that concepts are being translated from one system of information to another, but changing meaning in the process. Even where concepts are not undergoing translation and transformation, associations among visual, kinetic, and auditory and linguistic imagery are strengthened through juxtaposition. In *INADMISSLEABLE EVIDENTDANCE*, for instance, the whirling and circling in the dancing, with patterns based on circular matrices King imagined passing through the body, correspond to the interpenetrating circuits of the text's structure, which in turn is about interlocking spheres of political conspiracy. The underlying idea of circular interrelationships of bits of information is not only talked about but also given body in the formal structure of the dance itself. In *Time Capsule* (1974), what at first seem like totally isolated and disparate elements — a man whirling, films high overhead of King dancing along a linear path, King himself sitting at a small table and reading from his *Time Capsule* (*The Yellow Book*) after entering through a trap door, and later watering a pot of flowers, and the mysterious entry of another figure, dressed as an Arab — all ultimately interlock not because King draws connections between them, but because he gives us the framework for grouping them together in the title of the work. As if we had discovered a buried time capsule, we begin to look for rhymes and confluences, and we find them in our own construction of categories.

Nietzsche's philosophy has influenced King greatly, especially *Thus Spake Zarathustra.* He might say, along with Zarathustra,

> And let that day be lost to us on which we did not dance once! And let that wisdom be false to us that brought no laughter with it![14]

King has mentioned that he began work on *High Noon* (1974), his portrait-play of Nietzsche, partly as a result of studying whirling and reading about

Gurdjieff in P. D. Ouspensky's *In Search of the Miraculous: Fragments of an Unknown Teaching.* How does all that connect to Nietzsche? King felt that if one "pursued the circle long enough," one could discover all there is to know about dance. Similarly,

> Nietzsche was inspired by Zarathustra, and Zarathustra maybe even predates Buddha, and Zarathustra was a dancer, and dance was an integral part of what we now think of as yoga. Before there were just the positions, there was full animation of the body in dance.[15]

High Noon was performed in a small, cluttered room at the end of a small loft. It might have been any one of a number of small boarding-house rooms in which Nietzsche spent his time after his collapse in 1879, thinking, writing, perhaps talking and gesturing to himself. All this activity, the eruptions of Nietzsche's mind in solitude, King incarnated in a series of transformations from Nietzsche to Zarathustra to Dionysus, pacing from bed to trunk to desk. A quotation from R. J. Hollingdale's *Nietzsche: The Man and His Philosophy,* part of the program notes for *High Noon,* aptly describes King's electrifying performance:

> He is a man whose mind is full, overfull, of ideas; he is constantly finding ways of expressing them which, as he says in his letters, surprise and delight him; he spends much of each day walking, and at night he sits crouched over his table; and all the time he is talking to himself. He loves his own company, for with no one else can he enjoy such entertaining conversation . . . He argues, he grows angry, he laughs at himself; he postures and exposes himself as a posturer; he announces he is the freest of free-thinkers, and retorts that free-thinking is mere destructiveness. Gradually a philosophy emerges . . .[16]

King also states, in the program notes, that in Nietzsche lie the seeds for "all of 'Theater of the Absurd,' Beckett, Kafka, Dr. Caligari, existentialism, Artaud, etc. etc." but that perhaps no one had yet made a play about the philosopher because it would take a dancer to presume such an attempt. "Nietzsche doesn't need an actor, but rather a rhapsodist or an 'animateur' . . ." Yet *High Noon* showed that King is a consummate actor as well as a dancer. King and company, that is, for the cast included Mr. Pontease Tyak as The Voice of Zarathustra, Kenneth King as Nietzsche, and Mr. Paeter Nostraddos as The Figure of Dionysus. The credits for direction named Pontease Tyak and Zora Zash.

The text of *High Noon* was selected and arranged by King from Nietzsche's writings, especially from *Thus Spake Zarathustra.* Of course, King would identify with many aspects of Zarathustra's preaching and identity: the concept of man as a poet and reader of riddles, the notion of eternal recurrence, the need for masks, and so on. But the main point in Nietzsche's philosophy that King reiterates is nihilism, "as a complicated style and philosophical sensibility."[17] It is this nihilism, this "transvaluation of values" that King assimilates to his own broad notions of the " 'nihilation' of choreography."[18] In *SuperLecture* King had spoken of how the tape recorder and electricity did away with steps and positions, indeed, with choreography. And, in an article in *Dance Magazine* the following year, he wrote:

> Past knowledge or information about dancing is reducible via mathematical or symbolical formulations to codes . . . Perhaps the Master Choreographer of All Time will be the computer who will undoubtedly be able to synthesize all of history . . . The "Most Perfectly Imaginable Dance" no doubt will eventually be programmed.[19]

He has referred to his own choreography since 1969 as programmed movement, allowing for openness of form. And in 1975, he was still considering the scientific possibilities or superfluity of choreography:

> I think improvising is a science. I also think that sooner or later choreography as we now think of it will be redundant. You see we can move faster than we think so why think how we should move! Why try and set something that is already spontaneous and indeterminate? . . . Choreography is over. Which doesn't mean we should stop doing it. Quite the contrary. We're trying to see the options.[20]

King approaches improvisation as systematically as he approaches other aspects of dancing. It seems that there is a science or code of improvisation that King works at discovering, breaking down movements the way a chemist breaks down organic elements. He begins with a set of movements, a vocabulary, for a particular piece, and then sets up a framework within which the flow of those movements happens, based on intuitive choices, but also on rigorous practice, combining them in various ways. His model derives from a linguistic one. Out of the code, or system of elements, and the rules for combining them, come a variety of messages, or specific dance actions. Whether or not a grammar as rigid as that we use for language could evolve for dance

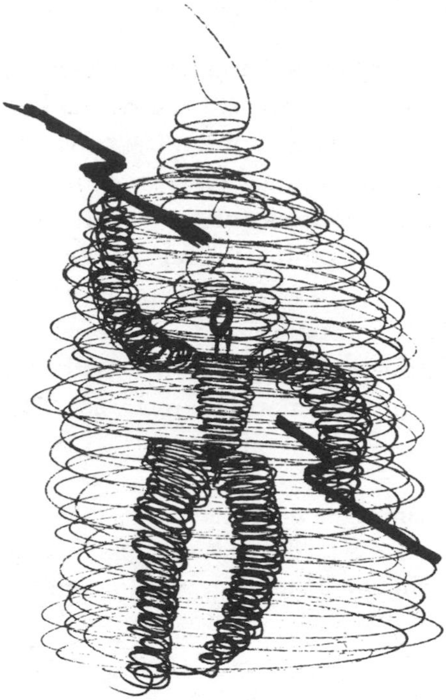

Coiled Man (Kenneth King)

is not important to King (i.e., whether movements would have to be done in a particular order to mean a particular thing). What does matter is the process by which he attempts to arrive at a grammar, or meta-grammar: the persistent analysis of movement from kinetic, theatrical, and poetic points of view. At times, movements will have an associational meaning that is significant for King in terms of conveying to his dancers the thought behind the movement, or even in terms of expressing that associated concept in the dance whenever the movement is performed. For instance, with a series of lunges he calls "The Clocks," King feels he has found a key to Merce Cunningham's elastic use of time. The "Marcel Duchamp Tendu" is actually a series of tendus, or stretches of the foot, from parallel to turned-out, expressing a theory of constant change and creating a visual perception of fragmentation and axiality of planes in space inspired by Duchamp's *Nude Descending a Staircase.* "The Orbits" involve three people running forward with small steps while rotating their paths around each other in complexly interchanging patterns. The private meaning of the various gestures, steps, and patterns may not be understood specifically by the spectator, but in terms of King's associative montages, they add more links to the loosely knit chains of significant elements.

In *Battery* (1975–76), the linguistic analogy is especially suggestive, since the dance is a tribute to the philosopher Susanne Langer, to whose theories on language and dance as a prelinguistic conceptualizing and expressive mode King feels especially close. Langer's thesis that language originated in certain physical processes, including ritual, communal dances, corresponds to King's own aesthetic which embraces the use — perhaps, the necessity — of spoken language within the dance event. In regard to *Battery*, he told critic Deborah Jowitt:

> I know dance is nondiscursive but we process our perceptions linguistically. Language is bound up with how we see in ways we're not even aware of. And often when I do a movement, words come to mind — not because the movement *means* them, but because the gestures, the act of dancing, become a reflective device.[21]

Battery was made in three parts over the course of about a year. The first was done as a quartet in New York City, the second a group piece in Chicago, the third a larger group piece in New York. The spoken score comprised excerpts from Langer's writings, including *Mind, Philosophical Sketches*, and *Feeling and Form*. In the first version, the dancers repeat simple movement patterns, primarily the circling of arms and leaning torsos. In the second and third versions, the accumulating gestures and signals — incarnating and illuminating Langer's thoughts on the expressive gesture as the unique, basic element of dance — are augmented by slides of artworks, enormous frames moved around by the dancers which foreground parts of the action, and a small shrine constructed of a large chair, candles, flowers, and Langer's books.

According to Langer, dance is related to, and may use as its materials, aspects of music, visual arts, and drama. But ultimately dance is neither music made visible, nor a moving series of pictures or sculptures, nor a silent drama (i.e., pantomime). Dance is an art consisting of expressive gestures. But the gestures are expressive in a special sense: they are imagined by the dancer or choreographer rather than symptomatic, becoming free symbolic forms that express the idea or structure of feeling, rather than a specific emotion immediately felt. Unlike pure gesticulation, the symptomatic expression of subjective conditions, a dance, according to Langer, sets forth logically expressive symbols, making concepts visible. The felt experience of physical forces are made palpable in the dance. But what we see in the dance is not a set of forces, but an appearance, an illusion of those powers in action — in much the same way that when we see water flowing downhill we don't speak of seeing gravity per se, but of seeing gravity in action. Dance forces, according to Langer, are "virtual Powers," apparitions, dynamic images. But dance is different from other dynamic images, like rainbows and reflections in mirrors, because it is an art form which, like the other arts, treats of the nature of human emotion.

It seems to me that the invisible powers Langer refers to are not spirits or transcendental powers, but the "vital rhythms" (as she calls them) of growth, decay, development, and motion. These vital rhythms are connected to Langer's notion of the "life of the mind" — the mental processes of emotion, imagination, sensation, recollection, and reasoning. In this respect, the mental processes that take form in King's dances are intimately related to the rhythms of the movements. King writes that Langer's ideas about language and dance are key to his work:

> Man's ability to separate language and symbolic mentality could only have transpired because of the kinetic activation of the body, and the organization of motor responses that grow directly out of ritual and dance. In other words, the dialectic-process of culture and human evolution, dance — being the oldest art, precedes and actually prepares the way at each stage for speech, the necessary symbolic thought patterns and reflexive mappings that negotiate each complex phase of culture.[22]

Thus it seems appropriate that the movements in *Battery* follow the dynamic patterns Langer sees as essential to dance: a gathering and dispersing of forces, an accumulation of symbolic gestures — salutes, swiveling of the torso with the hands flat on the head, hieroglyphic bendings of the forearms, spiraling paths that traveled the length of the deep performance spaces, intersecting with the spiraling paths of other dancers, like cogs in a machine or planets in a system of galaxies. Or does the dancing look appropriate because Langer in fact correctly analyzed dancing itself, or because her analysis of the constituent factors of the dance is the soundtrack to the performance? Never exactly illustrating the points in Langer's writings, the loose correspondences between the two systems (the words and the dancing) also seem to gather and disperse, making meaning when the analogies are strong, and dissolving it when they diverge.

King has composed several other tributes to philosophers whose writings have inspired his choreographic work. Besides *Battery* and *High Noon, Metagexis* (1973) celebrated Nietzsche (as well as Gertrude Stein and Isadora Duncan), *Praxiomatics* (*The Practice Room*) (1974) was dedicated to Edmund Husserl, and several works have names that might be mistaken for philosophical tracts, including *Being in Perpetual Motion* (1968–70) and *The Phenomenology of Movement* (1969). I have heard people refer to King as either a philosopher or a mystic, but I think he is neither of these, even though his dances use and perhaps illuminate (though they just as often veil and reinterpret) philosophical concepts and may use physical techniques (like whirling) to evoke prophetic visions or hint at a mystical interconnectedness between the spheres of experiences. Inner and outer, mental and physical, past and future, at times become indistinguishable. And with his shrines, icons, and hagiography, King's performances at times seem like the ritual celebrations of a theosophist.

Yet I believe that King's goal in performance is neither that of the mystic — to transcend control and gain divine wisdom in a changed consciousness — nor the philosopher — to carry out rational discourse — but that of the artist. He brings his philosophical and scientific inspiration with him into the performance, but his art works are not didactic. They are visions and meditations made possible by a refined theatrical sensibility.

King is tall and thin and moves with extraordinary speed and lightness. His body always seems to be a reservoir of nervous energy, yet he expends that energy with an easy flowing pliancy. At times I think of his dancing, as well as his style of creating, as scattered, diffuse. He moves rapidly from idea to idea, from place to place, from gesture to gesture. Yet more often I realize that what seemed indirect actually consisted of many quick, direct changes of focus. He breaks movements down minutely and meticulously, bending the spine one vertebra at a time, making a contraction of the chest or back a sequential ripple. Yet the movement is never choppy or abrupt, but smooth, fluent. His long arms and legs open generously from a secure center, thrusting, jabbing, winding, and skittering through space with a keen but silky attack and sustained momentum. His dancing at times reminds me of sparking electrical charges, of water-driven motors, of machines producing action that moves the dancer. His gestural patterns and configurations of pathways seem to relay impulses between groups of dancers, between the dancer and the environment. When he partners a woman — I am reminded especially of his duets with Carter Frank in the various versions of *RAdeoA.C.tiv(ID)ty* (an ongoing choreographic project dedicated to Marie Curie, 1976–78) and in *Dance S(p)ell* (1978), or in his duet with Diane Jacobowitz at the Cooper-Hewitt Museum in 1978 — he seems to hover around her, guiding her but barely touching her, at times like a halo or a moth with a flame, but at times like a Dr. Coppélius or Frankenstein manipulating a creature of his own making. When I see him dancing outside, he looks at ease, holding his own against the grandeur of nature and architecture, skimming along the ground in tennis shoes, jogging pants, sweat shirt and suspenders, with an irrepressible lilt in his body that belies the bumpy surface of the earth, making large, clear gestures that carve out an impression in the space.

Like many of King's dances, *RAdeoA.C.tiv(ID)ty* has been performed in several versions over the course of several years. There is a solo video version for King, made in 1976 at University of Maryland, a developing series of gestures and postures beginning with pliés, and continuing to test the relationships of the torso, arms, and legs to the center of the body. The hands pull apart as if stretching a wire. The torso and legs form one extreme angle, then having found the tension between the two lines of the angle, readjust to find the opposite tilt. The body bends over to frame one leg crossed at the knee of the other; the hand scoops over the head in a rhyming gesture, curling forward sharply. Performed first in silence and then to the chants of Tibetan Buddhist monks, the dance is a resilient testing of the body's bending and straightening motions. It speeds up and slows down, but overall the dynamics seem soft and even. As the legs test one kind of activity, the chest and arms do something quite different. Occasionally a gesture seems literal and specific: King cups a hand over his eyes, as if looking out a great distance. Holding his hands flat, he points his fingers against his temples and rotates his hands back and forth, as if screwing his hands into his head. He makes winding, wrapping motions with his hands, or pulls them downward diagonally across his face. His gestures are so sharply and clearly articulated that when some small detail changes — the wrist bends, or the fingers curve — the shift seems enormous. As he advances, marking off a corridor of space, the scale of his gestures magnifies.

The next version of *RAdeoA.C.tiv(ID)ty* (Prologue/Part I) — performed at Dance Theater Workshop in New York in 1976 — involved four dancers, working out the same movement themes, and a separate duo who sat at a table behind a curtain that was occasionally parted, revealing them reciting "t-e-l-e-g-r-a-p-h-i-c s-o-n-g-s" and other texts. Over the course of the next year, King, Carter Frank, and Jumay Chu performed the dance themes in various spaces, sometimes accompanied by the videotape of King's solo version, and in 1978, King presented a version of the piece at Brooklyn Academy of Music. Here twelve dancers expand the gesticulation and breakdown and isolation of movements, moving along highly geometric paths, emphasizing the diagonals in their bodies as they travel perpendicular to the audience. A melodious voice (Amy Taubin's) reads excerpts from Marie Curie's *Radioactive Substances,* and slides tell of the unpredictable horrors that would issue from the Curies' momentous discoveries, while human dancers seem to dance out analogues to the microscopic movements and processes described on the audio track. Finally, a huge white tent descends from the ceiling to engulf the figures. The "synapsulated" movements of the dancers correspond to the described processes of the breaking down chemical elements. And, later in the same program, the Telaxic Synapsulator appears, a gleaming, light-refracting machine with spinning parts. A duo of booming voices describes the marvelous uses of the machine, while King, waving a glowing penlight like a wizard's wand, and Carter Frank advanced down the long performance space with the machine, as if dancing it into being. *The Telaxic Synapsulator* was performed simultaneously with *Dance S(p)ell,* inspired by the life and work of Nikola Tesla, the American inventor who worked with high-tension electricity. To electronic music by William Tudor, who also composed original electronic scores for *Battery* and *RAdeoA.C.tiv(ID)ty,* eight dancers trace geometrical shapes contained within a large rectangle, with whirling steps and small, light leaps and jumps. With music that sounds halfway between Renaissance melodies and a science-fiction movie and with gentle, harmonious, and geometrically ordered dance figures, *Dance S(p)ell* somehow seems like an allegorical court ballet of the future. Though King partly covered it up with *The Telaxic Synapsulator, Dance S(p)ell* is pure movement, King's tribute to the classical elements of the dance: turnout, elegant line, graceful carriage. Perhaps the title is partly ironic, signaling a rueful concession to the demands of the marketplace.

Together, the lovely, peaceful dancing of *Dance S(p)ell* and the tongue- and mind-twisting future shock of *The Telaxic Synapsulator* continue to advance the intertwined cultural concerns that occupy King's thought and art: a faith in human inventiveness, expressed in the hope that technology, leading us further and further out, is leading us some place better, and is related to the human body through parallel structures and actions; and the equally visionary image, moving further and further in, of the galactic pattern, mystically bracketing the operations of the universe with the workings of the microcosmos — the human body.

Kenneth King, from Print-Out[23]

!(cele((CERE))bration: WORTS & EXEORCISES-fir-tHEdie(EYE)ing:KING)

YOU ARE staySHUNED to WOM 68.9 on your DIE-l. PEEPholes of the WEREld here this BROODCAST. THIS IS AN e-MERGERency. RADIORA-TION is causing MUTANYtations ((like NATCHoral SEAelection)) and perverOVERTy-stricken WHIZZ KIDS are having the FREEkiest d-REAMS — re:DIREemptERECTIONS for civilSIBLINGization.

I spEND my DAZE lyEYEing HEAR IMMObileIVINGIZED, sus(PEND)ing SUM inDEAF(finite) duRADIATEion foCUSSing skyWARTS: SEAing the clo(WOW)ds flow(WOE)ting overHEAD and fee(EEL)ing the MOOn pul-(LULL)ing the orgONEs embeDEAD in my skein.

At dawn the briHEIGHT yelLOW sun riIRISzes over the hoeRISEon, im-PERCEPTionably ILLUMIN(nascent)MATEing EVEre:Things. enTOT(err)ing the mountAIMS I abanDOOMED ART(tickle)uLAYERting CONTRA-die(STINK)tions, which meth(ODD)ically charACTOReyesIZES all exTER-MINAL ph(PNEUMA)onon.

As I get out of bed I REALwhyZE how PSYCHE(soma)ATTIC I HAVE GROAN TO BE. My TRANCEmi(grain)RATIONAL headACHES are ob-SURDviously newEROTIC proCRASS(agnos)TYPEcations, INsprite of the disCORE(RAGE)ing disPAIR whitch SEEzes me.

((SIGHTmullRETAIN(eons)LY)) I am A-MUSEd by wild OWWtbursts of e-MOTION and my CONCEPTcentRATION is disINTERurbanED THEEse DAZE by the roarORAL exCURSEtions thru upper LOCOCATIONS, wONE-anderring thru VEILeeys and wild birds CHATTERIRPING veheMENEVio-lently, MUSEically HIP(notate)IZING me by thAIR EELecCLECTRIC SOW-(WOW)UNDS which are DEIFYiantiveLY messSAGEmyrrEYEzing.

I no longer enCOUNTer CIVILsiblingIONized peepWHOLES. UPHEAR EVEre:THING exPYRES backVERBwarts. evi(ADVENT)denseLY my dif-FIGHTiOCCULTy SPEECHing WORTS IS SYNC(roam)maTHEMEattic with my in(TEAR)FEARior de(RE:ARRANGE)MEANT.

The impre(PLACATE)ations of cheMECHANical sub(STRATA)stances mACHE me con(SIGH)dribbleLY MORONbund because my PRIME-i(TIME)ive inSTINKS are BEEing META(morpho)surFACEwise-D.

enDURING the DAZE I COLLICect ANIMULS and in-SECTS, and I NO-testeIATE the cataTONICgoryICAL de:TAILS in a jourNIL under "OB-SURDVATIONS." whEARin I make an at(TEMPO)tempt to ((proph-(FETISH)ically)) ex-PLACATE the SENSE-ations of my NERV(VERVE)-OUS SYSTEM.

((assertAIMly)) I am not TREPIdreadIC SINce I am HELLpleaseLY de-viWISEiating a system whAIRby ((logisTI(MIME)ically)) I sepPREPaRA-DIATE the in-SECT-ins-IDES and ex(HUME)TRAPolate the cheMYSTICAL POT(ent)IONS which I difFEARwrenchIATE from the cheMECHANical exAPPEARiences.

Douglas Dunn: Cool Symmetries

DOUGLAS DUNN'S oeuvre is small but beautiful. He has made seven major pieces since leaving Merce Cunningham's company where he danced from 1969 to 1973. Four of the works are solos and three are group pieces. Besides dancing with Cunningham, Dunn danced with Yvonne Rainer from 1968–1970, and for six years (1970–1976) was part of The Grand Union. And, over the past six years, he has collaborated with other dancers and with film makers, and he has written about dancing and about words. Two film collaborations exist: *Mayonnaise* (1972) by Charles Atlas and *101* (1974–1977) by Amy Greenfield.

Born in 1942, Dunn grew up in California and did not begin dancing until he was in college, though he had been active in sports since childhood. He started taking ballet classes after he and a friend at Princeton went to visit a dying professor, who recommended studying classical dancing; the professor recovered, but Dunn was already on his way to dance addiction. He eventually went to New York to study dance and was soon working with Yvonne Rainer and soon after with Cunningham.

Some striking aspects of Dunn's choreography make it as difficult to characterize and write about as it is significant. One immediate difficulty is the absence of any one particular style. Although certain issues, themes, and elements recur throughout his work, the dances seem mostly to share a stubborn resistance against conforming to any single style or genre. Just when one thinks he is a master of pure movement invention, juxtaposing abstract movements against pure word play (*Nevada*), he comes up with a piece that consists of theatrical images and no words at all (*Time Out*). Then, after fabri-

Douglas Dunn in *Solo Film & Dance*. Photograph © Nathaniel Tileston, 1977.

cating complex, difficult, changing tableaux (*Time Out*), he makes a piece that is only stillness (*101*). But this stillness is framed by the silent residue of activity, because in *101* the dance consisted of his lying motionless on top of a maze he had built in his loft. At times his performance attitude is one of withdrawal, even apparent trance (*101, Time Out, Nevada*). But other dances are veritable catalogues of ways to make contact with the audience (*Octopus, Gestures in Red*).

Another problem in writing about Dunn's work is his subject matter. His dances are almost entirely about themselves and their choreographic processes. This self-revelation in the dance comes about frankly, yet subtly. Movements, images, situations excite associations. But what is emphasized finally is the very form and stuff of the dance itself. So closely bound together are form and content in Dunn's work that they almost can't be unglued.

I intend to trace here some of the motifs — designs and ideas — that emerge in the work, primarily in the two long solos (*Time Out* and *Gestures in Red*). But first I'll describe the seven major pieces briefly.

Nevada, first performed at the New School in New York City during the Choreoconcert series in 1973, was a solo in three parts. Dunn, dressed in a black cowboy outfit, came out on the small stage, and advanced toward the audience with face and body gestures suggesting a bashful confrontation. He kept opening his mouth as if to speak, lowering his hands as if to dig them into his pockets, looking at the audience and then lowering his gaze. The gestures were all small and uncompleted.

In the second section, he performed a variety of manipulations on a triangular piece of wood. The third part of the dance happened during the "critique" section of the concert, when each choreographer commented on his or her dance. Dunn fitfully sat on a chair and stood up, while his taped voice chanted a series of statements — positive, negative, and double negative — about dancing and talking. "Talking is talking. Dancing is dancing. Not talking is not talking. Not dancing is not dancing. Talking is talking & not talking. Dancing is dancing & not dancing. Not talking is not talking & not not talking . . ."[1] Then he crawled around on the floor and howled.

In *Nevada,* Dunn set out the basic elements and structures that thread throughout his work. The piece played off the given social situation and the format of the concert — a short dance work-cum-comment, on a stage in an auditorium, on a program with other choreographers. Dunn here had to perform two roles: that of the dancer performing the work and that of the author commenting on it. The piece resolved the split by knitting the two roles together, using formal means — repetition, reversal, inverse, illustration, and negative illustration. The dance presented a crazy symmetry in an upside-down mirror. When Dunn danced, he looked for a while as though he were about to give a lecture. Then he reversed the audience's expectations by breaking into pure dance. During the commentary, on the other hand, he danced, and his taped voice spoke about dancing and talking. The commentary itself was structured as a repetitive, symmetrical series of statements, tautologies, and inversions.

Four for Nothing (1974), the title of which is a pun on the dancer's method of counting rhythm before actually moving, was a piece for four dancers who had almost nothing — minimal movement — to do during the dance. It became, for both the dancers and the spectators, an investigation of weight and gravity.

101, subtitled "A Performance Exhibit," took place four hours a day, six days a week, during two months in the spring and two weeks in the fall of 1974. *101* had the audience exploring a massive maze in Dunn's loft (a labyrinth built of rough wooden slatted cubes, stacked to a height of about fifteen feet and filling the entire loft space), finally discovering him (or perhaps not) lying motionless on top of the structure, dressed in a white jumpsuit with red and blue bandanas tied around various parts of his body. His eyes were closed, and his lips were painted blue; red, white, and blue makeup lined his face.[2]

This piece shows once again Dunn's curiosity about social expectations in performance: what happens when an audience arrives at a performance and nothing happens? (The concept of *Four for Nothing*, but even more extreme.) But it also illustrates this formal concern with what finally constitutes dancing, proposed in the *Nevada* commentary, which was tested in *101* at one end of the spectrum. If, in *Nevada*, dancing could consist of talking, dancing, and not dancing, in *101* dancing was an entire four hours — repeated daily — of not dancing.

Octopus was performed at the New School, in the Choreoconcert series of 1974. In the first section, Dunn came out in the costume from *101* and stripped down to a red bathing suit. Then, as he began to walk through the audience on the backs of the spectators' seats, two couples (a man and a woman, one clothed and one nude in each pair) came out and quickly traded clothing, one passively and one actively undressing and dressing.

In the critique section, Dunn came out and said, "Hi, today is my birthday." The audience spontaneously sang "Happy Birthday." Dunn then went on to explain that the first section of the dance had been called "Whale," and that there was another section, "Hubbahubba & the Boohoos," which they, the audience, had not yet seen. Whether or not they would see it was left open; in fact, that section was going on at that moment. Red balls were handed out to the audience, and the five dancers established a simple movement pattern on stage. The audience completed the piece by throwing the balls back onto the stage.[3]

Using the same format as *Nevada, Octopus* humorously linked the dancing with the commentary, using a pleasing, rhymed series of repetitions, reversals, and completions. But unlike the previous Choreoconcert piece, *Octopus* involved the audience much more intimately, relying on them to participate, and invading their space.

Time Out, Dunn's first evening-length solo, was performed a year before *Octopus,* in 1973, at the Exchange Theater in New York. *Time Out* was a series of quite disparate tableaux, in which Dunn silently acted out different characters doing different activities. There was no narrative plot, and no other use or development of the characters. In each scene, he simply explored one movement strategy, generated either by a prop, a costume, or a system of repetition or reversal. Although there was no narrative cohesiveness, the piece was tightly structured in terms of its formal elements.

The first scene, for instance, began as follows: Dunn, totally covered (except for his face) by a navy blue sweat shirt, pants, mittens, and socks, fitted his body into a freestanding white corner; he faced into the corner with his feet forming a 90-degree angle — toes meeting and heels apart. After a string of long poses, which eventually became shorter and shorter, he ended up with a pose that was the exact inverse of the first one: facing out of the corner, his feet forming a right angle, with heels meeting and toes apart. The freestanding white corner was the reverse image of a freestanding black curtain, which formed a corner that jutted out toward the audience. This curtain, which served to mask the performer as he changed costumes between scenes, fell over in the final scene. It revealed Dunn in a passive, vulnerable stance — the opposite of his aggressive relationship with the white corner in the initial section. It disclosed, too, the detritus of every scene that had preceded it: worn clothing, used props, and a hanging skeleton. Its purpose (revelation of structure and material) was also the antithesis of the first scene (concealment of the body and of events to come).

In the intervening scenes, movement sequences were displayed, then reversed or repeated according to mathematical schemes. Musical interludes — tapes of rushing water, an orchestra warming up — were interrupted and repeated. In one section, the accompaniment was the tick of a metronome, in another the incessant whirring of a movie projector that, unloaded, flickered white light on a screen. In their utilitarian style, the movements — whether they involved handling a prop, lying down, or abstract dance steps like jumps — were analogues to the sounds.

Time Out is packed with theatrical detail that is relatively easy to remember. The movement material in it is sometimes complex, but it is everywhere announced, framed, and sorted by clearly built, discrete sections, with specific and apprehensible shapes, different costumes, sounds, and moods.

Gestures in Red, first performed in 1975, a year and a half after *Time Out* (with *Four for Nothing, 101,* and *Octopus* intervening), explores many of the same issues as *Time Out,* but in a different format. Without props, musical interludes, or costume changes, the movement is the only dynamic element, and much harder to see distinctly or to remember.

Gestures in Red has four parts. The first, done mainly on the floor or low in space, explores backward movements. The second section, in which Dunn stands in one place, successively lays out six different activities using various parts of the body. The third section first sets up a limited space in which to move, while Dunn articulates his shoulders and feet, then the space expands and the rules for movement encompass the entire torso and legs. In the fourth part, Dunn covers the entire space (I have seen it ranging over the spacious floor at MoMing, in Chicago, and in a wide loft space in New York), using movements that rarely repeat.

Here we see clearly that Dunn's basic formal strategy is one of systematic exploration. This piece seems to leave no movement possibilities uninvestigated, yet the inquiry is conducted with an intelligent, pleasing economy of method.

Lazy Madge, begun in the spring of 1976, and (as of the winter of 1978–1979) continuing as an ongoing, evolving project, is a group piece that has been performed in a variety of spaces. It has involved a stable group of eight to ten people (the number changes as some leave New York or come to town temporarily). *Lazy Madge* was originally generated by the following procedure: Dunn choreographed solos composed of short movement phrases for the dancers one by one; he choreographed duets for himself and some of the dancers; and then he put all the solos and duets in the same space (Lucinda Childs' loft), giving the performers the responsibility of choosing when to enter and initiate a sequence. Since then, other duets, group sections, and solos have been made, and the duets may now be performed in halves — by individuals without their partners. This causes an element of improvisation to creep into the dance, because if a duet is started with a partner who does not know the other half, that partner has to ad lib a response. The rules for performing *Lazy Madge* shift slightly as the group decides what is dangerous, what feels comfortable, what is appropriate for a new space, and various other issues.

One very large and obvious distinction between the two long solos, *Time Out* and *Gestures in Red,* is the texture of their appearance. In *Time Out,* the surface is built by the accumulation of images rather than movements. The small scenes contain movements, but the overall quality is one of stasis. The image of a man in various postures in a corner becomes etched in our brains, not the movement details of how he got from one position to the next. The image of a man lying on the floor in a sleeping bag while a light (cast by an unloaded movie projector) flickers on the screen; a tableau of a man with a sweater stuffed full of crumpled newspapers; the apparition of a man standing frozen in formal dress behind a fallen curtain, flanked by a skeleton and a pile of used clothing.

Gestures in Red has exactly the opposite appearance. Here movement prevails, and even when one can't recall specific motions or phrases, one is struck by the complicated, changing movement details. Even the stillnesses seem to be movements. They are negative movements, just as in *Time Out* even the movements seem to be components of the larger static images.

101 carries to its logical conclusion the notion that not moving is still dancing. Yet quite literally the maze structure supports the stillness. It is a constant silent testament to the active labor in the dance — the work it took to build the maze — which is part of the performance physically though not temporally. That is, the traces of past vigorous work linger in the present immobility. Also surrounding the stillness is the motion of the spectator, magnified and heightened in contrast to the performer's motionlessness.

So it becomes clear that in Dunn's aesthetic program, movement possibilities run the gamut from utter stillness to rapid, constant, protean motion. "Dancing is dancing and not dancing," as he said in *Nevada.* But narrowing the movement down to zero only emphasizes the fact that there is no time during which our bodies are not in some kind of motion; in *101,* Dunn's heart still beat, blood still flowed, thoughts still continued. There really is no zero point in motion, only asymptotes. One extreme on the movement spectrum becomes less clearly defined, and in this dance Dunn has given us information that perplexes our perceptions.

In *Gestures in Red,* he complicates the opposite limit, finally stuffing as many movements as he can into each fraction of a second. The other end of the continuum also becomes asymptotic. If Dunn can do so many movements (apparently more than most people), maybe next time he'll be able to do even more . . . and more. *Gestures in Red* widens human gestural limits as surely as *101* attenuates them.

Underlying all of Dunn's work is a frank disclosure of his decision-making process. Any artist has to make choices, and Dunn's selections celebrate that fact. They assert themselves, become authoritative, emerge sharply even when their origins are not spelled out for us. At times, Dunn thrusts the decision making back on the audience, as if to show us, by involving us directly, just how hard and richly exciting those choices can be. In other dances, he runs through a range of options and we witness, at more of a distance, a compendium of structural or material limits.

In *101* the outcome of the performance was particular to the experience of each viewer, and rested almost entirely in his or her hands. Whether you chose to climb to the top of the maze, whether you discovered Dunn at all, how you related to his inert body, and even how long the performance lasted, were all open-ended questions with no single correct answer. In *Octopus,* only certain elements came under the control of the audience — the singing and the throwing of balls — and the setting (an auditorium) molded the spectators more clearly into a group. Although people were confined to their seats, they still could elect to look at either the action on stage or the action moving through their own space; or, they could try to do both. The audience altered the timing of the piece by adding their own material (singing, throwing balls), but this kind of manipulation could only result from collective action.

In both *Time Out* and *Gestures in Red,* the choices offered to the spectators remained strictly within the limits of the conventional passive/receptive role. Dunn did not encourage the audience to participate in decision making in these two solos. That is, the dances were for the most part fixed and the viewers had no hands in the order or outcome. In *Lazy Madge,* too, the viewer watches a presentation of choreographic process.

Time Out was a sampler of possibilities. As I have noted, there was no narrative informing the decision to perform one particular action rather than another. No drama unfolded, and no characters were fleshed out. Instead, events were governed, delineated and generated by a sensuous curiosity, and by an inquiry conducted through such formal devices as repetition, reversal, symmetry, and inversion. The space of the performance was complete, insular, and cushioned from the larger, permanent theater installation — because audience seating, props, scenery, and movement were carefully kept from making contact with the walls of the theater space until Dunn placed a placard, announcing the end, against one wall. Similarly, the events within the space were sealed off from the world, separate from external meaning. The possibilities for movement arose not from any literary or emotional reference, but from the inevitable carrying out — or interruption — of a given situation. If you have a sleeping bag, unroll it and get inside it; if you have a corner, stuff your body into it in all conceivable ways.

In *Gestures in Red* the choreographic process was shown through a systematic investigation of the restraints movement invention can bear. This analysis began very slowly, with a narrow focus, and expanded in speed, scope, and complexity. In the first part, every aspect of backward movement was plumbed, mostly on the floor. The second part was a list of movement qualities and different body parts: hips thrusting, arms rotating, back rounding, every part vibrating. But it all happened as Dunn stood in one spot. This section of the dance also catalogued the different methods of repeating an action: at the same time on separate limbs; at different times; regularly; irregularly; continuously; by sustaining the movement. In the third section, the movement choices were limited only to certain body parts and certain areas of the stage. These limits were made clear in retrospect, once they were broken to allow for more of the body to move and more of the floor to be covered. The fourth part, as I have said, absolved Dunn of limits altogether. So the dance offered not only the results of the investigation, in terms of invented movements, but also a look at methods: how restraints are applied, systematically tested, and dissolved.

What is irreducible about dance, *Gestures in Red* asked, if one can simplify it to one extreme and complicate it to another? How can one pin down a definition if one can tighten the limits narrowly and then expand them infinitely? Slow, medium, or fast speed; standing in one place, making specific floor patterns, moving in a limited area, moving all over the place; repeating, varying, reversing, distilling, compressing movements — all these choices applied not just to make a pleasing composition (which they do), but to criticize and illuminate the design of that composition. When the choices list themselves, they become explicit. And the possible range of choices in this dance implicitly becomes infinite. This is in direct contrast to *101*, where only one kind of restraint was used, and was the subject of the entire performance.

Octopus was constructed in a pleasing, symmetrical pattern of repetition and interruption, tension and release, series and reversal. Actions and movements complemented, completed, and answered each other, each new event provoking a response. Resembling *Gestures in Red* in the symmetry and systematism of its structure, *Octopus* set up expectations only to subvert them or, sometimes, to satisfy them. The two actions in "Whale" — four dancers changing clothing, and Dunn walking through the audience — happened at the same time and for the same length of time. They created tension, however, as they separated spatially — a tension that was released by the logical conclusion of both activities. The action of two couples switching clothes was a rhyme of the initial strip performed by Dunn. And another repetition, this one without any elaboration or reversal, was the double lecture, with the corresponding double song by the audience. The delayed response to the march through the audience in "Whale" came in "Hubbahubba & the Boohoos" when the spectators tossed red balls onto the stage; this egress balanced out the previous ingress. Two actions in "Hubbahubba" were twins in intention: the lecture which provoked the singing, and the quick gait — resembling that of shooting gallery animals — which provoked the throwing.

Lazy Madge offers the audience no unusual behavioral choices. But since the dancers create a dense field of activity through their decisions about when to enter and what material to perform, the spectators are forced to decide which of the performers and which of the material to watch. There is no single focus of attention clearly marked for exhibition.

Not only must the dancers determine when and where to dance (based on their own sense of the space and timing, or on limited rules they may have previously set up together, or on considerations of danger), but they — and thus the viewers — are constantly shifting the range of attention. The material is choreographed to occur — or at least to begin — at specific sites on the stage. But any side of the performing area, which is usually a room or loft rather than a proscenium stage, can serve as "front" for any sequence, so that traffic can become unruly. When one person is dancing a solo, he or she must also pay attention to what else is going on in the room, thus frequently altering a path to avoid collision or responding to another's initiation of a duet. But a dancer involved in a duet or group action has to pay attention not only to his or her own movements, but also to the partners; attention to activity outside the immediate group is much more difficult. In this dance, Dunn is the author: he invented the movement material, tailoring each solo to suit the individual dancer. Yet the dancers also participate in each performance's choreography, by exercising their choices.

Although Dunn started out by simply making up the movements for *Lazy Madge* without prior rules or limits — a more difficult approach than he used in the earlier pieces — certain movements and tendencies do recur throughout. There is a constant contrast of actions done in relevé (at a high level) or in plié (at a low level); there are broad sweeps across the space, performed jumping or turning; there is an unusual disclosure of support systems — for example, a lifted leg is held up with the hands. There are frequent oppositions of diagonally placed limbs and spiraled backs, and juxtapositions of different body parts executing disparate actions. There are also idiosyncratic gestures that look almost pantomimic. And there appears that strange Dunn phenomenon, seen also in *Nevada,* of gestures that signal emotional effect to the viewer but that are generated in a motor, rather than a behavioral, context. For instance, the head, when tilted a particular way, looks tender for a moment. The overall impression of the movements is of a workmanlike physical economy. Body parts are used efficiently: those not used are often, where possible, simply placed out of the way. And movements are strung together without regard for an externally imposed sense of polish or harmony; the line of flow is chunky, not smooth.

Surprise and interruption pop up in almost every Dunn dance. *Nevada*'s first section was entirely composed of arrested gestures. It was an abstract movement study that, because it involved primarily the face and hands, finally assumed an emotional appearance — a mixture of surprise and anxiety. *Time Out* not only included that same study of interruptions intact within it, it also was structured overall as a discontinuous series of images. The musical sections in *Time Out* often consisted of repetitive sounds, regularly broken by splices in the tape. The collapse of the black curtain shattered the space, and also turned a private domain into a public one. The shocks from the subversion of expectation in *Time Out* were psychological as well as kinesthetic.

In *101* the first surprise came when the spectator arrived to find that the performance was as passive as a sculpture exhibit, since the only immediately visible object was the maze. Then the spectator discovered the body atop the maze. Theatrical expectations were upset further by the way the viewer, and not the artist, determined the duration and decorum of the event. The spectator decided how close, how intimate, and how provocative to be with the performer, once the body had been discovered.

In *Lazy Madge*, interruption is structurally integral to the choreography, since any solo or duet can be subject to the introduction of more movement material. But even the types of movement are checked by the other types. Said Dunn of his method in *Lazy Madge*, "I'm thinking of movement in an imagistic way — images that interrupt the line of movement."[4]

Closely connected to Dunn's use of interruption, in terms of both movement and social expectations, is his architecture of tension. Interruption is one way to resolve that strain. *Four for Nothing*, based on a minimal exploration of our purely physical opposition to gravity that is weight, made physical tension the very subject of the dance. *Nevada*, in which the movement material was a series of halted gestures, seemed to be about psychological stress: the nature of the gestures themselves, the fact that their relationship consisted in shattering each other, and their location, all contributed to the steadily increasing, palpable sense of anticipation. In *Octopus*, I have noted how excitement built kinesthetically, intellectually, and emotionally by the interrupted stripping; by the geographical divergence of the two actions in "Whale"; by the perceptual choices offered to the audience; and by the invasion of the audience's space.

In *Time Out*, tension built both through the suspense of seeing physical tasks carried out, and via the psychological response evoked by certain situations — for example, a pointed gun. The accumulation of body positions in the corner during the first tableau created a rhythm of anticipation as it became more and more rapidly realized. Fear when the gun was pointed and a rather shameful sense of voyeurism when the curtain fell or when Dunn lay in the sleeping bag, both deepened the audience's perception of vulnerability — in the first example, our own, and in the second two cases, Dunn's. Finally, the perception of a special kind of tension arose — the stimulation and pressure of experiencing vulnerability, epitomized in performance.

The first part of *Gestures in Red*, through its slowness, generated a weightiness in time and space, a gestation where shapes and durations formed and converged. The kind of excitement the final section created was precisely the opposite; a shattering and quickening of movements over time and space, a congestion that was practically orgasmic.

In *Lazy Madge*, energy builds and releases through the variation of attention required, as foci collect and disperse on stage, and the short solos and duets and group actions overlap, intervene, or simply coexist.

But interruption is not the only resolution for the tension Dunn constructs. Sometimes the dilemma is brought to a satisfying closure as an action is completed, as in the movement qualities section of *Gestures in Red,* where each activity simply ran its course; or as in *Octopus,* when the changing of clothes was accomplished and the end of the auditorium reached; or as in *101* when the spectator had enough and decided to leave.

Sometimes the intense expectation is relieved by a reversal, although reversals can also function to complicate tension. The stress that seemed like apprehension at speechmaking during *Nevada* was reversed when the lecture was authoritatively delivered in the critique. This reversal was elaborated further by the form and meaning of the lecture: a chain of inversions. The apparent involvement with the audience in the first section of that same dance — with facial gestures focusing outward — was reversed in the next part of involvement with the prop and a withdrawal of focus. In *Time Out,* movement sequences were repeated in reverse order; the final pose in the first part was the opposite of the initial pose; the white corner was the contrary of the black corner; and with the fall of the black curtain, the progression of Dunn's exits was inverted, as *our* gaze entered *his* space.

Sometimes the reversal is one of protocol, of audience-performer roles, or of the audience's expectations. Reversal is like surprise and interruption, but also like completion. It is precisely this kind of intricate, mirrorlike, sturdy structure I have been describing that gives Dunn's works the feeling of gems, hard, cool, and sparkling.

The elegance of his work is inimitable. It does not only have to do with the complicated architecture of the choreography — although that is certainly important — but also with his body, its classical look and proportions, the easy, precise, and lively way he moves, his polish and grace.

Dunn's gracefulness is quintessential. Everything boils down to a certain host-guest relationship with the audience. And in this, as with everything else, he examines the entire spectrum of modes of contact — from absolute withdrawal in *101* to the benign manipulation of *Octopus.* In between, there are all the balances and nuances of the normal relationship between audience/voyeur and performer/exhibitionist.

There is even, in *Nevada,* something that looks like anxiety at the prospect of making contact. For the audience, there is ambiguity about the presentation. Is this man *really* nervous, you think — so nervous that he's cracking his performance presence? Or is he so cool he can act out this particular emotion with precision as part of the show? Or is he simply performing a set of movements to which I am attaching meaning?

The continuum that all these aspects of contact constitute joins at the end to become a circle, since Dunn's withdrawal from his normative role in *101,* his negative presence, is no less an assault on the audience than his invasion of their space in *Octopus.*

Yet his relationship with the audience is not aggressive or hostile, but cooperative, assuming an intelligent and sensitive spectator with whom he initiates a dialogue on structure and decision — embellished with humor, surprise, elegance, economy, and, most of all, grace.

Douglas Dunn, "Talking Dancing"[5]

Talking is talking
Dancing is dancing

Not talking is not talking
Not dancing is not dancing

Talking is talking & not talking
Dancing is dancing & not dancing

Not talking is not talking & not not talking
Not dancing is not dancing & not not dancing

Talking is not dancing
Dancing is not talking

Not talking is not not dancing
Not dancing is not not talking

Not talking is not dancing
Not dancing is not talking

Talking is dancing
Dancing is talking

Dancing is talking
Talking is dancing

Not dancing is not talking
Not talking is not dancing

Dancing is talking & not talking
Talking is dancing & not dancing

Not dancing is not talking & not not talking
Not talking is not dancing & not not dancing

Dancing is not dancing
Talking is not talking

Not dancing is not not dancing
Not talking is not not talking

Not dancing is not dancing
Not talking is not talking

Dancing is dancing
Talking is talking

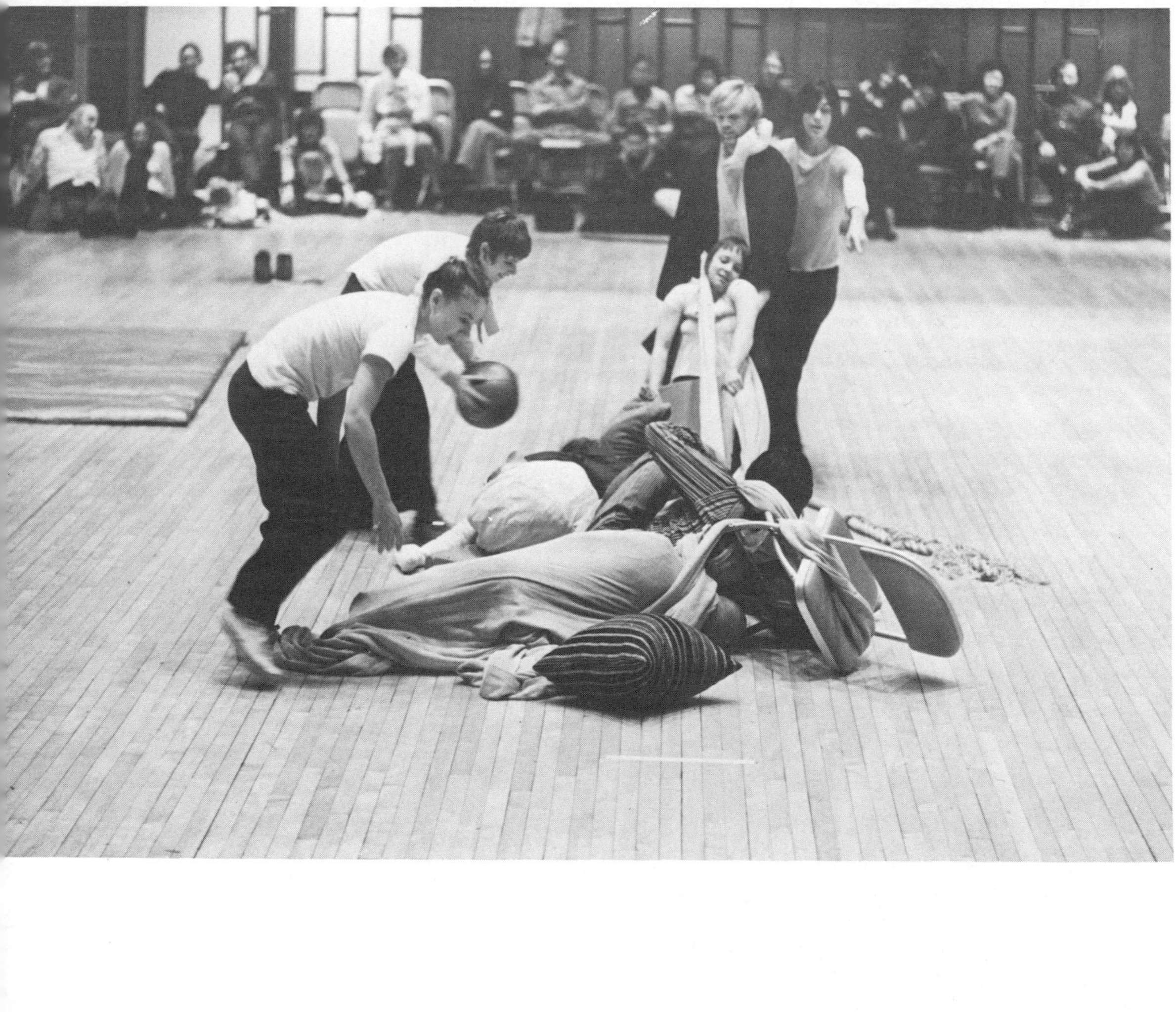

The Grand Union: The Presentation of Everyday Life as Dance

THE GRAND UNION was a collective of choreographer/performers who during the years 1970 to 1976 made group improvisations embracing dance, theater, and theatrics in an ongoing investigation into the nature of dance and performance. The Grand Union's identity as a group had several sources: some of the nine who were its members at different points had known each other for as long as ten years when the group formed. They had seen and performed in each other's work since the Judson Church days. Most had studied with Merce Cunningham, and three had danced in his company.

One rich and important source of the group's genesis was Yvonne Rainer's work *Continuous Project — Altered Daily* (abbreviated *CP — AD*). To understand the course of the Grand Union's work, it is useful to look first at the changing nature of *CP — AD*. Rainer began work on the piece in 1969, and in March 1970 presented a definitive version at the Whitney Museum. The performers were Becky Arnold, Douglas Dunn, David Gordon, Barbara Lloyd (Dilley), Steve Paxton, Yvonne Rainer, and various readers.

CP — AD took its name from a sculptural work by Robert Morris in which the daily alteration of the work — an arrangement of earth and metal in a garage — was put on view (after being altered) for spectators. In *CP — AD*, Rainer's concern was to make an ongoing performance that would change during and between performances, using various aspects of the working process of dance-making: learning, rehearsing, marking (a dancer's term for executing a movement at a low energy level); working out and running through material; and dancing the material in a finished performance style. Given these categories, the performance itself could include behavior that was, according to Rainer, "actual" (spontaneous) or "choreographed"

The Grand Union, improvisatory performance (to benefit the Committee to Defend the Black Panthers), 1971. Left to right: Becky Arnold, Nancy (Green) Lewis, Barbara (Lloyd) Dilley, Douglas Dunn, Yvonne Rainer (standing); Steve Paxton, David Gordon (on floor). Photograph © Peter Moore, 1971 (learned, edited, stylized). Rainer wanted, as well, to show the dichotomy between "professional" dancing behavior, and "amateur" (ordinary) gesture and deportment.[1]

Another concern was to include within the performance the different relationships between the performer and the material, which Rainer systematized according to "levels of performance reality." On a primary level, the performer does original material in a personal style; on a secondary level, the performer works in a recognizable style, or performs someone else's material in the original style; on a tertiary level, the content and style of the material are not coordinated — i.e., the performance is a transformation, a deliberately "bad secondary performance."[2]

The piece was an assemblage of "chunks" and "insertables" of movement material — solos, duets, group sequences — that could be put in any order determined by the performers. Some of the material was already known and polished, some actually rehearsed, some marked, some learned during the performance. The dancers could initiate a section by calling out its name, or by bringing out the requisite prop, or by putting on the appropriate music. Discussion between the performers about the work as it progressed — comments and tactical analyses — created a casual, rehearsal-like atmosphere.

The movement sequences often focused on the manipulation of a prop or a "body adjunct," including: five pillows, a large pair of wings, a stuffed round object with a leg and foot attached to it, two pieces of 8½ x 11-inch paper, one 2 x 6-foot strip of foam rubber, an object that when strapped on the back transformed the dancer into a hunchback. Many of the routines also involved manipulating, hoisting, and carrying other performers. Some of the bits used music: "Chair-Pillow," for example, was performed to the tune of Ike and Tina Turner's "Mountain High, River Deep"; a section called "Here Comes the Sun" was accompanied by the Beatles' song of the same name. At other times, the movement activity was accompanied by reminiscences of film stars and directors (mostly taken from Kevin Brownlow's *The Parade's Gone By*), recited by several people at a microphone — an element that added more information about the nature of performance to the performance. Films, including one of the Connecticut College rehearsal of *CP — AD*, the previous summer, were shown in other rooms in the museum.

When one looks at the silent film *Connecticut Rehearsal* by Michael Fajans, one sees a spartan, condensed version of the later variations on *CP — AD*. One can also see the groundwork that would clear the way for the Grand

Union's style and material. In the following description of segments of *Connecticut Rehearsal,* my description of the action is in *italics;* Yvonne Rainer's commentary[3] is enclosed in quotation marks; and my **boldface** markings signal conceptual seeds that are important for the work of the Grand Union.

The group walks around in the gym, **dressed casually,** *in T-shirts, pants or shorts, and sneakers. They toss a large cardboard carton* **from one to another as if it is a ball.** *Now they hoist Becky Arnold, and running in a large circle all together, pass her around as if she's the box. They pass both the box and Arnold. Dunn tries to lift Dilley to pass her; she resists slightly, sliding her feet from side to side, shifting her torso as Dunn holds on to it.* **The attempted hoist turns into a pas de deux.**

Rainer runs over to Dunn and Gordon, **looking as if she's about to block a pass.** *The three turn to catch Arnold, who is jumping toward them, apparently* **without warning.** *They walk in single file, carrying Arnold on top of their heads. Dilley runs alongside them carrying a large screen. Now the box is on top of Arnold who is on her back on top of the three heads. They lower her gently.*

People are balancing pillows on their heads, then throwing them on the floor. Some stomp on their pillows with triumphant smiles. Dunn throws his pillow to the floor, then **punts** *it and* **laughs. "It was a study in what's funny** — put your foot down, then look at it or at the pillow; then step, **thwarting the expectations of the group."** *Dilley pulls the pillow down over her face, puts a hand over one breast.*

The group runs around the periphery of the gym, ducking each other in slow motion **as if they're playing in the water.** *Dilley runs and runs, holding on to a pillow. As she falls to the floor,* **Dunn breaks her fall** *with a pillow. Everyone runs and falls with pillows.*

Rainer and Gordon take turns standing at a distance from the box and leaning toward it to reach a sheet of paper on top of it. "I was interested in the size of the box and **the interchangeability of the box and the body,** in **doing something with the box that changes the movement.** Here the body is revealed in the extreme stretch — like the paper on the box. The final result is minimal: taking the thing or moving it slightly."

"Those three people in the circle are **seeing how far they can** move their feet out while leaving their arms entwined."

As people turn their attention from one activity to the next, they jog around **like football players between plays;** *they make* **boxing movements,** *kick backward. Now it looks like* **a game** *of hot potato with the box.* **"If you called someone's name they got supported. If you called 'box' it got passed around."**

Dunn, standing, is hoisted on Rainer's back as she stoops over **in a kickoff position.** *Now Dunn is lying on the backs of Rainer and Arnold as they crawl. Gradually they turn over and roll him off. Rainer revolves Dilley in different directions by turning her own body against Dilley's. People are doing* **gymnasts' flying angels, or using each other's weight to lean, stand, and sit.**

The group sits on the floor. **They talk.** *They extend their hands and clasp each other's arms. Then* **they try to stand.** *Arnold has her back to everyone; all stand except Arnold.* "I kept changing the arms around. It was an hour's work just sitting there and getting up. Becky's arms were in back of her so **she couldn't get up, so I used that.** It's the final movement of this sequence and it ended up being a very spectacular lift. **Now we're discussing how** to get Becky off her back in one fell swoop. **Then I have to try it to see what it feels like."**

"We had three performances at the Whitney. The first night was raucous; I felt like we'd had a party the audience hadn't been invited to and I felt queasy. The second night we seemed to pull back on the freedom, and it was solemn. The third night we got a mixture, a nice **balance of subdued formal carrying out of tasks and informality."**

When one examines the conceptual groundwork as it emerges from this description, one notices certain salient features: the atmosphere and dress are casual; the dancers stop to discuss the activity or to try it out themselves, with variations. Often, references are made to sports, games, and gymnastics. Objects are transformed by a particular kind of use into other objects. People's bodies are sometimes treated as objects, also to be transformed by using them in unusual ways. Gags are investigated. Physical feats are attempted and, if they fail, are tried over and over.

As *CP — AD* progressed during performances on tours, Rainer struggled with her ambivalence about hierarchy and democracy, freedom and limits, her role as "boss-lady" (as she put it) and her desire for cooperative work. She sought some kind of balance between "unevenness and diffusion . . . *and* the tight focus of a lot of my imagery." She experimented with the possibilities of choice on the part of the performers, giving them options to break a prescribed section, to repeat or continue a section, or to "do your own thing" — and to veto, as a group, the choice of an individual. (The group could rarely reach a consensus on vetoes, however.) By the time of the Whitney performances, "doing your own thing" was limited to one chance per person per performance.[4]

The account of how the Grand Union evolved out of the loosening structure of *CP — AD* varies according to which member of the group one consults. Those who did not perform in *CP — AD* have a radically different view of the group's origins. And although *CP — AD* was a work concerned with process, the dancers in the piece were not as involved in the struggles of defining the process as Rainer, the choreographer, was. With the decision to form the Grand Union, the process deeply involved nine choreographers instead of one. The various members of the group had disparate experiences with improvisation, performance, training, and choreography. Each one also had his or her own ideas and expectations of what the Grand Union would be and how it would function. (See "Grand Union, Q & A.")

In the fall of 1970, Trisha Brown, who had been experimenting with improvisation for over ten years, was invited to join the group. Friendly with most of the Grand Union members, Brown nevertheless had misgivings about sacrificing her independence as a choreographer and diverting time and attention from her own work. Brown brought not only her knowledge of improvisation, but also her concerns with structure and her intelligent humor into the Grand Union performances.

Many of the issues and elements in *CP — AD* had been influenced originally by the early work of other choreographers. When those features resurfaced in the Grand Union's performance, audiences sometimes saw them as Rainerisms, yet they were contributions by the others, filtered through Rainer's use in *CP — AD*. For instance, the interchangeability of objects and people, or of two different objects, was used by Paxton in *Proxy* and other dances. The balance of formality and informality had precedents in the work of Simone Forti, Paxton, Brown, and others. The humor in dances by Brown and Gordon was one aspect of *CP — AD* and the Grand Union. But many other concerns in Brown's and Forti's choreography have been cited by Grand Union members as influencing all of them. Ann Halprin's experiments and teachings are also valued as a source.

Two other performers — Dong (Lincoln Scott), an actor and dancer, and Nancy Lewis (Green), who had danced with Lucas Hoving, Anna Sokolow, José Limón, and Twyla Tharp — joined the Grand Union in 1970 as well.

Still, early Grand Union performances were often based, for many of its members, on the concept of the group as a "repertory dance company with an inheritance from *CP — AD*."[5] They created evenings of dance with partially improvised organizational structures, using much material from the Rainer work. Members of the group took turns as temporary leaders and choreographers. Barbara Dilley contributed a follow-the-leader structure; David Gordon used the group in his *Sleepwalking* a number of times in 1971, 1972, and 1973, including performances at Oberlin College and The Walker Art Center. Though the early concerts were not necessarily political in content, the group was aware of its political nature as a struggling collective. Early in 1971, the Grand Union gave three benefit performances for the committee to defend the Black Panthers.

In the early years, some people referred to the group by its corporate name, The Rio Grande Union, and some mistakenly identified it as Yvonne Rainer's troupe. But Rainer was quite consciously submerging her ego in the Grand Union's democratic process, and simultaneously reasserting directorial authority in her own pieces.[6] The tendency of many critics to attribute the work of the group to a leader, and to choose Rainer as the most convenient candidate, prompted her to write at least one letter in public protest.[7] In fact, the group was working out its relationship to authority. The members found that they were less comfortable performing in each other's work than they were performing together. By late 1972, with Rainer's position as an equal member clarified, and with two years of experiments in structure and power relations behind them, they had evolved a flexible, open, generous improvisatory format. It allowed for invention, commentary, teaching, repetition, imitation, and all the other possibilities for handling material that *CP — AD* had unearthed. The situation allowed any member to discover new performance modalities. It also provided room for any member to assume control — or at least, to attempt to do so — for part of an evening, and although any new material could be introduced, there was also the alternative of hanging on to favorite bits. But the format was not totally without limits. Certain things — audience participation, for example — were for the most part discouraged.

With its aspirations to collectivity, equality, and spontaneity, the Grand Union was unconventional in comparison to mainstream dance companies, but it certainly was not alone. Members of the group on their own, and colleagues like Deborah Hay and Simone Forti, as well as teachers like Ann Halprin, had been working for years to find alternatives to the established power structures of the dance world. During those years, American culture generally expressed themes of concern with cooperation, collective living and working situations, and attention to process over finished product. In politics and social situations as well as in the fine arts, people began to look to spontaneity and improvisatory methods to provide a life better than that which a rigidly constructed, individual-oriented, hierarchical society had created. Water beds, Earth Shoes, interest in physical disciplines like yoga, rolfing, the Alexander technique, health food fads — all indicated an obsessive anxiety about the body, a concern that reflected deeper anxieties about our body politic. The Open Theater, the Living Theater, and the San Francisco Mime Troupe were among the many theater groups looking for collective forms in both the working process and the content of the plays they performed. Conceptual artists rejected the notion of displaying and preserving art works as commodities, cooperative galleries were formed, and in several cities art workers' collectives got together to take political action. It seemed necessary to "let the world in again," as Leo Steinberg said of Robert Rauschenberg's work.[8] For the Grand Union, the added dimension of theater and dance as social forms meant that a social as well as aesthetic world invaded the stage. The Grand Union used some of the same strategies that Marcel Duchamp, the other Dadaists, and later, Happenings had: stretching the material and formal limits of their art by incorporating objects (and gestures) from everyday life, using imagery (including sounds) from popular culture, and making long, rambling works in a flexible format with a constantly changing stream of images and meanings.

Just as their concerns varied, the persona each member of the Grand Union projected in performance could shift enormously from one night to the next, from one section of a single performance to another. The Grand Union, as I knew it from 1973 to 1976, was: Trisha Brown, Barbara Dilley, Douglas Dunn, David Gordon, Nancy Lewis, and Steve Paxton. Six people with widely divergent styles and concerns, working within a framework that encouraged provocation, as well as cooperation. During the Grand Union's last years the group was sometimes criticized for having evolved predictable characters and situations — they were likened to soap-opera characters, lovable and familiar, though stereotypes, or to a children's serial on TV.[9] It is tempting to characterize Lewis as the floppy clown, Gordon as the flamboyant rock star–provocateur, Dilley as the humorless mystic, Brown as the deadpan punster in words and movement, Paxton as a gentle Jesus, and Dunn as a cross between Fred Astaire and John Wayne. All stock characters. But to do so is to limit and flatten the richness of a Grand Union performance. The concerts were not about playing characters, but about interaction, contact, behavior. The roles, characters and personae transformed easily to accommodate to the changing flow of situations. At times the characters were utterly fictional, at times parodies of real people, at times the "real" performer, at times amalgams of everyday and fantasy roles. The possibility that in performance the characters could change from one frame of experiential reality to another created an unstable, surrealistic context where both content and tense were constantly subverted. For instance, a "real" Dilley interacting with a "fabricated" Gordon, or a Lewis who has been instructed by Brown to imitate Paxton no matter what anyone might then say to the contrary, were people who seemed to operate outside any established rules for reality — ordinary, dramatic, or fictional. And a "real" Dilley or a "real" Paxton could also play any one of a number of roles, since both on stage and off they are complex, changeable people, playing many real-life roles in a variety of interactions.

Sociologist Erving Goffman's observations about how we organize experience and "manage impressions" are telling in this regard. In *The Presentation of Self in Everyday Life,* Goffman analyzes social life in work situations, using a dramaturgical perspective. He describes how workers "perform" — for each other, for the boss, for outsiders. He observes that different people associated with a workplace team up to collaborate on certain performances and he analyzes how different settings, routines, and roles influence behavior. According to Goffman, working life — in fact, all of everyday life — is a process of self-production, of engineering communication to create — to stage — certain impressions. As in the theater, sometimes we are "onstage," with all the conventions and limitations that implies. Sometimes we are "offstage" — able to relax from the strenuous demands of the role. The dramatic strategies we use in daily life, Goffman suggests, are the same sorts of techniques dramatists use on stage — although the moral and social results of those techniques when applied in real life are more profound.[10]

Goffman distinguishes between onstage and "backstage" behavior and lists some of the characteristics of backstage conduct. These include acts that are symbolically offensive, hostile, impolite, and intimate (often unspoken) — such as "reciprocal first-naming, co-operative decision-making, profanity, open sexual remarks, elaborate griping, smoking, rough informal dress, 'sloppy' sitting and standing posture . . . mumbling and shouting, playful aggressivity and 'kidding' . . . minor self-involvements such as humming, whistling, chewing, nibbling, belching, and flatulence."[11] These are the sorts of acts, for example, that factory workers can engage in in the foreman's absence, while in the foreman's presence a totally different performance code is followed. Features in Grand Union performances sometimes seemed to be drawn from that list; they literally invoked backstage behavior during performance. We often saw Grand Union performers do things on stage which normal dance concert behavior would not permit: they ate, hummed, walked away from a group activity, explained to the audience what was going on, consulted their partner during a lift about his or her comfort or state of mind. Similarly, there was room in Grand Union performances for what Goffman calls "discrepant role-playing," "communication out of character," and for switching roles and regions. There was freedom to express all the faux pas dancers must repress and mask in "normal" performances — such as stumbling or forgetting. What's more, there was freedom to explore further and expand these faux pas as material. Grand Union performances, by sabotaging the performance work process, by showing people out of whack with conventional rules for working and for other social behavior, seemed to pry open those rules. During Grand Union performances, one felt a compensatory satisfaction in seeing them break the rules, have social adventures — in a realm where such acts suffer no permanent repercussions. It was a different kind of satisfaction from that which we feel when antisocial acts are committed in conventional dramas, however. Because the Grand Union's art was so close to life, the subversions felt closer, more dangerous. And because the subversions often had to do with the nature of performance itself — someone called out "intermission!" when a situation became overloaded, or announced that they were tired and then said "The End" — they were unfamiliar and unsettling.

Goffman once again provides a clear system for understanding such variations on reality in his *Frame Analysis.* Here he categorizes different experiences of reality, based partly on the amount and type of information available to participants in an interaction. Goffman's "frames," "fabrications," and "keyings" correspond strikingly to Rainer's analysis of levels of performance reality (primary, secondary, tertiary). A "keying" of a particular activity, for instance, is a conscious transformation of that activity into something quite different, although modeled on the original activity. Keying is systematic transformation, openly acknowledged as such by the participants. It is usually signaled with cues of some sort. Examples of keyings are fantasies, daydreams, drama (that is, make-believe); contests and certain sports (imitating combat but different in crucial ways); ceremonies such as weddings or coronations; re-doings, such as rehearsals, practice, or re-runs. Turning a novel into a play is a process of keying. Turning that play into a film is a keying of a keying. Fabrications are another type of transformation, in which the information about the transformation is partly hidden from some of the people involved. Fabrications, in short, are deceptions, running the gamut from the benign — practical jokes — to the exploitative and criminal — blackmail, espionage, or perjury.[12]

Frame Analysis was published in 1974. It seems no accident that the work of a sociologist should parallel the investigations of a contemporary performance group, especially since both used consciously theatrical language and metaphors to communicate their findings. A standard Grand Union device was to switch frames, although this was never their conscious purpose. And since they were a group of individuals with constantly clashing objectives, their inquiries were rarely systematic. Certain narratives emerged, only to be destroyed. A collective agreement was reached about the frame currently in operation, and collapsed in an instant.

For instance, David Gordon and Nancy Lewis have been acting out a B-movie scene: they are tenant farmers, worried about the rain and the crops. He is lying on his back, obviously incapacitated, and she is begging him to get up just this once to help her handle the crisis. They break character to discuss who is supposed to sing the climactic song, behaving as though this had all been scripted already — Lewis objects to singing it all by herself, Gordon assures her he'll join in on the chorus. He promises to turn over when she comes to the line about the water — an overt hint that whatever she now invents should contain that cue for him. Then, they're on, reassuming the frame of the keying, "really" acting the scene they've just been discussing. Steve Paxton has been assigned the role of the thunder, and as Lewis sings he carts a chair, a bucket of water, a tall standing fan, and a long silk scarf closer to them. Barbara Dilley moves in to sprinkle water from the bucket, as Paxton holds the billowing scarf in front of the fan. The group cooperates to make the scene develop . . . and suddenly Gordon gets up and says, "I want to turn this into an up moment. Forget the farm; forget the crops; forget the drought. Let's think about surfers and sand . . ." A Beach Boys record comes on. Paxton and Dilley move over to where Douglas Dunn has been dancing on top of a tall stool, they wrap the scarf around him, and now Dunn looks like he's riding waves. The frame shifts easily from one moment to the next. The physical activities and props are transformed — keyed — by the words and the music from one meaning to another.

Often the keyings referred to other modes of performance, sometimes with an ironic connotation. The Grand Union poked fun at itself as a group of artists by transforming actions into athletics, or vaudeville, or TV commercials. In another adventure with the blue silk scarf, Gordon has just finished artfully arranging an exquisite tableau of dancers and drapery, when Brown turns to look at the drape — the scarf — and says, "What kind of detergent do you use? Somehow my laundry never turns out white." Or an action would be given more weight, become more solemn, suggesting a religious rite or a psychological obsession that has different rules than art. Dilley, weighted down with backpacks and scarves, is dancing a solo, while Dunn calls to her from across the room, "Barbara . . . Barbara . . ." She answers curtly: "How many times have I told you that when I'm dressed like this my name is not Barbara!" Brown, tangled up with long cardboard poles, becomes Joan of Arc. At times it seemed the whole Grand Union format referred archly to vaudeville, as a dance number broke for some patter, and gags interrupted the dancing, which in turn interrupted the songs. But this was surrealistic vaudeville, as the free-associative method of adding new music, new props, new ideas prompted new frames of reference in a stream of rapid change.

In *Frame Analysis,* Goffman specifically analyzes the frame structure and process that govern conventional theatrical events.[13] He names eight characteristics that sharply mark off a dramatic performance from everyday face-to-face interactions. Again, we can see the Grand Union's systematic assault on normal theatrical practice more clearly by contrasting their method. First, he points out, there are spatial boundaries which arbitrarily divide the stage world from the "real" world. With the Grand Union it depended on where they were performing. They did not perform on the street, for instance, and they did respect boundaries between performers and audience — more so than other radical theater groups have. Yet by making themselves at home on whatever stage they occupied for the evening or for the week, by using its lights, ladders, wings, anterooms, winches, and curtains familiarly as props, they deflated the illusory qualities of the stage territory. They treated the stage as if it were the real world, erasing the borders somewhat.

Second, in conventional theater, the doings of the characters are exposed without any compensatory or protective adjustment. The characters can dispense with normal psychological defenses. The Grand Union's invocation of backstage behavior eliminated this rule. So did the narratives they introduced about the problems of performing. It is Gordon's turn to get up and dance. Instead he wails into the microphone, à la Bob Dylan, "Do you know what it's like to be next — do you know what it's like not to know what you're going to do in a minute — do you know what it's like to be in a strange city and — DO YA KNOW WHAT IT'S LI-KE!?" To turn nervousness into bravura performance was one way of coping. So was confessing one's confusion, or hostility, or need to be watched and loved. So was the option of turning one's back to the audience, standing outside of the performance for a rest, or repeating a familiar movement phrase.

A third rule, according to Goffman, is that spoken interactions do not occur in normal physical configurations (that is, with two or more speakers facing each other), but angled toward the audience. With the Grand Union, conversations or monologues were often mumbled, whispered, or repeated. Two performers carried on a conversation while doing separate dances on opposite sides of an enormous stage. Or one would be lying on top of the other. Normal physical configurations were rare in any case for more than a few minutes, whether talk occurred or not.

Fourth on Goffman's list is the fact that normally in theater the focus tends to center on one person at a time, with the rest of the characters remaining out of focus. Fifth, the timing of conversation is made artificial in that turns at talking are respected by other performers to the end, and the audience response is allowed before the next turn is taken. Sixth, interaction is systematically managed to supply the audience incidentally with various kinds of information about the character's history, the story, et cetera. Seventh, expression is unlike normal conversation in its excessive length and grandiloquence. Eighth, no action goes unobserved by the audience, since so little is known to begin with about the characters; but the characters sometimes act as though they ignore each other.

The Grand Union stubbornly challenged the limits of performance by breaking all of these rules. As I've said, they were not alone in testing the limits of theater; besides the groups mentioned above, Richard Foreman's Ontological-Hysteric Theater, Meredith Monk and The House, The Performance Group, Robert Wilson, Structuralist Workshop, and others have experimented with fragmenting plot, character, and locale information, with using more movement than words, with presenting ordinary conversation, often inaudible, on stage, and with providing an overload of foci among which the audience must make choices. But the Grand Union was unique in its ability to express a broad range of material — from social life, work life, and from art, in words, action, and dance movement — passing from one medium to another with ease and mobility in an evening's work.

A typical Grand Union evening was never predictable. It would perhaps begin with quiet dance warm-ups by four or five of the group: stretching and bending joints systematically but according to individual systems, boogying gently to blues or Cajun music, quietly testing movement material that the choreographer was concerned with in his or her own work. Gradually interactions would come about: people imitated each other, or did variations on one another's movement styles, or engaged in movement dialogues. Or they talked — quietly conversing, or loudly commenting, or running a separate channel of information in speech that altered the perception of the movement material. The missing performers would make their entrances. Suddenly the entire group would coalesce into a single activity, and then a duet would break off into separate solos in separate corners. Someone would put on a new record, and the whole scene would change. Two people would step aside for a moment, and the scene changed again. The performance ebbed and flowed. Logic was invented, then discarded. A process was begun, examined, dropped, or carried through to its limits — or past its limits into something new. A familiar bit was put into gear. Maybe this time it rambled on and on, without any conclusion in sight, or maybe it took on new twists, with brilliant inventions.

There were no answers, no goals, no expectations. Just two hours or so to look at some things. To try out some things. Making choices individually, collectively, then dealing with the implications and repercussions. Finding out how the others respond. Using the presence of the audience as another feedback mechanism. If someone felt hostile, it came out. If someone was hurt or surprised by someone else's actions, that had to be dealt with. If two people were picking up readily on each other's signals one night, the performance worked differently from when no one was connecting.

What is preference? What is choice? What, in fact, is improvisation? Is this competition? What facilitates cooperation? Is this particular behavior authoritarian? What is illusion? What is real? Is it repetition if something is remembered in a different way? How is time experienced? How are patterns made over time and over space? What is performance? The questions did not get answered, but they were constantly raised in an evening's work.

The performances were without plan, without script, without a single preplanned structure. There was no focal climax, no particular order, no illusions that were allowed to stand for more than a moment. And yet the performances were always about illusion, order, climax, focus, presence, repetition, logic, and structure no matter what the surface material was. And somehow the performances were at their most magical when everyone on stage seemed intent on figuring out what magic is, precisely, and on deliberately denuding magic for themselves and for the audience. When the performance suddenly "clicked," one was tempted to describe the sensation with that old standby of impressionistic criticism: magic. Yet theatrical magic was not the goal of the Grand Union. Rather, they aimed at displaying the social and psychological conditions that make the "magic" of performance possible.

They investigated the structure of dance. "We'll throw Steve and Barbara in the air. They'll clasp bodies in the air, change places, and come down in our arms again," Gordon explains to Brown. Or Dunn discourses on his method while starting a very long sequence. He falls, gets up, turns around, falls, turns over. "Right now I'm starting a very long sequence." He continues dancing. "I don't think I'll do the whole thing. This is the end," doing some jumps and quick footwork. "This is the middle," he says, running back to a point near where he started, and falling again. Or, the lights dim, the dancing slows down, someone's singing softly about rain . . . "This looks for all the world like an ending," Gordon announces. "Wait," says Paxton. He motions for a new record, the lights come up, a new action rolls into gear.

One favorite narrative theme was that of the doctor-patient encounter, a sketch that had its origins in a visit by the rest of the group to Paxton, seriously ill in St. Vincent's Hospital in 1971. It was invoked almost ritualistically, when someone was lying down, or had transformed his or her body with an object, or acted in some way marginal to the group. In a concert in Minneapolis, Rainer stuck a broken hippopotamus sculpture into her blouse. Gordon, with a German accent, suggested removing the lump surgically. In Chicago, Dilley, who really had a cough, became the patient. The others tried to exorcise the cough, which they began to talk about as a being or spirit, or at least to try to dislodge "her" into another region of Dilley's body. In Iowa, the three men had been playing with mirrors, and suddenly they swooped down on Dilley, lying at the side of the stage. "Who referred you to us?" they asked. "When did the pains begin?" It was unclear whether the problem was physical or metaphysical. As the doctors and patient argued, Dilley commented bitterly, "This is just like the inside of my head." When she solemnly requested that the doctors give her some answers to her dilemma, and show her a way out, Gordon asked Lewis, now playing the nurse, to show Dilley the way. Lewis pointed dramatically to the door.

Sexual innuendo crept in whenever possible. "Is this the best you've ever had it, Trisha?" was a frequent question as Brown perched on top of another person who was balanced on a ladder or beam, or as she was carried upside-down. "Is this your first time?" someone would be asked pointedly.

All these themes and narratives — those conveyed in words, those given in movement and action — told, either directly or metaphorically, about the work of the group. They called attention to the body, the special problems dancers have with their physical equipment, the risks they take and the adventures they have. And the special wisdom and mastery over the body they acquire during the years they train and use the body as an instrument. The doctor-patient *shtick* was redolent of formulaic popular drama, like vaudeville, soap opera, and melodrama, as well. The stories the characters told provided an accompaniment to the movement, which clarified and identified the elements of performance, and the processes of the group — its means, its methods, and its fragility — as the movement was invented and performed for the audience, i.e., put to the ultimate test. The occasional ambiguity of the text (is Dilley really sick or is this part of the routine? is Brown calm or terrified?) underscored the fact that the borders between illusion and reality were tangled, at best, in this particular theatrical event. The stories made us focus on particular actions, or attach particular meanings to an event. Then a new story made us notice other details, or see other, sometimes contradictory, meanings. Finally, we were forced to consider the impossibility of achieving a single, fixed way of looking at facts and behavior.

Ultimately, the Grand Union's work was about the kinds of contact we make in the world, through language and behavior. Through conscious, reflexive performance, the group provided an aesthetically abstracted image of life in the modern world: at work, in groups, among friends, among strangers. Physical contact can be one-sided — a solo dance, an imitation of another person's actions, manipulations of an object or of another person as object. Or, physical contact can be mutual — teaching, sharing, balancing, supporting, responding, collaborating on movement. In terms of verbal content, having a conversation is mutual; punning, playing with words or sounds, delivering monologues is one-sided. Private-public: whispers/shouts; touching/gesturing; interaction/display. The contact changes, of course, because of the context. Intimate mutual relations are not so private when there's audience sitting on all sides, after all. And public behavior not normally found in the theater becomes a kind of double performance when done on stage. Normal interactions metamorphose in an unconventional setting. But with the Grand Union, strange behavior transmuted just as easily into banal readings — for instance, a dancer pretzeled into a strange position and balancing at great height would be tagged as expressing illness or social deviance rather than simply as inventing fantastic movement. Or someone hanging upside-down from a beam would act in every other respect as though that were a perfectly normal posture.

Flux was a characteristic Grand Union quality, not only in the ever-changing moods and interests of the cast of characters, but in the structure of the performance itself, and as a way of regarding the work over the six years of its life. The accumulation of dramatic crises in a single night, mirroring the operations of memory, washed the performance with an overall quality of consistency and neutrality. The performance ebbed and flowed, flickered and changed, like life, like thought. Sometimes an evening seemed just like yesterday's installment. Sometimes it looked totally new. A quiet, fluctuating rhythm pervaded the work, gluing together the brilliant humor, the drudgery, the shocks and enchantments, the floundering and the flying. People turned from self-involvement to interest in another or in the group. Some stopped in the middle of an activity to check things out. Others sulked, or worried about getting tired, or getting old.

What is a dance? What could the outer limits of dance art be? At a lecture-demonstration in Minneapolis in 1971 — similar to a "regular" Grand Union performance, but with room for questions from the audience — someone asked "Why don't you all do something together?" and someone else asked "When are you going to begin?"[14] At each Grand Union performance I've seen, I had the distinct gut feeling that this was the last dance and the most all-encompassing dance possible. The Grand Union would have to disband tonight, I would think each time, because now they've said it all, done it all, no more invention is imaginable. Expectations, assumptions, memory, freedom had been tested and pried open. A new world of possibilities for dance, performance, art had come into being. But this new special world, created by six individuals working together — with more power together, and of a different sort, than any of them had working individually — was so inextricably interwoven with the "real" world I live in, and they live in, that the world could never be the same again.

The Grand Union, Q & A

Respondents: Becky Arnold (BA); Trisha Brown (TB); Barbara Dilley (BD); Douglas Dunn (DD); David Gordon (DG); Nancy Lewis (NL); Steve Paxton (SP); Yvonne Rainer (YR)[15]

1. Why did you join Grand Union and what were your choreographic concerns at the time you joined?

BA: When Yvonne disbanded her company in late 1969–1970 and suggested the members work collectively, I decided to try the experience — "Sure, why not," I said. "Should be interesting."

My choreographic concerns were embryonic — I had done little composing.

TB: In 1970, Yvonne Rainer asked me to join an improvisational dance company called the Grand Union. This new group would replace her former company and eliminate her role of leader/choreographer. Equality was in the air. A few others were invited; the final package included David Gordon, Stephen Paxton, Barbara Dilley, Nancy Lewis, Lincoln Scott, Becky Arnold and Douglas Dunn.

Prior to this invitation, I had choreographed and produced *Trillium, Falling Solo with Singing, Lightfall, Target, Rulegame 5, Motor, Homemade, Inside, A String, Skunk Cabbage, Salt Grass, and Waders, Medicine Dance, Planes, Snapshots, Falling Duet, Ballet, Dance with a Duck's Head, Yellow Belly, Skymap, Man Walking Down the Side of the Building, Clothes Pipe, The Floor of the Forest, and Other Miracles, Etc.,*

Leaning Duets and *The Stream.* Those dances, some of them appearing during the Judson collaboration, had not been either witnessed or reviewed by a New York critic with the exception of perfunctory mention by Jill Johnston. I was, therefore, leery of submerging my unrecorded choreographic identity in a second collaborative venture that would perpetuate a lack of recognition for my own work.

At the initial meeting of the Grand Union, I expressed my grave reservations about throwing in with them and Yvonne said, "What you want is a concert of your own at the Whitney Museum," to which I responded, "Yes," although self-elevation was not in the air.

Walking on the Wall, Leaning Duets, Falling Duets and *Skymap* were performed at the Whitney Museum on March 30 and 31, 1971. See Deborah Jowitt, *Village Voice,* Anna Kisselgoff, *New York Times,* Marcia Siegel, Boston *Sunday Herald Traveler,* and Sally R. Sommer, *The Drama Review.* Six months before this, I had joined the Grand Union.

BD: I didn't join . . . as such. The Grand Union evolved out of work by Yvonne Rainer. In particular, *Continuous Project — Altered Daily.* I worked with Yvonne from 1968 through this transmutation and it was, in a word, outrageous. There was a contagiousness to the explosion of spontaneity that started slowly, then grew and grew and grew till we just "did it" without even a word necessary.

A very elemental question of concerns — what did I want to make, if I did? Where did one come from, anyway, to come on . . . basic hesitation, self-doubt and insecurity.

DD: Politics.
Stillness.

DG: At the beginning there was no process. There were a number of people who had functioned as the Yvonne Rainer Company and had continued to make work independently. Not me. I had stopped in 1966.

Yvonne didn't want to be boss anymore and I can't think why we were continuing to attempt to work together at all except that probably we were still working for Yvonne. What I mean is that now that we were no longer a group the only reason that we stayed a group was because Yvonne told us to and told us to find some new way of working and she would work with us.

Anyway, I can't remember whose idea it was that we could do group choreography but we tried several ways. People brought in whole phrases or pieces of material and we all tried to learn them. Barbara Dilley was doing her circle dances then and we all worked on them for her and mostly made her angry because we took liberties with her material. After all weren't we free and equal?

We tried a peculiar method of alternating a movement or short phrase donated by each member in a linear fashion and random order. That was a disaster. We were not fond of each other's choices.

We dealt most badly with Yvonne's material input. Now that she was not boss, and none of us were, it was very difficult to stick to anything in rehearsal and more difficult to stick with her material. But peculiarly the Y. R. Co. kept having places to perform. We began to bring some of that under-rehearsed and unrealized material into performance which still had as its basis the material from *Continuous Project.* People would then begin improvising around this new material and also around their self-consciousness about being in performance without much material. I clung desperately to the old material refusing to improvise. I thought they were all crazy and the audiences that sat through what we were dishing out were crazier.

I performed Y.R.'s *Trio A* in most of those performances as slow as I could, as fast as I could, to music, while singing, while talking and any other goddamned way I could think of.

At some point Yvonne went to India and someone had the idea to keep performing, even more often, in New York City while she was gone, to establish our identity as an entity without Yvonne as boss. Becky, who was even more against the improvisational performances than I was, showed up for few or maybe none of those performances, which took place in a loft on 13th Street for many weekends in a row, two or three nights each weekend.

At those performances I began to learn to improvise. Some things that happened during those performances: we learned some material Steve made — the smallest head, eyes, mouth, neck gestures while sitting side-by-side on a bench or a rolled up mat. We did Barbara's circle material often, many nights, sometimes to Terry Riley music, sometimes I did fake stripping while moving around in the circle, sometimes we moved as a group, sometimes as separate people working at the same time. I began to understand the difference. I had begun working on something that came to be called *Sleep Walking.* The people who were learning the material came to the performances and sometimes performed it while we worked. Steve had been operated on and we had all visited him in the hospital prior to those performances.

There was somebody old there propped up in a chair sliding down as we visited saying over and over "Oh Lord, help me, I'm slipping, help me Lord." At one performance I began being followed by Barbara. She was extraordinary at picking up on someone's material and reinforcing it by lending her body and her mind to the action, stretching the ideas as well as following them. I began to realize my material by watching her participation in it. I began to roll over on the mat. She was following. I began to speak. "Oh Lord, help me, I'm slipping, help." She was saying what I was saying. Then Trisha was there too. Rolling over and saying "Oh Lord, I'm slipping." I began to slow down the talking, like a recording at the wrong speed and they did it too. It was amazing to me and I date my active participation in the Grand Union's improvisations from that point.

I suppose we were the Grand Union by then. I can't remember. I know that the name came right after a performance of the Y. R. Co. in Philadelphia for the B'nai B'rith. Yvonne and I took a walk the next day. I think we went to the Rodin Museum or to see the last Duchamp or maybe both. I remember sitting in a park for a while and talking about a new name . . . one that would not have a dance connotation. Like a rock group, I remember saying. Yvonne was hot for the Body Shop. I suggested Grand Union. The next day in New York, Yvonne called and said she thought Grand Union was a good idea. I don't remember a vote on it. There surely must have been one. After that we began fighting the battle to be known as the Grand Union and not as Yvonne's company. That was harder than any of us suspected it would be and more important to us eventually than any of us suspected it would be.

Again, probably not in order of time, I remember a rehearsal or a working session at Yvonne's loft. Trisha was there, testing out whether or not she wanted to be around. She had not been a member of the company. She was the first person invited to join us. I remember conversations with Yvonne about getting her to join. Anyway, Trisha suggested a format for that afternoon. It was something about a journey and took place around the perimeter of the space and at some point ended with Trisha lying on the floor and talking about a house and what was happening on the first floor and the second floor and the third floor and so on. I think then for some reason she was dead and we began to mourn her and I introduced some kind of spiritual singing and then crying and then turned the crying to laughing and we all did it or I led it while they clapped the rhythms. After that Trisha knew I could talk and sing and make noise and pushed the material in that direction. Steve and

Barbara had been dancing together at most performances and the direction seemed to be toward the kind of dancing that they did. We didn't speak much, mostly to give instructions or pass information. With Trisha pushing for verbal material and me more comfortable with verbal material than with Steve and Barbara's organic dance material, and more aggressive with that material, we slowly began moving in that direction. Barbara complained and said she couldn't do it. By the last years of the Grand Union Barbara was the one who always insisted on a mike for herself and in the last performances we had to rent a body mike for her.

At some point we were invited to participate in the American Dance Festival or something like that taking place in New York and we chose to perform at the Y on 14th Street. There had been a lot of talk about performing in the tunnel in the 40s on Park Avenue but it never came about. I was not interested in performing outdoors. There was also at that time, I believe, a performance at Prospect Park which I didn't attend — partly because it was outdoors and partly because something had happened to piss me off and I can't remember what except that when they came back from performing in the park they called me to come over to Trisha's house for a meeting to discuss it and we all kissed and made up. At those performances on 14th Street I asked the Grand Union to perform in the now completed version of *Sleep Walking* along with the people who had been working on it. I shared a program with the Grand Union. It was the first and last time that such an arrangement was attempted. They gave me a very difficult time during rehearsal and clearly did not want to do the work. Yvonne also did *Grand Union Dreams* during those performances and we all gave her a hard time during those rehearsals, not wanting to do that work either. I think after that we kept our personal work very separate from the Grand Union. Yvonne was beginning to withdraw. Steve was developing Contact Improvisation, which he had begun teaching during Grand Union residencies as his share of the teaching workload. I had nothing to teach so I began making more pieces during the residencies. We often did two Grand Union performances and several performances of our own work using students during residencies.

NL: I've always believed in improvisation as an art form (as well as a life form) — and here was a choice group wanting to perform in this way, also. The time was right. I had shaken my early teachings, now it was time to shake Merce Cunningham's technique. This was an opportunity I could not refuse.

Choreographic concerns? Set limits and boundaries, but they are only meant to be left. One has to be highly sensitive and skilled in spontaneous behavior as an art form — both intellectually and physically — for a more articulate work. There is a lot of junk around — some good. It is not always a blind act. This is what I learned from the Grand Union. I went in blind and good, and came out aware and better. It was the most intellectually stimulating combination of artists with whom I have ever had the pleasure (and difficulty) of working. The physicality was also obviously brilliant and thrilling but it was the minds between the lines — Who instigated this part? Who responded this way? And why? "Why did you do that? Why did you leave? What does that mean?" was the fascination of the thing for me.

SP: In terms of personalities and compositional adventures of the individuals in the group, there was promising electricity, chemistry, endurance, and daring.

In 1970–1971 I was walking and throwing my body off the ground.

YR: Some of the contradictions that pushed the Grand Union toward where it eventually went were present at the very beginning of *Continuous Project —Altered Daily.* There seemed to be an innate contradiction between — or we weren't aware of the difficulty of — improvising and talking casually, and performing material in a very professional, perfect way. I wanted to have not just a totally improvisatory look, or a totally unrehearsed look, or a totally casual behaviorist look. I wanted *CP-AD* to go from one thing to another, making clear that the things were very different. But the process of democratization and disintegration had already, I think, from the first moment, begun its inexorable progress and I just went with it. There was no way of my getting back in control. It would have meant that I had to demand that my material be done in a certain way. And that was one of the key psychological factors that started the momentum.

I could improvise by myself. I did it years before, in 1963. But with other people, I remember always feeling I was doing predictable things, obvious things. It wasn't the right atmosphere for me. I withdraw from that kind of competitiveness.

2. How did the Grand Union's process develop and change over the six years of its existence? How did Grand Union affect your own work?

BA: I don't know how the Grand Union's process developed and changed over six years because I moved to Massachusetts in 1972 after two years of working with them.

The greatest effect on my own work was confidence in performance and use of improvisation.

TB: When we began working together, only three or four members of the group knew how to improvise, the others did not and therefore relied on a dance in the Rainer repertory titled *Continuous Project — Altered Daily.* I did not learn that dance, it was my intention to deliver an unpremeditated performance each time. The blank slate approach. At Rutgers on November 6, 1970, my first performance with the Grand Union, I worked alone, unable and unwilling to participate in "known material." This self-imposed isolation caused extreme discomfort, there were so many of them throwing pillows in unison and so few of me looking awkward. Luckily, Steve stepped into my dilemma and asked, "Would you like to dance?" as he extended his arms in the traditional ballroom position of the male lead and we were off . . . for about five years.

There was no way to do something wrong in the Grand Union, improvisation includes error. In the beginning, we were raw and the form unformed and I never knew what was coming next. Steve Paxton arriving with a burning candle installed on his hat symbolizes that period for me. That and the night we verbally reduced a foam-rubber mattress to a kitchen sponge. I pressed for verbal expression (*Yellow Belly, Skymap*) because I liked the state of mind that that exposure produced. In time, all members became multi-voce and could reach cacaphonic heights at the drop of a hat. If you said "Drop a hat," everyone threw them in the air. Subversion was the norm. Everything was fair game except fair game. We were ribald, they were ribald. Too daring. In Tokyo, Steve and David brought a spotlight down to a pinpoint on my face and then hidden by darkness plied my features to music while using the spotlight to "get this." Hilarity pervaded and pervaded and pervaded. There were time lapses, empty moments, collusion with the audience, massive behavior displays, pop music, outlandish get-ups, eloquence, bone-bare confrontations, lack of concern, the women's dance, taking over, paying deference, exhilaration, poignancy, shooting one's wad, wadding up one's wad, making something out of nothing, melodramarooney, cheap shots, being oneself against all odds and dancing. Dancing and dancing and dancing.

BD: It seems to me now that each shift of process was directly related to any single mind's shift, as perception, intelligence rubbed against each other and sparked . . . *something*. The moves included: from ruler to democracy to anarchy to dissolution from practiced forms, to variations, to take-offs, to spoofs, to sarcasm to the unknown; from simple single image of self to multiphrenic kaleidoscope of personages shifting in and out of body; a child, growing up through adolescence to responsibility, to death.

Very deeply. Indeed, most of my understanding and subsequent development of disciplines of improvisation came from Grand Union's magic. A fascination with the mind and how it is manifested in art has become a constant. Delight with objects and their power.

DD: We made great strides developing a theatrical image-model of a possible ideal world, a viable heterogeneous social organism, one accommodating a wide range of individual rights, one knit together by a mutual search for appropriate levels of tacit contractual tolerance.

No influence.

DG: As for the process that was developing, it seems to me to have been a very passive process if one at all. Nancy and Dong were brought to a rehearsal to see if they might be able to work with us and it was never discussed whether or not they would stay and they did. Dong left after a while at his own choosing. To me he never seemed comfortable with the work we were doing but we never discussed it with him. Becky had been uncomfortable from the beginning and never adjusted . . . but also never went away. I think she kept waiting for the moment Yvonne would reassume authority and it never came. In small groups we discussed the difficulties we were having with some of the people but it was impossible ever to sit down as a large group and work things out. Everyone tread very carefully so as not to hurt anyone. Becky finally moved to Boston and relieved herself of having to quit or come to terms with us and the work. Even then, we continued the fiction that, Boston not being all that far, Becky could commute to perform and I think she even did once or twice at the beginning.

Part of the strange democracy we were functioning in produced the problem of whether or not we were all committed to any given performance. Steve clearly wanted a more flexible structure in which whoever was available or who wanted to would participate. I held out for compulsive performing. I am like that. Steve tested out his method by helping to schedule a series of performances and not showing for one of them. Instead he went to see a performance of Batya Zamir and came along afterward to Yvonne's place where we were holding a small postperformance talk. He seemed so reasonable and so guiltless (a state I was not too familiar with in myself) that his direction seemed the one we would take. Also logistics seemed to make that direction necessary. We were not always all available. Sometimes, I remember at 14th Street, the audience would be coming in and there would be two or three of us hiding in the kitchen wondering if anyone else would show up to perform and sometimes they didn't and we held the fort.

An important residency took place at the Walker Art Center. It was, as I recall, the first big paying job we had and also a blueprint for the way we treated residencies after that. We all made pieces of our own or showed old work of our own there and concluded with Grand Union performances. We also did one of the two lecture-demonstrations we ever did, there. We could never figure out what the difference was between a lecture-demonstration and a performance and avoided them. It was also the first place we had to wage an active battle against being known as the Rainer Company, about which Yvonne felt both guilty and uncomfortable, I think. Guilty because perhaps she had not made it clear strongly enough and uncomfortable because indeed the job never would have come about without her name and reputation. She also had an agent then who took 10 percent of the fee, which made everyone angry because he had done nothing to get the job and we had handled most of the preliminary work for it. We were not yet associated with Artservices. There was no Artservices. During that residency we established another pattern . . . that of seeming to be in support of each other's work. We attended each other's performances conspicuously at all ungodly hours and en masse. To all outward appearances we seemed to be a happily married group (people asked us if we had sex with each other) when in fact I believe we were continually uncomfortable with the work choices of each other (or some of us were, certainly) and the fact that we all seemed to stand for everything that each of us did. This got worse as time went by.

In the beginning performances we were very high at the end of an evening. We could barely leave each other when the performance and the after-performance meal were over. We often piled into one of our hotel rooms and on one bed and went step-by-step over the material that had occurred and a great deal of which we had missed by doing something else simultaneously. We would talk for hours and hours until dawn. One night Douglas had to go to bed because he was supposed to fly out early in the morning to perform the next night with another company. He left us and soon came back and threw himself on the bed in our midst and said he couldn't leave us. We felt that way too. In the beginning we often shared rooms (two people). At the end we all wanted singles.

It took quite a while for personal patterns of behavior to develop — in performance, that is. When they began to be visible some were interesting and some were irritating to me. Time made the interesting ones more interesting and so forth.

The material and the props and the music we used were becoming codified. We would hook onto a record and it would appear all through a series of performances. We would continuously invent new ways of dealing with the same music or the same prop. At the Dance Gallery we did seventeen performances. There was a large metal barre. We used it as a barre, as a gymnast's bar, as a tightrope, as a bar that served liquor and one night as a huge telephone standing on its side.

Who worked with whom in duets was becoming very clear. I worked rarely with Doug, consistently with Trisha, Steve, often with Barbara and less frequently with Nancy than reviews would have one believe. Doug was often a soloist, worked most frequently with Barbara or occasionally with Nancy or Steve. Also at the Dance Gallery we tried to incorporate guest performers more than at any other time. Simone Forti, Carmen Beuchat, Lisa Nelson, Yvonne at one performance. It never worked. We had turned into a closed shop somehow.

I think we did some of the most interesting theater I know about. I think the lack of clarity of the process and the fact that we did not have common goals helped to make it interesting for a while. Then, I think, that these same things helped to end it.

NL: Grand Union was fresh and amazing in the beginning. It just got a bit old. Individual interests were heading toward individual work. "It" had dwindled to five, though no less puzzling and amazing — even in Missoula, Montana, where an audience member gasped "You get paid for this?" as Steve offered him a chunk of grapefruit. "Home art" went home to do the next thing.

It hasn't affected my work, although the people and the way they move have. Every now and then, while working on something, as I suddenly find myself flying — prone — across the room, I have to say, "Oh no. This is not original. This is Paxton . . . splat." Or if I start talking about my work in this working repetitive way — while the work works its way to a working result, the result works in an identification of the worker with whom I worked while working in the working works of the Grand Union — here I go again "Oh no, this is not original — these origins come from the original orange — David Gordon." I don't think I have an original bone left. Maybe the timing is mine?

SP: The electricity (imagination and thought in leaps and bounds) became modified by the chemistry (a ceaseless, underlying, dim awareness of what is perceived as real about a relationship or person — a passive understanding of another person including an impression of what that person thinks of one).

Grand Union set out to explore uncharted territory and discovered they *were* that territory and began to discover it.

Grand Union set up a laboratory to examine improvisational phenomena and they saw backward through the microscope into each other's eyes: found they were the phenomena looking back, and the lab as well. Set out in a storm and found they were the storm *and* the set. Set out across a desert and found they crossed themselves. In the heat, took refuge in shade. Of course, they were the shade, and also, distant mountains beckoning through the heat.

There were encounters with savage beasts and private pools in which to swim after dust-filled afternoons.

There was jet lag, there was influenza, there were babysitters. There were lovers in the audience. There were past lovers, near future lovers.

Adventures of the mind ruled by appetites of the muscles. Antipathies influencing formal concerns, now for the better, now for the worse.

The vision of Contact Improvisation was in part provoked by the constant flowing forms we encountered when Grand Union was cooking.

Grand Union provided a constantly changing view of possibilities of form, performance, space, audience. A perception of flux.

Grand Union provided working time and space to focus on intriguing elements of the flux; provided stimuli, energy, money, and companionship in adventure.

YR: When there's no boss, there are new problems and these should be discussed as much as the material, but we didn't discuss them. I remember that at one performance — the benefit for the Committee to Defend the Black Panthers, at Loeb Student Center — we had learned a series of poses that we'd all contributed to — cheesecake, muscle man, dance photos, et cetera.

We were to do just that, in order, almost in unison. It was obvious to me that people had forgotten the sequence. Since we'd spent so much time learning it — and maybe I'd had a large part in making up this material — I got very mad in the performance and began a monologue about how if you learn something, you ought to do it! And then that became a funny Grand Union bit. Grand Union was the result of total social breakdown! Your chapter gives it much more dignity than it had.

There were never votes, or anything like democratic process. When we named the group Grand Union, I think I called a couple of people. Barbara liked it. Steve was some place or other. No one objected, or everybody liked it. A lot happened through individual conversations which then were relayed to other people. We didn't have meetings to decide on certain important issues.

I never did much in Grand Union performances. From the time that my material was let go of, I was never comfortable with the Grand Union. I'm not a good improviser. I don't easily get involved in these interactions, especially talking. I got involved in a lot of solo movement things, or movement with Steve.

The Grand Union was full of incompatibilities and hostilities; these were an essential part of its nature and I think that the ways in which they were worked out and acted out and enacted was one of the most fascinating things about the group.

3. Why did the Grand Union end?

BA: I can only guess why Grand Union ended, since I wasn't involved then. My guess is that each individual movement interest had formalized to the extent that it couldn't be realized in this type of group process. A certain continuity in work development was not possible with the Grand Union process because each performance created itself. Although a member might want to work on some special material, the direction of work and how each member dealt with that material varied each time they performed.

The Grand Union probably helped its members learn what they really wanted to work on.

TB: I left the Grand Union in 1976 to address full attention to my own choreography after many months of discomfort at not being able to edit or control the contents of a Grand Union concert. Not long after that, they all stopped.

BD: We collectively outgrew the need to stretch ourselves apart from the place we had been stuck to; we had no discipline to see us through the turmoil of heightened constant change; we each found things we really wanted to do and began questioning the indulgence of the form we had created; we were more and more separated by time and space; we came to know each other, perhaps too well; we were in danger of having a solidified notion of what it was that we did, which made it awful when we didn't do it; any and all of the above fit.

The magic that was present is still with me and escapes an easy pigeonhole as all good magic does. I learned, past all other educations, things I had not known and continue to go on from that place with my own personal journey. There is genuineness and honesty in what we were up to that was unmistakable for those who watched and made whatever we did unique and desirable to follow, somehow. It is a bigger thing than performance and extends deeply into the lives of people who open to it. It requires a discipline of awareness and intelligence as the forces of spontaneous *anything* are very powerful and often the world reacts directly to what you have just done.

DD: Enlightenment
1970 — sudden
1976 — gradual
War over
Dick out
Those who needed to view us
had done so
Two members experienced severe drops
in their levels of tacit contractual
tolerance

DG: More and more we were involved with our own work and more importantly our own lifestyles. We couldn't or wouldn't work together in between performances. When we came together to perform we were more and more strangers depending upon past experiences to pull it all together. Worse yet, some of the things we were doing in performance were becoming more and more unpalatable to each other. I clearly made Barbara very uncomfortable. She was searching for a serenity in performance and I was offering vulgarity. I would tear into the preciousness of her material. One night back at the Walker I made Steve very angry and we spent the whole evening after the performance discussing it, he and I, and I thought I could really not work with these people anymore because they were putting constraints on my performance behavior and I thought of quietly going to the airport and waiting for the first plane in the morning back to New York. We were due to leave for Chicago to perform at MoMing the next day and I decided it was too dramatic an action and instead I would go and give very quiet performances making no active decisions about material during the performances but following anything any one set up or staying quietly alone. It was Barbara who drew me out about five minutes into the performance and turned me or helped me turn myself back into the overactive blithering idiot that so afforded me the pleasure that for me was inherent in the Grand Union.

More and more, however, there were postperformance recriminations. They took different forms. We would go off in splinter groups. Somewhere in California Doug and I went to a local thrift shop to buy some records to use in these performances. We came back with the sort of eclectic junk we always seemed to prefer at the cheapest prices for as many as we could carry. Barbara was furious after the performance because we had used music she could no longer tolerate.

We none of us seemed capable of setting up any positive way of dealing with problems . . . only complaints about things after the fact. Occasionally, as also happened in California, an accidental afternoon's social sitting and talking in someone's room brought out a serious conversation about the difficulties we were personally experiencing but no actual confrontation could take place because we were performing that evening and on tour with each other and had to keep a peaceful front.

More and more, however, at the end of a series of performances I began to contemplate leaving the Grand Union. Trisha was talking about leaving and not showing for certain performances and not fully participating in those that she was at. She was a crucial person in the Grand Union for me. My relationship with Barbara was strained. In Japan I really blew up at her at a personal warm-up session in front of Trisha's company and the rest of the Grand Union. In the final New York performances I blew up at her in performance. Nancy was getting on my nerves more and more. Her performance persona, which never changed, was as irritating as anything I could imagine. The popularity of that persona was more irritating than it was . . . and the fact that we were continuously being linked together by people who wrote about the Grand Union made me angry. Although there could be and still were moments in performance that surpassed anything I could have thought of on my own they were becoming rarer.

I met privately with Steve. I said that I could not see the Grand Union changing either personnel or material. I said that I wanted out or I thought I did although I still couldn't just leave. Steve, who was better at taking the bull by the horns than I said why didn't we make the upcoming California tour and New York performances the last and disband. Trisha was gone by that time. We called the others and put it to them and they agreed. I was relieved and uncomfortable, both. The Grand Union had been my active fantasy world for a lot of years and I didn't know how I would get along without it. Yet, there was an enormous sense of relief at not having to come in contact at all with some of its members for a while, or never again.

The last G.U. performances were in Missoula, Montana. The last night we were all staying in a motel near the theater. We had separate rooms. I was watching a Fred Astaire and Eleanor Powell film on T.V. in my room prior to performance. They all came to my room to get me to go with them to the theater. In retrospect it was a kind of solidarity that I foolishly and obstinately refused to respond to. I was glad it was all over and I said that I would stay and watch the film some more and be along later. As soon as they were gone I felt uncomfortable about what I had done. I packed my bag and headed for the theater. I went up to the dressing room. They were all on the stage already. I very slowly began to make up and dress. I put on very elaborate Japanese make-up with two pairs of eyelashes on each eye and an elaborate white and blue costume, kimono, something tied around my head . . . my armor. Still, I could not quite get myself to go downstairs to the stage. I looked around and saw a plastic-covered window frame as tall as I am. I picked it up and carried it downstairs and stood in the wings for a minute sizing up what was going on on stage. Barbara was moving around quietly by herself. Doug had a black dress form and he was trying to get the audience to give it a first name. Steve, I think, was working with Nancy at stage left. I moved on stage, holding the plastic screen in front of me. I was not clearly visible behind it. I moved along the back of the stage to center and sat down propping the screen at an angle against the wall and sitting under it invisible to the audience. Doug had gotten the audience to name the figure Elizabeth. He was searching for a second name now. It was a difficult battle. They were not very responsive. There were not very many of them out there. Steve wandered over and suggested to Doug that a good second name was Attila the Hun . . . Elizabeth Attila the Hun. Nancy said, in her quavery voice, that she wished that her name was Elizabeth Attila the Hun. At that moment I stood up, pushing the door down in front of me so that I could walk forward on it and said "Hi, Hun, I'm home" and I was in . . . like jump rope, waiting for the perfect time to jump in without tripping on the rope . . . I was in. And I knew then, and I know even better now that that was what it was all about and that it could never have happened any other way and it is the essence of the Grand Union that those openings occurred and that someone took them or in not taking them, that not taking them became the material and if there was no material, then no material became the material.

I try to remember those things when I am making my own work now.

NL: Like any 250-watt bulb — it burned out.

SP: It became a hibit.

YR: To be taxed to the limits of one's inventiveness creates terrible pressure. That may be one reason Grand Union ended . . . there was just too much pressure.

Chronology

Selected Bibliography

Notes

Index

Chronology

1960

Forti: *See–Saw; Rollers*

Gordon: *Mama Goes Where Papa Goes*

1961

Forti: Five Dance Constructions and Some Other Things: *Slant Board, Huddle, Hangers, Platforms, Accompaniment for La Monte's "2 sounds" and La Monte's "2 sounds," From Instructions, Censor, Herding;* Solo Improvisation; Structured Improvisations with Trisha Brown and Dick Levine

Rainer: *Three Satie Spoons; The Bells*

Paxton: *Proxy*

Brown: Structured Improvisations with Simone Forti and Dick Levine

1962

Rainer: *Satie for Two; Three Seascapes; Grass; Divertissement; Dance for 3 People and 6 Arms; Ordinary Dance*

Paxton: *Transit*

Brown: *Trillium*

Gordon: *Mannequin Dance; Helen's Dance*

Hay: *Rain Fur; 5 Things; Rafladan* (with Alex Hay and Charles Rotmil)

1963

Rainer: *We Shall Run; Word Words* (with Steve Paxton); *Terrain; Person Dance; Room Service* (with Charles Ross); *Shorter End of a Small Piece*

Paxton: *English; Word Words* (with Yvonne Rainer); *Left Hand David Hayes; Music for Word Words; Afternoon*

Brown: *2 Improvisations on the Nuclei for Simone by Jackson MacLow; Improvisations on a Chicken Coop Roof; Falling Solo with Singing; Lightfall; Part of a Target*

Gordon: *Random Breakfast; Honey Sweetie Dust Dance*

Hay: *City Dance; All Day Dance; Elephant Footprints in the Cheesecake—Walk: For Shirley* (with Fred Herko); *Would They or Wouldn't They?*

Childs: *Pastime; Three Piece; Minus Auditorium Equipment and Furnishings; Egg Deal*

Monk: *Troubadour Songs; Resonance; Me*

1964

Rainer: *At My Body's House; Dialogues; Some Thoughts on Improvisation; Part of a Sextet; Incidents* (with Larry Loonin); *Part of a Sextet no. 2 (Rope Duet)*

Paxton: *Flat; First; title lost tokyo; Jag ville görna telefonera*

Brown: *Target; Rulegame 5*

Gordon: *Silver Pieces* (aka *Fragments)*

Hay: *All Day Dance for Two; Three Here; Victory 14; They Will*

Childs: *Cancellation Sample; Carnation; Street Dance; Model*

Monk: *Timestop; Diploid; Break*

King: *cup/saucer/two dancers/radio*

1965

Rainer: *Parts of Some Sextets; New Untitled Partially Improvised Solo with Pink T-Shirt, Blue Bloomers, Red Ball, and Bach's Toccata and Fugue in D Minor* (later called *Untitled Solo*)

Paxton: *Section of a New Unfinished Work; The Deposits*

Brown: *Motor; Homemade*

Hay: *Hill*

Childs: *Geranium; Museum Piece; Screen; Agriculture*

Monk: *Cartoon; The Beach; Relâche; Radar; Blackboard*

King: *Spectacular; Self-Portrait: Dedicated to the Memory of John Fitzgerald Kennedy*

1966

Rainer: *The Mind is a Muscle, Part 1* (later called *Trio A*); *The Mind is a Muscle* (first version); *Carriage Discreteness*

Paxton: *Section of a New Unfinished Work* (augmented); Improvisation with Trisha Brown; *A.A.; Earth Interior; Physical Things*

Brown: *A String* (including *Motor, Homemade,* and *Inside*); Improvisation with Steve Paxton

Gordon: *Walks and Digressions*

Hay: *No. 3; Serious Duet; Rise; Solo*

Childs: *Vehicle*

Monk: *Portable; Duet with Cat's Scream and Locomotive; 16 Millimeter Earrings*

King: *m-o-o-n-b-r-a-i-nwithSuperLecture; Blow-Out; Camouflage*

1967

Forti: *Face Tunes; Cloths; Song*

Rainer: *Convalescent Dance*

Paxton: *Satisfyin Lover; Love Songs; the sizes; The Atlantic; Somebody Else; Some Notes on Performance Walkin' There* (later called *Audience Performance #1*)

Brown: *Skunk Cabbage, Salt Grass, and Waders; Medicine Dance*

Hay: *Flyer; Group I*

Monk: *Blueprint/Overload*

King: *Print-Out: (CELE((CERE))-BRATIONS: PROBElems & SOULutions for the dyEYEing: KING)*

1968

Forti: *Book; Bottom; Fallers; Sleepwalkers; Throat Dance*

Rainer: *Untitled Work for 40 People; The Mind is a Muscle* (final version); *Performance Demonstration no. 1; North East Passing; Body and Snot; Two Trios*

Paxton: *State; Untitled Lecture; Beautiful Lecture; Audience Performance #1; Audience Performance #2; Salt Lake City Deaths*

Brown: *Planes; Snapshots; Falling Duet; Ballet; Dance with the Duck's Head*

Hay: *Group II; Ten*

Childs: *Untitled Trio*

Monk: *Co-op*

King: *A Show; Being in Perpetual Motion*

1969

Rainer: *Rose Fractions; Performance Fractions for the West Coast; Connecticut Composite*

Paxton: *Smiling; Lie Down; Pre-history*

Brown: *Yellowbelly; Skymap; Man Walking Down the Side of the Building; Clothes Pipe, the Floor of the Forest, and Other Miracles, Dance for a Dirty Room, Everybody's Grandmother's Bed, the Costume, Adam Says Checkered Sea; Leaning Duets*

Hay: *Half-Time; 20 Permutations of 2 Sets of 3 Equal Parts in a Linear Pattern; Deborah Hay with a Large Group Outdoors; 26 Variations on 8 Activities for 13 People and Beginning and Ending; Whale Piece II; A Dance to Be Seen Several Times on One Concert*

Monk: *Title: Title; Untidal: Movement Period; Tour: Dedicated to Dinosaurs; Tour 2: Barbershop; Juice; Tour 4: Lounge*

King: *exTRAVEL(ala)ganza; Conundrum; Phenomenology of Movement*

1970

Rainer: *Continuous Project—Altered Daily; WAR;* Judson Flag Show *(Trio A);* Street Protest *(M-Walk)*

Paxton: *With Rachel, Suzi, Jeff, Steve & Lincoln; Roman Newspaper Phrase; Niagara Falls At; Intravenous Lecture*

Brown: *The Stream*

Hay: *Deborah Hay and a Large Group of People from Hartford; 20-Minute Piece*

Monk: *Tour 5: Glass; Tour 6: Organ; Tour 7: Factory; Needle-Brain Lloyd and the Systems Kid; Raw Recital*

King: *Secret Cellar; Carrier Pigeon; Christmas Celebration*

Grand Union: Improvisational Performances

1971

Forti: *Buzzing; Illuminations* (later known as *Sheila in Progress,*) with Charlemagne Palestine, ongoing until 1975

Rainer: *Grand Union Dreams; Numerous Frames*

Paxton: *St. Vincent's Hospital At; Collaboration with Wintersoldier*

Brown: *Walking on the Wall; Leaning Duets II; Falling Duet II; Rummage Sale and the Floor of the Forest; Accumulation; Roof Piece*

Gordon: *Sleepwalking*

Hay: *Deborah Hay and the Farm*

Monk: *Tour 8: Castle; Vessel; Key* (record album)

King: *INADMISSLEABLE EVIDENTDANCE; Perpetual Motion for the Great Lady; Christmas Celebration*

Dunn: *One Thing Leads to Another* (with Sara Rudner); *Dancing Here* (with Pat Catterson)

Grand Union: Improvisational Performances, including benefit for the Committee to Defend the Black Panthers

1972

Rainer: *In the College; Performance; Lives of Performers* (film); *Inner Appearances*

Paxton: *Magnesium* (Contact Improvisation); *Benn Mutual* (with Nita Little, Contact Improvisation); Contact Improvisation (ongoing)

Brown: *Accumulation* (55″ version); *Primary Accumulation; Theme and Variation*

Gordon: *Liberty; The Matter* (first version); *The Matter* (second version, including "Oh Yes," "Men's Dance," "One Part," and "Mannequin 1962"); *Co-Incidents* (with Douglas Dunn)

Hay: *Wedding Dance for Sandy and Greg;* Circle Dances (ongoing)

Monk: *Education of the Girlchild* (Part I); *Black Room; Paris* (with Ping Chong)

King: *Simultimeless Action* (containing "The Dansing Jewel" and "The Great Void"); *Solstice Event; Christmas Event*

Dunn: *Co-Incidents* (with David Gordon); *Eight Lanes, Four Approaches* (with Sara Rudner); *Mayonnaise* (film, with Charles Atlas); *Pas de Two* (with Sheela Raj)

Grand Union: Improvisational Performances

1973

Rainer: *This is the story of a woman who . . .*

Paxton: *Dancing* (ongoing); *Air*

Brown: *Woman Walking Down a Ladder; Accumulating Pieces; Group Accumulation I; Group Primary Accumulation; Roof Piece II; Group Accumulation II; Announcement; Spanish Dance; Structured Pieces I: Sticks* (first version), *Scallops, Discs, Bug, Mistitled (5″ Clacker), Leaning Trio, Falling Duets, Circles; Accumulation with Talking*

Childs: *Untitled Trio* (revised); *Calico Mingling; Particular Reel; Checkered Drift*

Monk: *Education of the Girlchild* (final version); *Our Lady of Late*

King: *Metagexis; Patrick's Dansing Dances; Mr. Pontease Tyak; INADMISSLEABLE EVIDENTDANCE* (revised)

Dunn: *Nevada; Orange My Darling Lime; Time Out*

Grand Union: Improvisational Performances

1974

Forti: *The Zero; Crawling*

Rainer: *Film About a Woman Who . . .* (film); *Kristina (for a . . . novella)*

Paxton: *With David Moss* (ongoing); *Roming (Aroma)*

Brown: *Figure 8; Split Solo; Drift; Spiral; Pamplona Stones; Structured Pieces II: Spanish Dance, Leaning Duets I & II, Mistitled (5" Clacker), Discs, Falling Duet, Sticks* (3 versions), *Tracing*

Gordon: *Spilled Milk; Spilled Milk Variations; Chair, Alternatives 1 through 5; One Act Play*

Monk: *Paris/Chacon* (with Ping Chong); *Our Lady of Late* (record album)

King: *Praxiomatics (The Practice Room); Time Capsule; High Noon (A Portrait–Play of Friedrich Nietzsche); The Telaxic Synapsulator*

Dunn: *Four for Nothing; 101; Octopus; 101* (film, with Amy Greenfield)

Grand Union: Improvisational Performances

1975

Forti: *Untitled; Fan Dance; Four Story; Big Room* (later known as *Home Base*), with Peter Van Riper, ongoing until 1980); *Red Green*

Brown: *Locus; Structured Pieces III: Leaning Duets II, Clump; Pyramid*

Gordon: *Times Four*

Childs: *Reclining Rondo; Congeries on Edges for 20 Obliques; Duplicate Suite*

Monk: *Small Scroll; Roots; Plateau #1; Anthology* (music for voice and piano)

King: *The Ultimate Exposé; Battery* (Bicentennial dance events celebrating Susanne K. Langer)

Dunn: *part one part two* (with David Woodberry); *Gestures in Red*

Grand Union: Improvisational Performances

1976

Forti: *Planet*

Rainer: *Kristina Talking Pictures* (film)

Paxton: *Scribe*

Brown: *Solo Olos; Structured Pieces IV:* two reversals of *Solo Olos* with caller; *Duetude; Line Up*

Hay: *Solos (ongoing)*

Childs: *Transverse Exchanges; Radial Courses; Mix Detail; Cross Words; Figure Eights; Solo: Character on Three Diagonals* (from *Einstein on the Beach* by Robert Wilson and Philip Glass)

Monk: *Quarry; Venice/Milan* (with Ping Chong); *Plateau #2*

King: *Battery* (Part 3); *RAdeoA.C.tiv(ID)ty* (ongoing 1976–78)

Dunn: *Lazy Madge* (ongoing); *Early and Late*

Grand Union: Improvisational Performances and Disbandment

1977

Paxton: *Backwater: Twosome* (with David Moss, ongoing)

Brown: *Line Up* (final version)

Gordon: *Wordsworth and the motor + Times Four*

Hay: *The Grand Dance* (ongoing)

Childs: *Plaza; Interior Drama; Melody Excerpt*

Monk: *Plateau #3; Tablet* (music); *House of Stills; Quarry* (film)
King: *Video Dances; Labyrinth*
Dunn: *Celeste; Solo Film and Dance; Relief*

1978
Forti: *Phoenix; Garden; Fountain Huddle; Lake Bass*
Paxton: *Solos; The Reading*[3]
Brown: *Splang; Water Motor*
Gordon: *Not Necessarily Recognizable Objectives; What Happened*
Childs: *Katema; Work in Progress with Philip Glass*
Monk: *Plateau Series; Recent Ruins* (in progress)
King: *RAdeoA.C.tiv(ID)ty* (final version); *Dance S(p)ell* with *Telaxic Synapsulator; Wor(l)d (T)raid* (in progress); *The Run–On Dance; WORD RAID* (in progress)
Dunn: *Rille; Coquina; Palm*

1979
Forti: *Proceeding; Estuary; Umi Aui Owe*
Paxton: *PA RT* (with Lisa Nelson); *Come to Pass; Going On and Going On Two*
Brown: *Accumulation with Talking Plus Water Motor; Glacial Decoy; Decoy*
Gordon: *An Audience with the Pope, or This Is Where I Came In; The Matter (plus and minus); Close Up; Song and Dance; Broom; Solo Score; Lifting Duet*
Childs: *Dance*
Monk: *Recent Ruins; Dolmen Music; Ellis Island* (film; short version)
King: *Wor(l)d (T)raid* (premiere); *WORD RAID*
Dunn: *Foot Rules; Echo* (solo version); *Relief*

1980
Rainer: *Journeys from Berlin/1971* (film)
Paxton: *Raft: Freelance Dance* (with Danny Lepkoff, Lisa Nelson, Nancy Stark Smith, Christina Svane)
Brown: *Opal Loop/Cloud Installation #72503*
Gordon: *By Two; Untitled Solo* (as a trio); *Dorothy and Eileen;* untitled solo with unlimited backup group; *Double Identity Part One; Soft Broil*
Hay: *HEAVEN/below; The Genius of the Heart; Leaving the House; Heavily Laden Fruit*
King: *Blue Mountain Pass; Stand–Up Comedian; Space City; GENERATOR* (with David Moss)
Dunn: *Suite de Suite; Echo* (group version); *Pulcinella*

1981
Forti: *Jackdaw Songs; Bird Bath; Moves*
Paxton: *Bound;* choreography for *Titus Groan* (Peter Huston and Gordon Jones); performances with Freelance Dance
Brown: *Son of Gone Fishin'*

Gordon: *Pas et Par; Big Eyes* (Grote Ogen); *Phone Call; Double Identity Part Two; Profile; Counter Revolution*

Hay: *Grace; Shaking Awake the Sleeping Child*

Childs: *Mad Rush; Relative Calm*

Monk: *Specimen Days: A Civil War Opera; Dolmen Music* (record); *Turtle Dreams (Waltz); Ellis Island* (film; 30 minute version)

King: *The PHI Project; Dancing Words; SPACE CITY* (film, with Andrew Horn and Robyn Brentano); *Casablanca; Straw Boss*

Dunn: *Cycles; Walking Back; Holds; Chateauvallonesque; Skid; View; Hitch*

1982

Forti: *Door Studies; 222* (with Steve Paxton)

Paxton: *Temporary I; Temporary II; Temporary III; 222* (with Simone Forti)

Gordon: *T.V. Reel; 10 Minute T.V.* (video); *Trying Times; Big Eyes II*

Hay: *Tribute to Growth; Promenade; Three Meditations* (with Pauline Oliveros)

Childs: *Formal Abandon* (Parts I and II)

Monk: *View #1;* music for *A.M./A.M.* (Ping Chong); *Paris* (video, with Ping Chong)

King: *Bridge; COMPLETE ELECTRIC DISCHARGE; S–C–A–N; DANCE MOTOR; In the Labyrinth*

Dunn: *Game Tree; Secret of the Waterfall* (video version)

1983

Forti: *Spring; Board Game; Course*

Paxton: Improvisations with Simone Forti and Nancy Stark Smith; *Oono Home Permanent; Memoirs of My Nervous Illness* (with Anne Kilcoyne); produced Contact at 10th and 2nd (with Cynthia Hedstrom)

Brown: *Set and Reset*

Gordon: *Passing Through; Limited Partnership;* movement for *The Photographer* (JoAnne Akalaitis, Robert Coe, and Philip Glass); *Framework* (1983–84); *Short Order; Passing Sentence; Changing Horses*

Hay: *The Well; The Light of the Body; The Movement of Light; Midnight Well Water*

Childs: *Available Light; Formal Abandon* (Part III)

Monk: *Turtle Dreams: Cabaret; Turtle Dreams* (record); *Turtle Dreams (Waltz)* (video); *Mermaid Adventures* (film); *The Games* (with Ping Chong)

King: *Annexialics; Flextime; Lucy Alliteration; SCREAM AT ME TOMORROW*

Dunn: *Secret of the Waterfall; Second Mesa*

1984

Forti: *full moves; Face*

Paxton: *1984* (with Anne Kilcoyne); *Improvisation*

Gordon: *Negotiable Bonds; Field Study; Field, Chair and Mountain; A Plain Romance Explained; My Folks* (1984–85)

Hay: *A Performance in Four Parts;* Solo with B.L. Lacerta

Childs: *Cascade; Outline; Premier Orage; Field Dances* for *Einstein on the Beach* (Philip Glass and Robert Wilson)

Monk: "Graduation Song" for *A Race* (Ping Chong); *City Songs* (music)
King: *COMPLETE ELECTRIC DISCHARGE II* (for Nikola Tesla); *Moose (On the Loose); STRUNG-OUT NEWSCASTERS*
Dunn: *Elbow Room; Pulcinella: Ballet in One Act; 1st Rotation; Futurities; 2nd Rotation*

1985
Forti: *Full Moves; Jamberoo Dawn*
Rainer: *The Man Who Envied Women* (film)
Paxton: *Excerpt; Improvisation to CBC radio news and interviews; Ave Nue; Ankle On*
Brown: *Lateral Pass*
Gordon: *Piano Movers; Offenbach Suite*
Hay: *Tasting the Blaze; Entertainment; A Love Song Study*
Monk: *Book of Days* (in progress); "Window Song" for *Nosferatu* (Ping Chong)
King: *PLANET X; CRITICAL PATH* (for R. Buckminster Fuller)
Dunn: *Jig Jag; 3rd Rotation*

Selected Bibliography

General and Background

Ballet Review vol. 1, no. 6 (1967), Judson Issue.
Banes, Sally. *Democracy's Body: Judson Dance Theater 1962–1964*. Ann Arbor: UMI Research Press, 1983.
Banes, Sally, and Noël Carroll. "Cunningham and Duchamp." *Ballet Review* vol. 11, no. 2 (1983): 73–79.
Battcock, Gregory, ed. *The New Art*. New York: E. P. Dutton, 1966.
———, ed. *Minimal Art*. New York: E. P. Dutton, 1968.
Cage, John. *Silence*. Middletown, Conn.: Wesleyan University Press, 1961.
———. *A Year from Monday*. Middletown, Conn.: Wesleyan University Press, 1967.
Carroll, Noël. "The Return of the Repressed: The Re–Emergence of Expression in Contemporary American Dance." *Dance Theatre Journal* vol. 2 no. 1 [1984]: 16–19, 27.
———. "Post–Modern Dance and Expression." In *Philosophical Essays in Dance*, edited by Gordon Fancher and Gerald Myers. Brooklyn: Dance Horizons, 1981, pp. 95–104.
Carroll, Noël, and Sally Banes. "Working and Dancing: A Response to Monroe Beardsley's 'What Is Going On in a Dance?' " *Dance Research Journal* 15/1 (Fall 1982): 37–41.
Cohen, Selma Jeanne. "Avant–Garde Choreography." *Criticism* 3 (Winter 1961): 16–35. Reprinted in three parts in *Dance Magazine* 36 (June 1962): 22–24, 57; (July 1962): 29–31, 58; (August 1962): 45, 54–56.
Copeland, Roger. "Postmodern Dance and the Repudiation of Primitivism," *Partisan Review* 50 (1983): 101–121.
———. "Postmodern Dance/Postmodern Architecture/Postmodernism." *Performing Arts Journal* 19 (1983): 27–43.
Croce, Arlene. *Afterimages*. New York: Alfred Knopf, 1977.
Cunningham, Merce. *Changes: Notes on Choreography*. Edited by Frances Starr. New York: Something Else Press, 1968.
Denby, Edwin. *Dancers, Buildings, and People in the Streets*. New York: Horizon, 1965.
———. *Looking at the Dance*. New York: Horizon, 1968.
Erdman, Jean, and Trisha Brown, Bill Dixon, Judith Dunn, Deborah Hay, Meredith Monk, Constance Poster, and Yvonne Rainer. "Conversation in Manhattan." *Impulse* (1967, The Dancer's Environment): 57–64.
Festival International de Nouvelle Danse catalogue. Montreal: Parachute, 1985.

Foster, Hal, ed. *The Anti-Aesthetic: Essays on Postmodern Culture*. Port Townsend, WA: Bay Press, 1983.
Howell, John. "No to Homogenized Dancing." *Performing Arts Journal* 2 (Fall 1977): 3–12.
Jackson, George. "Naked in Its Native Beauty." *Dance Magazine* 38 (April 1964): 32–37.
Jameson, Frederic. "Postmodernism, or the Cultural Logic of Late Capitalism." *New Left Review* 146 (1984): 53–92.
Jencks, Charles. *The Language of Post-Modern Architecture*. New York: Rizzoli, 1977.
Johnston, Jill. *Marmalade Me*. New York: E. P. Dutton, 1971.
______. "The New American Modern Dance." In *The New American Arts*, edited by Richard Kostelanetz, pp. 162–193. New York: Collier Books, 1967.
______. "Which Way the Avant-Garde?" *New York Times*, August 11, 1968, p. II–24. Reprinted in *Marmalade Me*, pp. 94–97.
Jowitt, Deborah. *Dance Beat: Selected Views and Reviews, 1967–1976*. New York: Marcel Dekker, 1977.
______. *The Dance in Mind*. Boston: David R. Godine, 1985.
______. "The Return of Drama," *Dance Theatre Journal* Vol. 2 no. 2 [1984]: 28–31.
Judson Dance Theater: 1962–1966. Exhibition catalogue. Bennington, VT: Bennington College Judson Project, 1981.
Kendall, Elizabeth. *Where She Danced: The Birth of American Art Dance*. New York: Alfred A. Knopf, 1979. Reprint ed., Berkeley: University of California Press, 1984.
Kirby, Michael. *Happenings*. New York: E. P. Dutton, 1966.
______. *The Art of Time*. New York: E. P. Dutton, 1969.
Kirstein, Lincoln. *Dance: A Short History of Classic Theatrical Dancing*. New York: G. P. Putnam's Sons, 1935; Reprint. Dance Horizons, 1969.
Klosty, James, ed. *Merce Cunningham*. New York: E. P. Dutton, 1975.
Kostelanetz, Richard. "Metamorphosis in Modern Dance." *Dance Scope* 5 (Fall 1970): 6–21.
______. *The Theatre of Mixed Means*. New York: The Dial Press, 1968.
______, ed. *The New American Arts*. New York: Collier Books, 1967.
Livet, Anne, ed. *Contemporary Dance*. New York: Abbeville Press, 1978.
Lyotard, Jean-François. *The Postmodern Condition: A Report on Knowledge*. Minneapolis: University of Minnesota Press, 1984.
McDonagh, Don. *The Complete Book of Modern Dance*. Garden City, NY: Doubleday, 1976.
______. *The Rise & Fall & Rise of Modern Dance*. New York: New American Library, 1971.
New Dance USA. Festival catalogue. Minneapolis: Walker Art Center, 1981.
Newman, Charles. *The Post-Modern Aura: The Act of Fiction in an Age of Inflation*. Evanston: Northwestern University Press, 1985.
Schneemann, Carolee. *More Than Meat Joy*. New Paltz, NY: Documentext, 1979.
Shelton, Suzanne. *Divine Dancer: A Biography of Ruth St. Denis*. Garden City, NY: Doubleday, 1981.
Siegel, Marcia B. *At the Vanishing Point*. New York: Saturday Review Press, 1973.
______. *Watching the Dance Go By*. Boston: Houghton Mifflin, 1977.
______. *The Shapes of Change: Images of American Dance*. Boston: Houghton Mifflin, 1979. Reprint ed., Berkeley: University of California Press, 1985.
Sohm, H. *Happening and Fluxus*. Cologne: Koeinischer Kunstverein, 1970.
Tomkins, Calvin. *The Bride and the Bachelors*. New York: Viking Press, 1968.
Tomkins, Calvin. *Off the Wall: Robert Rauschenberg and the Art World of Our Time*. Garden City, NY: Doubleday, 1980.
Trachtenberg, Stanley, ed. *The Postmodern Moment*. Westport, CT: Greenwood Press, 1986.

Periodicals

Alive
Artforum
Avalanche
Ballet Review
Ballett International
Contact Quarterly (formerly *Contact Newsletter)*
Dance Chronicle
Dance Magazine
Dance Perspectives
Dance Scope
The Drama Review (formerly *Tulane Drama Review)*
East Village Eye
Eddy
Hudson Review
Live
New Dance
New York Magazine
Performing Arts Journal
Soho Weekly News
Village Voice

Simone Forti

Works by Simone Forti

Forti, Simone. *Angel*. New York: By the Author, 1978.

______. "Bicycles." *Dance Scope* 13 (Fall 1978): 44–51.

______. "A Chamber Dance Concert Translated." *The Drama Review 19* (T–65, March 1975): 37–39.

______. "Dancing at the Fence." *Avalanche* (December 1974): 20–23.

______. "5 pieces." In *An Anthology,* edited by La Monte Young and Jackson MacLow, unpaged. New York: Something Else Press, 1963; Reprint. Cologne: Heiner Friedrich, 1970.

______. *Handbook in Motion*. Halifax: Press of the Nova Scotia College of Art and Design; New York: New York University Press, 1974.

______. [Performance Score.] *Women's Work,* edited by Alison Knowles and Anna Lockwood, unpaged. New York: By the Authors, 1975.

______. "Theater and Engineering—An Experiment." *Artforum 5* (February 1967): 26–30.

Liss, Carla, with Joan Jonas and Simone Forti. "Show Me Your Dances . . ." *Art and Artists* 8 (October 1973): 14–21.

Sorell, Walter, with drawings by Sorell, Vaslav Nijinsky, Mary Wigman, Alwin Nikolais, Simone Forti, Frances Alenikoff, and Carolee Schneemann. "Notes on Dancing, Writing and Painting." *Dance Scope 9* (Spring/Summer 1975): 41–49.

Works about Simone Forti

Celant, Germano. "Simone Forti." *Parachute* 11 (Summer 1978): 10–13.

Howell, John. "Performance." *Art in America* 63 (May–June 1975): 18–19.

Johnston, Jill. "Seated Forever." *Village Voice,* November 23, 1967, p. 20.

McDonagh, Don. "Simone Forti." *The Complete Guide to Modern Dance,* pp. 376–378. New York: Doubleday, 1976.

Mekas, Jonas. "Movie Journal." *Village Voice,* December 7, 1967, p. 41.
Morris, Robert. "Notes on Dance." *Tulane Drama Review* 10 (Winter 1965): 179–186.

Yvonne Rainer

Works by Yvonne Rainer

Rainer, Yvonne. "Don't Give the Game Away." *Arts* 41 (April 1967): 44–45.

______. "The Dwarf Syndrome." In *The Dance Has Many Faces,* 2nd ed., edited by Walter Sorell, pp. 244–245. New York: Columbia University Press, 1966.

______. "Film about a Woman Who . . ." *October* 2 (Summer 1976): 39–67.

______. "From an Indian Journal." *The Drama Review* 15 (T–50, Spring 1971): 132–138. Reprinted in Yvonne Rainer, *Work 1961–73,* pp. 173–188. Halifax: The Press of the Nova Scotia College of Art and Design; New York: New York University Press, 1974.

______. "Kristina (For a . . . Opera): Filmscript." *Interfunktionen* no. 12 (1975): 13–47.

______. "Notes on Deborah Hay." *Ikon* (February 1967).

______. "A Quasi Survey of Some 'Minimalist' Tendencies in the Quantitatively Minimal Dance Activity Midst the Plethora, or an Analysis of *Trio A.*" In *Minimal Art,* edited by Gregory Battcock, pp. 263–273. New York: E. P. Dutton, 1968. Reprinted in *Work,* pp. 63–69.

______. "Some Retrospective Notes on a Dance for 10 People and 12 Mattresses Called 'Parts of Some Sextets' Performed at the Wadsworth Atheneum, Hartford, Connecticut, and Judson Memorial Church, New York, in March 1965." *Tulane Drama Review* 10 (Winter 1965): 168–178. Reprinted in *Work,* pp. 45–51.

______. *Work 1961–73.* Halifax: The Press of the Nova Scotia College of Art and Design; New York: New York University Press, 1974.

Rainer, Yvonne, with Willoughby Sharp and Liza Béar. "The Performer as a Persona: An Interview with Yvonne Rainer." *Avalanche* no. 5 (Summer 1972): 46–59.

Rainer, Yvonne, with William Coco and A. J. Gunawardana. "Responses to India: An Interview with Yvonne Rainer." *The Drama Review* 15 (T–50, Spring 1971): 139–142.

Rainer, Yvonne, with Camera Obscura Collective. "Yvonne Rainer: Interview." *Camera Obscura* 1 (1976): 76–96.

Rainer, Yvonne, with Ann Halprin. "Yvonne Rainer Interviews Ann Halprin." *Tulane Drama Review* 10 (Winter 1965): 142–167.

Works about Yvonne Rainer

Anderson, Jack. "Yvonne Rainer: The Puritan as Hedonist." *Ballet Review* vol. 2, no. 5 (1969): 31–37.

Goodman, Saul. "Yvonne Rainer: Brief Biography." *Dance Magazine* 39 (December 1965): 110–111.

Hecht, Robin Silver. "Reflections on the Career of Yvonne Rainer and the Value of Minimal Dance." *Dance Scope* 8 (Fall/Winter 1973–74): 12–25.

King, Kenneth. "Toward a Trans-Literal and Trans-Technical Dance Theater." In *The New Art,* edited by Gregory Battcock, pp. 119–126. New York: E. P. Dutton, 1973.

Koch, Stephen. "Performance: A Conversation." *Artforum* 11 (December 1972): 53–58.

Levin, David Michael. "Performance." *Salmagundi* no. 31–32 (Fall 1975–Winter 1976): 120–142.

McDonagh, Don. "Yvonne Rainer." In *The Complete Guide to Modern Dance,* pp. 445–448. New York: Doubleday, 1976.

Michelson, Annette. "Yvonne Rainer, Part One: The Dancer and the Dance." *Artforum* 12 (January 1974): 57–63.

______. "Yvonne Rainer, Part Two: Lives of Performers." *Artforum* 12 (February 1974): 30–35.

Morris, Robert. "Dance." *Village Voice,* February 3, 1966. p. 8.

______. "Dance." *Village Voice,* February 10, 1966, p. 15.

Steve Paxton

Works by Steve Paxton

Paxton, Steve. "Contact Improvisation." *The Drama Review* 19 (T–65, March 1975): 40–42.

______. "Improvisational Dance: The Grand Union." *The Drama Review* 16 (T–55, September 1972): 128–134.

Contact Quarterly 1 (1975–present). Various letters and articles by Paxton and others, regarding Contact Improvisation.

Works about Steve Paxton

Banes, Sally. "Steve Paxton: Physical Things." *Dance Scope* 13 (Winter/Spring 1979): 11–25.

Luger, Eleanor Rachel. "A Contact Improvisation Primer." *Dance Scope* 12 (Fall/Winter 1977–78): 48–56.

McDonagh, Don. "Steve Paxton." In *The Complete Guide to Modern Dance*, pp. 429–432. New York: Doubleday, 1976.

Morris, Robert. "Dance." *Village Voice*, February 3, 1966, p. 8.

Rainer, Yvonne. "Paxton Untitled." *Soho Weekly News*, November 16, 1978, p. 31. Reprinted in *Dance Scope* 13 (Winter/Spring 1979): 8–10.

Trisha Brown

Works by Trisha Brown

Brown, Trisha. "Three Pieces." *The Drama Review* 19 (T–65, March 1975): 26–32.

______. "Trisha Brown." In *Contemporary Dance*, edited by Anne Livet, pp. 42–57. New York: Abbeville Press, 1978.

Brown, Trisha, and Douglas Dunn. "Dialogue: On Dance." *Performing Arts Journal* 1 (Fall 1976): 76–83.

Works about Trisha Brown

Banes, Sally. "Gravity and Levity: Up and Down with Trisha Brown." *Dance Magazine* 52 (March 1978): 60–63.

Copeland, Roger. "The 'Post-Modern' Choreography of Trisha Brown." *New York Times*, January 4, 1976. p. II-1.

Goldberg, RoseLee. "Performance: The Art of Notation." *Studio International* 192 (July 1976): 54–58.

______. "Space as Praxis." *Studio International* 190 (September 1975): 133–134.

Koch, Stephen. "Performance: A Conversation." *Artforum* 11 (December 1972): 53–58.

McDonagh, Don. "Trisha Brown." In *The Complete Guide to Modern Dance*, pp. 343–347. New York: Doubleday, 1976.

Sommer, Sally R. "Equipment Dances: Trisha Brown." *The Drama Review* 16 (T–55, September 1972): 135–141.

______. "Trisha Brown Making Dances." *Dance Scope* 11 (Spring/Summer 1977): 7–18.

Stephano, Effie. "Moving Structures: Effie Stephano Interviews Trisha Brown, Carol Goodden, Carmen Beuchat, and Sylvia Whitman." *Art & Artists* 8 (January 1974): 16–21.

David Gordon

Works by David Gordon

Gordon, David. "It's About Time." *The Drama Review* 19 (T–65, March 1975): 43–52.

Gordon, David, with Sally Banes. "An Interview with David Gordon." *Eddy* 9 (Winter 1977): 17–25.

Works about David Gordon

Banes, Sally. "David Gordon; or, The Ambiguities." *Village Voice*, May 1, 1978, p. 67.
Carroll, Noël. "Formal Dancing." *Soho Weekly News*, October 12, 1978, p. 73.
McDonagh, Don. "David Gordon." In *The Complete Guide to Modern Dance*, pp. 378–380. New York: Doubleday, 1976.
Morris, Robert. "Dance." *Village Voice*, February 3, 1966, p. 8.
———. "Dance." *Village Voice*, February 10, 1966, p. 15.
Smith, Karen. "David Gordon's 'The Matter.'" *The Drama Review* 16 (T–55, September 1972): 117–127.

DEBORAH HAY

Works by Deborah Hay

Hay, Deborah. "Dance Talks/Deborah Hay." *Dance Scope* 12 (Fall/Winter 1977–78): 18–22.
———. "Deborah Hay." In *Contemporary Dance*, edited by Anne Livet, pp. 120–133. New York: Abbeville Press, 1978.
Hay, Deborah, and Donna Jean Rogers. *Moving Through the Universe in Bare Feet: Ten Circle Dances for Everybody*. Island Pond, Vermont: Troll Press, 1974.

Works about Deborah Hay

Chin, Daryl. "Deborah Hay/A Brief Introduction." *Dance Scope* 12 (Fall/Winter 1977–78): 17–18.
Jeffers, Bill. "Leaving the House (Deborah Hay)." *The Drama Review* 23 (T–81, March 1979): 79–86.
Kirby, Michael. "The Objective Dance." *The Art of Time*, pp. 103–113. New York: E. P. Dutton, 1969.
McDonagh, Don. "Deborah Hay." In *The Complete Guide to Modern Dance*, pp. 385–389. New York: Doubleday, 1976.
Rainer, Yvonne. "Notes on Deborah Hay." *Ikon* (February 1967).

LUCINDA CHILDS

Works by Lucinda Childs

Childs, Lucinda. "Lucinda Childs." In *Contemporary Dance*, edited by Anne Livet, pp. 58–81. New York: Abbeville Press, 1978.
———. "Lucinda Childs: A Portfolio." *Artforum* 11 (February 1973): 50–56.
———. "Notes: '64–'74." *The Drama Review* 19 (T–65, March 1975): 33–36.
———. "Notes on Batya Zamir." *Artforum* 11 (June 1973): 71–73.
———. "Notes on Judy Padow." *Dance Magazine* 48 (November 1974): 30–31.

Works about Lucinda Childs

Banes, Sally. "Lucinda Childs: Simplicity Forces You to See." *Village Voice*, May 16, 1977, p. 68.
Carroll, Noël. "Whitney Museum and Larry Richardson's Dance Gallery, New York; Exhibit." *Artforum* 12 (March 1974): 83.

Goldberg, RoseLee. "Performance: The Art of Notation." *Studio International* 192 (July 1976): 54–58.
McDonagh, Don. "Lucinda Childs." In *The Complete Book of Modern Dance*, pp. 354–355. New York: Doubleday, 1976.
Mekas, Jonas. "Movie Journal." *Village Voice*, December 20, 1973, p. 81.

MEREDITH MONK

Works by Meredith Monk

Monk, Meredith. "Comments of a Young Choreographer." *Dance Magazine* 42 (June 1968): 60–64.

Works about Meredith Monk

Baker, Robb. "Landscapes and Telescopes; A Personal Response to the Choreography of Meredith Monk." *Dance Magazine* 50 (April 1976): 55–70.
Banes, Sally. "The Art of Meredith Monk." *Performing Arts Journal* 3 (Spring/Summer 1978): 3–18.
______. "Meredith Monk and the Making of *Chacon*." *Dance Chronicle* 1 (1977): 46–62.
Dorris, George. "Music for Spectacle." *Ballet Review* vol. 6, no. 1 (1977): 45–55.
Johnson, Tom. "New Dance/Music; New Directions in Music for Dance." *Dance Magazine* 48 (April 1974): 49–51.
Jowitt, Deborah. "Take a Trip with Meredith Monk." *New York Times*, January 13, 1974, p. II–9.
McDonagh, Don. "Meredith Monk." In *The Complete Guide to Modern Dance*, pp. 413–418. New York: Doubleday, 1976.
Metzker, Wendy Shankin, and Doris Seider. "An Interview with Meredith Monk." New York, May 24, 1976.
Poster, Constance H. "Making It New — Meredith Monk and Kenneth King." *Ballet Review* vol. 1, no. 6 (1967): 14–21.

KENNETH KING

Works by Kenneth King

King, Kenneth [Zora A. Zash and Sergei Alexandrovitch]. "Correspondence." *Ballet Review* vol. 2, no. 4 (1968): 34–37.
King, Kenneth. "Metagexis (Excerpts)." *Eddy* 8 (Spring–Summer 1976): 27–32.
______. "On the Move: A Polemic on Dancing." *Dance Magazine* 41 (June 1967): 56–58.
______. "SuperLecture." *The Young American Writers*, edited by Richard Kostelanetz, pp. 221–238. New York: Funk and Wagnalls, 1967.
______. *Time Capsule (The Yellow Book)*. New York: Zora A. Zash Enterprises, Ltd., 1974.
______. "Toward a Trans–Literal and Trans–Technical Dance–Theater." In *The New Art*, edited by Gregory Battcock, pp. 119–126. Revised Edition. New York: E. P. Dutton, 1973.
King, Kenneth, with John Howell. "Interview." *Performing Arts Journal* 3 (Fall 1978): 16–24.
Baker, Robb, with Kenneth King. "Dialogue with Kenneth King." *Soho Weekly News*, November 14, 1974, pp. 21–23.
Stephano, Effie, with Kenneth King. "Dance, Mesmex, and the Future . . ." *Art and Artists* 8 (March 1974): 16–19.

Works about Kenneth King

Banes, Sally. "Reflections on Kenneth King." *The Reader*, August 1, 1975: 26.
Battcock, Gregory. "Notions on a New Dance Program." *Film Culture* 43 (Winter 1967): 4.
Kronen, H. B. "King of the Mountain." *Eddy* 5 (Winter Solstice 1974): 45–47.
McDonagh, Don. "Kenneth King." In *The Complete Guide to Modern Dance*, pp. 398–400. New York: Doubleday, 1976.
Moore, Nancy. "New Dance/Criticism; Is It Whatever You Say It Is?" *Dance Magazine* 48 (April 1974): 57–60.
Perreault, John. "Inventions of the Unknown." *Village Voice*, November 9, 1967, p. 15.
Poster, Constance. "Making It New — Meredith Monk and Kenneth King." *Ballet Review* vol. 1, no. 6 (1967): 14–21.

Douglas Dunn

Works by Douglas Dunn

Dunn, Douglas [Fanny Logos]. "Hide & Seek." *Eddy* 7 (Winter 1975–76): 67–69.
———. [13]. "Not Bad, Not Bad." *Eddy* 3 (April 1974): 20–21.
———. "Notes on Playing Myself." *Eddy* 4 (Summer 1974): 22.
———. [Talking Dancing]. In *Merce Cunningham*, p. 39, edited by James Klosty. New York: E. P. Dutton, 1975.
———. [Fanny Logos]. *Tug Gut: Imaginary Writings of Douglas Dunn*. Photocopied. New York, 508 Broadway, n.d. [1975?]
———. [Fanny Logos]. "Words." *Eddy* 4 (Summer 1974): 38–40.
Brown, Trisha, and Douglas Dunn. "Dialogue: On Dance." *Performing Arts Journal* 1 (Fall 1976): 76–83.
Dunn, Douglas, Annabel Levitt, Lazy Madge. *Score*. New York: Vehicle, 1977.
Dunn, Douglas, with Sylvère Lotringer. "Interview." *Semiotext(e)* 3 (1978): 204–213.
Solomons, Gus, Jr., and Carolee Schneemann, Douglas Dunn, Amy Greenfield, Judith Scott, Rod Rodgers, Joan Jonas, Robert Wilson, Jean Erdman, Daniel Nagrin, Edith Stephen, Marjorie Gamso, and Jackson MacLow. "Thirteen Replies for a Video Editorial." *Dance Scope* 9 (Spring/Summer 1975): 8–10.

Works about Douglas Dunn

Banes, Sally. "Cool Symmetries: Douglas Dunn." *Dance Scope* 12 (Spring/Summer 1978): 50–62.
Carroll, Noël. "New School, New York; Exhibit." *Artforum* 13 (February, 1975): 73–74.
———. "308 Broadway, New York; Exhibit." *Artforum* 13 (September 1974): 86.
Denby, Edwin. "Edwin Denby on Douglas Dunn." Unpublished manuscript. New York, n.d. [1976?].

The Grand Union

Works by the Grand Union

Grand Union. "The Grand Union." *Dance Scope* 7 (Spring/Summer 1973): 28–32.
———. "Episodes from Grand Union Performances." Unpublished manuscript. New York, 1971.
———. "There Were Some Good Moments . . ." *Avalanche* 8 (Summer/Fall 1973): 40–47.
Baker, Robb, and Carolyn Brown, Kathy Duncan, John Howell, James Klosty, Deborah Jowitt, Andy Mann, Robert Pierce, Sara Rudner, Valda Setterfield, Marcia Siegel, and Trisha

Brown, Barbara Dilley, Douglas Dunn, David Gordon, and Nancy Lewis. "The Grand Union, Critics and Friends." *Soho Weekly News*, April 29, 1976, p. 22.
Paxton, Steve. "The Grand Union: Improvisational Dance." *The Drama Review* 16 (T–55, September 1972): 128–134.
Rainer, Yvonne. "Editors' Forum." *Dance Magazine* 46 (October 1972): 100.

Works about the Grand Union

Celant, Germano. "Dance: The Grand Union Is a Group." *Domus* 532 (March 1974): 54–55.
Foreman, Richard. [Observations on Grand Union.] Unpublished manuscript. New York, 1971.
Kendall, Elizabeth. "Grand Union: Our Gang." *Ballet Review* vol. 5, no. 4 (1975–76): 44–55.
Lorber, Richard. "The Problem with Grand Union." *Dance Scope* 7 (Spring/Summer 1973): 33–34.
Morris, Robert. [Observations on Grand Union.] Unpublished manuscript. New York, n.d. [1971].

Notes

Introduction: Sources of Post-Modern Dance, pages 1–19.

1. See Sally R. Sommer, "Loïe Fuller," *The Drama Review* 19 (T-65, March 1975): 53–67; and Loïe Fuller, *Fifteen Years of a Dancer's Life* (Boston: Small, Maynard, 1913; reprint ed. New York: Dance Horizons, n.d.).

2. See Isadora Duncan, *The Art of the Dance,* ed. Sheldon Cheney (New York: Theater Arts Books, 1969); and *Ballet Review* vol. 6, no. 4 (1977–1978), which has several articles on Duncan's art.

3. For information on St. Denis and Denishawn, see Ruth St. Denis, *An Unfinished Life* (New York: Harper and Brothers, 1939); Christena Schlundt, *The Professional Appearances of Ruth St. Denis and Ted Shawn* (New York: New York Public Library, 1962); Schlundt's "Into the Mystic with Miss Ruth," *Dance Perspectives* 46 (Summer 1971); and Jane Sherman, *Soaring* (Middletown, Connecticut: Wesleyan University Press, 1976). Also, for a cultural history of dance from the 1890s through the 1920s, centering on Denishawn, see Elizabeth Kendall, *Where She Danced* (New York: Alfred A. Knopf, 1979).

4. Jill Johnston, "The New American Modern Dance," in *The New American Arts,* ed. Richard Kostelanetz (New York: Collier Books, 1967), p. 166.

5. For Horst's theories of composition, see his *Pre-Classic Dance Forms* (New York: The Dance Observer, 1937; reprint ed. Dance Horizons, 1972), and Louis Horst and Carroll Russell, *Modern Dance Forms* (San Francisco: Impulse Publications, 1961).

6. For Humphrey's composition theories, see her *The Art of Making Dances* (New York: Rinehart, 1959; reprint ed. Grove Press, 1962).

7. This term was used by art critic Harold Rosenberg to describe the vanguard aspirations of modern art in *The Tradition of the New* (New York: Horizon, 1959).

8. Johnston, "The New American Modern Dance," p. 167.

9. Merce Cunningham, *Changes: Notes on Choreography,* ed. Frances Starr (New York: Something Else Press, 1968), unpaged [p. 133].

10. "Music," *Time,* April 25, 1960, p. 77.

11. Yvonne Rainer, *Work 1961–73* (Halifax: The Press of the Nova Scotia College of Art and Design; New York: New York University Press, 1974), p. 5.

12. Margaret H'Doubler was one of the first professors of dance in an American university — in the physical education department at the University of Wisconsin — and was influential in spreading dance throughout college curricula beginning in 1917. She had studied under Bird Larson, who used "Natural Rhythmic Exercises," and H'Doubler herself emphasized creative process over the discipline of physical exercises. She is the author of *Dance: A Creative Art Experience* (Madison, Wisconsin: University of Wisconsin Press, 1968).

13. Literature from Halprin's *Male and Female Ritual Honoring the Coming of Spring*, New York City, March 17 and 18, 1978. Halprin's ideas and experiences can be found in Anna Halprin et al., *Collected Writings* (San Francisco: San Francisco Dancers' Workshop, 1973); Anna Halprin et al., *Second Collected Writings* (San Francisco: San Francisco Dancers' Workshop, 1975); Anna Halprin, *Movement Ritual I* (San Francisco: San Francisco Dancers' Workshop, 1975); and Anna Halprin, James Hurd Nixon, and Jim Burns, *Citydance 1977*, ed. Buck O'Kelly (San Francisco: San Francisco Dancers' Workshop, 1977). Halprin began using the first name Anna instead of Ann in the early 1970s.

14. On Happenings and Cage's influence on the avant-garde, see Michael Kirby, *Happenings* (New York: E. P. Dutton, 1965). For several descriptions of John Cage's event at Black Mountain (some conflicting), see Martin Duberman, *Black Mountain: An Exploration in Community* (New York: Doubleday, Anchor Books, 1973), pp. 370–379.

15. Michael Fried, "Art and Objecthood," *Artforum* 5 (June 1967): 12–23. Reprinted in Gregory Battcock, ed., *Minimal Art* (New York: E. P. Dutton, 1968), pp. 116–147.

16. Rainer, *Work*, pp. 5–7, and my conversations with Rainer, Gordon, Paxton, Brown.

17. Judith Dunn, "My Work and Judson's," *Ballet Review* vol. 1, no. 6 (1967): 24.

18. David Gordon, "It's About Time," *The Drama Review* 19 (T-65, March 1975): 43–44, and my conversations with him, 1974–79. Also, see Gordon chapter.

19. James Waring, John Herbert McDowell, Judith Dunn, Arlene Croce, and Don McDonagh, "Judson: A Discussion," *Ballet Review* vol. 1, no. 6 (1967): 37.

20. "Judson: A Dance Chronology," *Ballet Review* vol. 1, no. 6 (1967): 54.

21. Rainer, *Work*, p. 8.

22. "Judson: A Dance Chronology," pp. 54–55.

23. Ibid., pp. 55–57.

24. Waring et al., "Judson: A Discussion," p. 35.

25. Jill Johnston, "Judson 1964: End of an Era," *Ballet Review* vol. 1, no. 6 (1967): 13.

26. Rainer, *Work*, p. 9.

27. "Judson: A Dance Chronology," and H. Sohm, *Happening & Fluxus* (Cologne: Koelnischer Kunstverein, 1970).

28. Johnston, "Judson 1964: End of an Era," p. 7.

29. See Simone Forti, "Theater and Engineering — An Experiment," *Artforum* 5 (February 1967): 26–30 for an inside view. For reviews see Erica Abeel, "Armory '66, Not Quite What We Had in Mind," *Arts* 41 (December 1966): 23–24; Dore Ashton, "Nine Evenings: Theater and Engineering at the 25th Street Armory," *Studio* 173 (January 1967): 40; and Doris Hering, "The Engineers Had All the Fun; Nine Evenings, Theater and Engineering, 69th Regiment Armory, N.Y., October 12–23, 1966," *Dance Magazine* 40 (December 1966): 36 ff.

Simone Forti: Dancing as if Newborn, pages 21–37

1. See Karl Groos, *The Play of Man* (New York: D. Appleton, 1901) and Konrad Lange, *Das Wesen der Kunst* (Berlin: G. Grote, 1901). A brief selection from Lange appears, as does a bibliography on Play and Art, in Melvin Rader, ed., *A Modern Book of Esthetics* (New York: Holt, Rinehart and Winston, 1966). Also, see Richard Schechner and Mady Schuman, eds., *Ritual, Play, and Performance* (New York: Seabury Press, 1976).

2. Interview with Simone Forti, New York City, Spring 1976. Unless otherwise noted, all quotations are from my interviews or informal talks with Forti, 1976–79.

3. Robert Motherwell, *The Dada Painters and Poets: An Anthology* (New York: George Wittenborn, 1951), p. xxi.

4. Ibid., pp. 62–63.

5. See Michael Kirby, *Happenings* (New York: E. P. Dutton, 1965), pp. 22–24.

6. Simone Forti, *Handbook in Motion* (Halifax, Nova Scotia: The Press of the Nova Scotia College of Art and Design; New York: New York University Press, 1974), p. 34.

7. *The American Moon* was a Happening by Robert Whitman, presented about ten times in No-

vember and December 1960. The audience was seated in separate compartments surrounding a central space in which many events took place, including the appearance of several figures costumed as a mouth, a tube, and a heap of cloth; a man swinging across the space on a rope; a man and a woman (Lucas Samaras and Simone Forti) rolling under a gigantic, transparent balloon. Each audience compartment had a front curtain, made of plastic and dotted with pieces of paper, on which films were projected. For a thorough documentation of *The American Moon*, as well as other Happenings that may have influenced the work of Forti and the other post-modern choreographers, see Kirby, *Happenings*.

8. Kirby, *Happenings*, pp. 28–29.
9. Ray Falk, "Japanese Innovators," *New York Times*, December 8, 1957; p. II-24.
10. Yvonne Rainer, "The Performer as a Persona: An Interview with Yvonne Rainer," *Avalanche* 5 (Summer 1972), p. 54.
11. Ibid.
12. Forti, *Handbook in Motion*, p. 44.
13. Ibid., p. 59.
14. For a complete description of this concert, including a floor plan, see Forti, *Handbook in Motion*, pp. 56–57. The performers were Ruth Allphin, Carl Lehmann-Haupt, Marnie Mahafey, Bob Morris, Simone Morris, Steve Paxton, and Yvonne Rainer (spelling according to the program notes).
15. See Jean Piaget, *Play, Dreams, and Imitation in Childhood*, trans. C. Gattegno and F. M. Hodgson (New York: W. W. Norton, 1962).
16. La Monte Young and Jackson MacLow, *An Anthology* (New York: Something Else Press, 1963; reprint ed. New York: Heiner Friedrich, 1970), unpaged.
17. H. Sohm, *Happening & Fluxus* (Cologne: Koelnischer Kunstverein, 1970), unpaged.
18. Simone Forti, "Theater and Engineering — An Experiment," *Artforum* 5 (February 1967): 26–30.
19. Jonas Mekas, "Movie Journal," *Village Voice*, December 7, 1967, p. 41.
20. Forti, *Handbook in Motion*, p. 16.
21. Ibid., p. 91.
22. Simone Forti, "Dancing at the Fence," *Avalanche* (December 1974): 20.
23. Ibid., p. 22.
24. Forti, *Handbook in Motion*, pp. 136, 118.
25. These *Animal Stories* by Simone Forti are previously unpublished.

Yvonne Rainer: The Aesthetics of Denial, pages 41–54

1. Liza Béar and Willoughby Sharp, "The Performer as a Persona: An Interview with Yvonne Rainer," *Avalanche* 5 (Summer 1972): 53.
2. Ibid.
3. Ibid., p. 54.
4. Yvonne Rainer, "Some Retrospective Notes on a Dance for 10 People and 12 Mattresses Called 'Parts of Some Sextets,' Performed at the Wadsworth Atheneum, Hartford, Connecticut, and Judson Memorial Church, New York, in March 1965," *Tulane Drama Review* 10 (T-30, Winter 1965): 168.
5. Alain Robbe-Grillet, "A Future for the Novel," *For a New Novel*, trans. Richard Howard (New York: Grove Press, 1965), pp. 21–23.
6. Rainer, "Some Retrospective Notes," p. 178.
7. Yvonne Rainer, "A Quasi Survey of Some 'Minimalist' Tendencies in the Quantitatively Minimal Dance Activity Midst the Plethora, or an Analysis of *Trio A*" was first written in 1966, and first published in Gregory Battcock, ed., *Minimal Art* (New York: E. P. Dutton, 1968), pp. 263–273. It also appears in Yvonne Rainer, *Work 1961–73* (Halifax, Nova Scotia: The Press of The Nova Scotia College of Art and Design; New York: New York University Press, 1974), pp. 63–69.

8. Ibid., p. 63.
9. Ibid., p. 68.
10. Ibid.
11. I use the word *virtuosity* here, as I suspect Rainer uses it, to mean technical brilliance for the sake of technique, without any accompanying artistic insight. Part of that brilliance is the signal that the movements performed are difficult, in tension with a contradictory perception that the movements are effortless. Virtuosity implies a climactic situation. Whereas post-modern dance might require equal stamina, precision, and difficulty, it eliminates virtuosity, in part because of *Trio A*'s precedent. I want to thank Selma Jeanne Cohen and the other members of her seminar on virtuosity, June 26–27, 1978, for some thoughts on this quality in dance.
12. Martin Heidegger, *Poetry, Language, Thought*, trans. Albert Hofstadter (New York: Harper and Row, 1975), p. 46.
13. Ibid., p. 78.
14. Ibid., p. 46.
15. Ibid., p. 40.
16. Ibid., p. 54.
17. Lincoln Kirstein, *Dance: A Short History of Classic Theatrical Dancing* (New York: G. P. Putnam's Sons, 1935; reprint ed. New York: Dance Horizons, 1969), p. 240.
18. Yvonne Rainer, *Work*, p. 75.
19. Ibid.
20. Conversation with Yvonne Rainer, New York City, August 1978.
21. Rainer, *Work*, p. 113.
22. Conversation with George Dorris, New York City, March 1979.
23. Rainer, *Work*, p. 77.
24. Conversation with David Gordon, New York City, March 1974.
25. Program note, *The Mind is a Muscle*, April 11, 14, 15, 1968. ("Statement," written March 1968.) Reprinted in Rainer, *Work*, p. 71.
26. William Butler Yeats, *The Trembling of the Veil* (1922), in *Autobiographies* (New York: Macmillan, 1927), pp. 348–349. Quoted in reference to George Balanchine's choreography by Lincoln Kirstein in "What Ballet Is About: An American Glossary," *Dance Perspectives* 1 (1959): pp. 10–11.
27. I would like to acknowledge Noël Carroll's suggestion that *Trio A* does away with the postural and architectural qualities of dance, leaving only motion. I would also like to thank both him and Yvonne Rainer for many valuable interpretations and insights.
A film of *Trio A*, danced by Rainer, was shot by Robert Alexander on August 12, 1978, and made possible my close study of the dance.
28. Reprinted from Rainer, "A Quasi Survey," in *Work*, p. 63.

Steve Paxton: Physical Things, pages 57–70

1. Steve Paxton, "Teacher Teaching," *Contact Quarterly* 3 (Fall 1977): 20.
2. Interview with Steve Paxton, Washington, D.C., June 30, 1975. Unless otherwise noted, quotations are from this interview or from my informal conversations with Paxton, 1974–79.
3. Steve Paxton, *"Satisfyin Lover," 0 to 9* no. 4 (June 1968): 27–30, and reprinted here, pp. 71–74.
4. Jill Johnston, "Paxton's People," *Village Voice*, April 4, 1968; reprinted in Jill Johnston, *Marmalade Me* (New York: Dutton, 1971), pp. 135–37.
5. Steve Paxton with Liza Béar, "Like the Famous Tree," *Avalanche* 11 (Summer 1975): 28.
6. Ibid., p. 29.
7. Robert Morris, "Dance," *Village Voice*, February 3, 1966, p. 8.
8. Paxton, "Like the Famous Tree," p. 28.
9. Victor Turner, "Passages, Margins, and Poverty," in *Dramas, Fields, and Metaphors: Sym-*

bolic Action in Human Society (Ithaca and London: Cornell University Press, 1974); see also Victor Turner, *The Ritual Process: Structure and Anti-Structure* (Chicago: Aldine, 1969).

10. Turner, "Passages, Margins, and Poverty," p. 252.

11. Jill Johnston, "Tornado in a Teacup," *Village Voice,* October 24, 1968; reprinted in Johnston, *Marmalade Me,* pp. 196–201.

12. Steve Paxton, "Contact Improvisation," *The Drama Review* 19 (T-65, March 1975): 40–42.

13. Danny Lepkoff [D.N.L.] "Letter," *Contact Newsletter* 1 (Summer 1976): 16.

14. Alan Potash, "Letter," *Contact Newsletter* 1 (Summer 1976): 11.

15. Lisa Nelson, "Cross Currents: What's New in Modern Dance?" *Contact Quarterly* 2 (Spring 1977): 27–28.

16. Reprinted from *0 to 9* no. 4 (June 1968): 27–30.

Trisha Brown: Gravity and Levity, pages 77–91

1. Interview with Trisha Brown, New York City, November 1974. Unless otherwise noted, quotations by Brown are from my interviews, conversations, and written correspondences with her, 1973–79.

2. Trisha Brown, "Trisha Brown," in *Contemporary Dance,* ed. Anne Livet (New York: Abbeville Press, 1978), p. 44.

3. Simone Forti, *Handbook in Motion* (Halifax: Press of the Nova Scotia College of Art and Design; New York: New York University Press, 1974), pp. 31–32.

4. Brown, "Trisha Brown," p. 45.

5. Jill Johnston, "Hay-Brown," *Village Voice,* April 7, 1966, p. 13.

6. Trisha Brown, Chronology, 1974, unpublished.

7. For an excellent documentation of the Equipment Pieces, see Sally R. Sommer, "Equipment Dances: Trisha Brown," *The Drama Review* 16 (T-55, September 1972): 135–41.

8. Effie Stephano, "Moving Structures," *Art and Artists* 8 (January 1974): 17.

9. I am thinking especially of Sol LeWitt's serial cubes and serial drawings, and also some of his writings on art: "When an artist uses a conceptual form of art, it means that all of the planning and decisions are made beforehand and the execution is a perfunctory affair. The idea becomes a machine that makes the art . . . Conceptual art is not necessarily logical. The logic of a piece or series of pieces is a device that is used at times only to be ruined . . . What the work of art looks like isn't too important. It has to look like something if it has physical form. No matter what form it may finally have it must begin with an idea. It is the process of conception and realization with which the artist is concerned." (Sol LeWitt, "Paragraphs on Conceptual Art," *Artforum* 5 [Summer 1967]: 80.) I am also thinking of Mel Bochner's diagrams, grids, works using measurements and other mathematical constraints and systems. Bochner points out that the use of mathematical thinking does not necessarily turn the art work into mathematics, but rather provides a set of external constraints that supplies order and turns the attention of the spectator to the structure of the information, rather than to the information itself. (Mel Bochner, "Problematic Aspects of Critical/Mathematical Constructs in My Art," excerpted in Lucy Lippard, *Six Years: The Dematerialization of the Art Object from 1966 to 1972* [New York: Praeger, 1973], p. 236.)

For information on other serial artists, see Bochner's article "Serial Art (Systems: Solipsism)," *Arts Magazine* 41 (Summer 1967): 39–43, reprinted in *Minimal Art,* ed. Gregory Battcock (New York: E. P. Dutton, 1968), pp. 92–102.

10. See Bochner, "Serial Art (Systems: Solipsism)," for a discussion of the qualities of Andre's works in terms of their material, low height, and matter-of-factness.

11. Lucy R. Lippard, "Eros Presumptive," *The Hudson Review* 20 (Spring 1967): 91–99; reprinted, revised, in *Minimal Art,* pp. 216–17.

12. Brown, "Trisha Brown," p. 54.

13. Trisha Brown Company, Program Notes, Brooklyn Academy of Music, New York, March 10–19, 1977.

14. Brown, "Trisha Brown," p. 54.

15. Sally R. Sommer, "Trisha Brown Making Dances," *Dance Scope* 11 (Spring/Summer 1977): 15.

16. *Skymap* was "choreographed" in 1969. It is a taped monologue which Brown "performs" by turning out the lights and turning on the tape recorder. The audience lies or leans back and visualizes the dance taking place on the ceiling.

David Gordon: The Ambiguities, pages 97–108

1. Valda Setterfield, who is married to David Gordon, trained in London with Marie Rambert and Audrey de Vos and danced in Merce Cunningham's company from 1960 to 1961 and 1965 to 1975, as well as having danced with James Waring, Katherine Litz, and Yvonne Rainer. She has appeared in films by Yvonne Rainer and in Brian de Palma's *The Wedding Party* (1966). In 1976 she performed with the Grand Union, and she continues to teach and to dance in Gordon's works.

2. David Gordon with Sally Banes, "An Interview with David Gordon," *Eddy* 9 (Winter 1977): 17–25, from interview, April 6, 1975. Unless otherwise noted, quotations from Gordon either come from this interview or from my informal conversations with him, 1974–79.

3. Gordon and Banes, "An Interview with David Gordon," p. 18.

4. For a description of *Mannequin Dance* and *Helen's Dance*, see David Gordon, "It's About Time," *The Drama Review* 19 (T-65, March 1975): 44–45. See also Jill Johnston, "Democracy," *Village Voice*, August 23, 1962, p. 9, for a review of their performance at Judson Church Dance Concert #1.

5. Gordon, "It's About Time," p. 44.

6. Ibid., pp. 45–47.

7. Robert Morris, "Dance," *Village Voice*, February 10, 1966, p. 15; Clive Barnes, "Dance: Village Disaster," *New York Times*, January 11, 1966, p. 20.

8. For a very detailed description of *The Matter*, see Karen Smith, "David Gordon's *The Matter*," *The Drama Review* 16 (T-55, September 1972): 117–127.

9. Gordon, "It's About Time," p. 43.

10. See especially Erving Goffman, *Frame Analysis: An Essay on the Organization of Experience* (New York: Harper and Row, 1974).

11. This response was written by Gordon after reading the chapter in March 1979.

Deborah Hay: The Cosmic Dance, pages 113–127

1. Deborah Hay and Donna Jean Rogers, *Moving Through the Universe in Bare Feet: Ten Circle Dances for Everybody* (Island Pond, Vermont: Troll Press, 1974), p. 5.

2. Annette Michelson, "Robert Morris: An Aesthetics of Transgression," *Robert Morris* (Washington, D.C.: Corcoran Gallery of Art, 1969), p. 57. Emphasis Michelson's.

3. Ibid., pp. 58–59.

4. Yvonne Rainer, "Notes on Two Dances by Deborah Hay," Unpublished manuscript. New York, August 22, 1966.

5. Marcia Marks, "Trisha Brown and Deborah Hay, Judson Memorial Church, March 29, 1966," *Dance Magazine* 40 (May 1966): 62, wrote: "It was called A Concert of Dance, but titles tend to be rather meaningless these days. Someone must have taken it seriously, however, for after the first number, Deborah Hay's *No. 3*, there was an explosive shout of 'Hoax!'."

6. Jill Johnston, "Hay's Groups," *Village Voice*, April 11, 1968: 34; reprinted in Johnston, *Marmalade Me* (New York: E. P. Dutton, 1971), p. 138.

7. Jean Erdman, Trisha Brown, et al., "Conversation in Manhattan," *Impulse: Annual of Contemporary Dance* (1967, The Dancer's Environment): 63.

8. Hay and Rogers, *Moving Through the Universe*, p. 4.

9. Chang Chung-yuan, *Creativity and Taoism* (New York: Julian Press, 1963; reprint ed. Harper and Row, 1970), p. 27.

10. The information on Tai Chi Chuan and Taoism comes primarily from Chang and from J. C. Cooper, *Taoism, The Way of the Mystic* (Wellingborough, Northamptonshire: The Aquarian Press, 1972); Al Chung-liang Huang, *Embrace Tiger, Return to Mountain* (Moab, Utah: Real People Press, 1973); and Richard Wilhelm, *The Secret of the Golden Flower*, Commentary by C. G. Jung, translated by Cary F. Baynes. (First published 1931; revised and augmented ed. New York: Harcourt Brace Jovanovich, 1962).

11. Hay and Rogers, *Moving Through the Universe*, p. 5.

12. Ibid.

13. Ibid., p. 6.

14. Ibid., p. 223.

15. Joann Kealiinohomoku, "Folk Dance," in *Folklore and Folklife*, ed. Richard Dorson (Chicago: University of Chicago Press, 1972), p. 387.

16. Ibid., p. 388.

17. Hay and Rogers, *Moving Through the Universe*, p. 231.

18. Deborah Hay, "Dance Talks," *Dance Scope* 12 (Fall/Winter 1977–78): 19.

19. Ibid., p. 21.

20. Notice for Deborah Hay's solo dance concerts, October 15 and 16, 1976, at Paula Cooper Gallery, New York City. Reprinted in "Dance Talks," pp. 21–22.

21. Hay, "Dance Talks," p. 21. See also Bill Jeffers, "Leaving the House (Deborah Hay)," *The Drama Review* 23 (T-81, March 1979): 79–86.

22. Deborah Hay, "The Grand Dance." Unpublished score. Austin, Texas, 1978.

Lucinda Childs: The Act of Seeing, pages 133–145

1. Interview with Lucinda Childs, New York City, March 21, 1977. Unless otherwise noted, quotations from Childs come from my interviews and conversations with her, 1975–79.

2. Lucinda Childs, "Lucinda Childs," In *Contemporary Dance* ed. Anne Livet (New York: Abbeville Press, 1978), p. 61.

3. Lucinda Childs, "Notes on Judy Padow," *Dance Magazine* 48 (November 1974): 30.

4. Louis Horst, "The Contemporary Dance, Inc., Kaufmann Concert Hall, April 25, 1963," *Dance Observer* 30 (June-July 1963): 88–89.

5. Jill Johnston, "The Object," *Village Voice*, May 21, 1964, p. 12.

6. Jill Johnston, "Morris-Childs," *Village Voice*, May 20, 1965, p. 21.

7. Lucinda Childs, "Lucinda Childs: A Portfolio," *Artforum* 11 (February 1973): 53. The dance is erroneously identified as *Screen.*

8. Lucinda Childs, "Notes: '64–'74," *The Drama Review* 19 (T-65, March 1975): 35–36.

9. Conversations with Lucinda Childs, January 1979.

10. Reprinted from Childs, "A Portfolio," p. 52.

Meredith Monk: Homemade Metaphors, pages 149–165

1. Antonin Artaud, "Manifesto for a Theater That Failed," in *Antonin Artaud: Selected Writings*, ed. Susan Sontag (New York: Farrar, Straus & Giroux, 1976), p. 160.

2. Program note, *Playbill*, Billy Rose Theater, February 3–8, 1969.

3. Some of this information comes from Wendy Shankin Metzker and Doris Seiden, "An Interview with Meredith Monk," May 24, 1976, unpublished. The rest—and any information or quotations not otherwise attributed—comes from my interviews and conversations with Monk, 1973–1979.

4. Ibid., pp. 6 and 8.

5. Jill Johnston, "Five for the Bridge," *Village Voice*, June 16, 1966, p. 20.

6. Deborah Jowitt, "Echoes and Reverberations," *Village Voice*, December 11, 1969, p. 33.
7. Bruno Bettelheim, *The Uses of Enchantment* (New York: Alfred Knopf, 1976).
8. For an account of the creation of *Chacon*, see Sally Banes, "Meredith Monk and the Making of *Chacon*," *Dance Chronicle* 1 (1977): 46–62.
9. Brooks McNamara, "VESSEL: The Scenography of Meredith Monk," *The Drama Review* 16 (T-53, March 1972): 87–103.
10. Program note, *Tour 4: Lounge*, Alfred University, November 19, 1969.
11. For the suggestion that *Education of the Girlchild* refers partly to Monk's grandmother's life in the *shtetl*, I am grateful to Arthur Sainer.
12. Monk's *Notes on the Voice*, written in 1973, are previously unpublished.

Kenneth King: Being Dancing Beings, pages 169–183

1. Kenneth King, "Toward a Trans-Literal and Trans-Technical Dance-Theater," in *The New Art*, ed. Gregory Battcock (New York: Dutton, 1966; new revised ed. 1973), p. 124.
2. Ibid., p. 119.
3. Allen Hughes, "Startling Dance Given in 'Village,' " *New York Times*, September 26, 1964, p. 17.
4. Jill Johnston, "Horizontal Baggage," *Village Voice*, July 29, 1965, p. 8.
5. Jack Anderson, "Judson Dance Theater, Judson Memorial Church, April 5–6, 1966," *Dance Magazine* 40 (May 1966): 87.
6. Constance H. Poster, "Making It New — Meredith Monk and Kenneth King," *Ballet Review* vol. 6, no. 1 (1967): 20–21.
7. Gregory Battcock, "Notions on a New Dance Program," *Film Culture* 43 (Winter 1967): 4.
8. Kenneth King, "SuperLecture," in *The Young American Writers*, ed. Richard Kostelanetz (New York: Funk and Wagnalls, 1967), pp. 223–230.
9. See Jill Johnston, "Where's Kenneth?" *Village Voice*, January 18, 1968, p. 24; reprinted in Johnston, *Marmalade Me* (New York: E. P. Dutton, 1971), pp. 119–21.
10. Kenneth King [Zora A. Zash and Sergei Alexandrovitch], "Correspondence," *Ballet Review* vol. 2, no. 4 (1968): 34–47.
11. Kenneth King with Effie Stephano, "Dance, Mesmex & The Future," Art and Artists 8 (March 1974): 19, and my conversations with King, 1973–79.
12. Kenneth King, *Time Capsule* (*The Yellow Book*) (New York: Zora A. Zash Enterprises, Ltd., 1974).
13. King, "Dance, Mesmex & The Future," pp. 18–19.
14. Friedrich Nietzsche, *Thus Spake Zarathustra*, trans. R. J. Hollingdale (Baltimore: Penguin Books, 1961), p. 228.
15. Robb Baker, "Dialogue with Kenneth King," *Soho Weekly News*, November 14, 1974, p. 21.
16. R. J. Hollingdale, *Nietzsche: The Man and His Philosophy* (Baton Rouge: Louisiana State University Press, 1965), pp. 139–141; quoted in program notes, *High Noon: Nietzsche Portrait-Play*, November 1, 1974.
17. King, program notes, *High Noon*.
18. King, "Dance, Mesmex & The Future," p. 16.
19. Kenneth King, "On the Move: A Polemic on Dancing," *Dance Magazine* 41 (June 1967): 58.
20. Kenneth King, in a letter to MoMing, July 10, 1975.
21. Deborah Jowitt, "Kenneth King: Our Only Dancing Philosopher?" *Village Voice*, July 5, 1976, p. 118.
22. Kenneth King, course outline, Dialogue & Dance: The Meta-Aesthetics of Movement and Composition, New York University School of the Arts, Fall 1973.
23. These excerpts from *Print-Out* are previously unpublished.

Douglas Dunn: Cool Symmetries, pages 187–199

1. This text, "Talking Dancing," was later published, untitled and slightly altered, in *Merce Cunningham,* ed. James Klosty (New York: E. P. Dutton, 1975), p. 39. The correct version is reprinted here, pp. 200–201.

2. For an excellent description and analysis of *101,* see Noël Carroll, "308 [sic] Broadway, New York; Exhibit," *Artforum* 13 (September 1974): 86.

3. For an analysis of *Octopus,* see Noël Carroll, "New School, New York; Exhibit," *Artforum* 13 (February 1975): 73–74.

4. Trisha Brown and Douglas Dunn, "Dialogue: On Dance," *Performing Arts Journal* 1 (Fall 1976): 80.

5. This is the original version of "Talking Dancing" as read at The New School, October 9, 1973.

The Grand Union: The Presentation of Everyday Life as Dance, pages 203–218

1. Yvonne Rainer, *Work 1961–73* (Halifax: The Press of the Nova Scotia College of Art and Design; New York: New York University Press, 1974), pp. 125–154.

2. Ibid.

3. Lecture to performance class, School of Visual Arts, New York City, December 3, 1973.

4. Rainer, *Work,* pp. 125–154.

5. Paxton, "The Grand Union" *The Drama Review* 16 (T-55, September 1972), p. 129.

6. In 1970, *WAR;* in 1971, after her return from six weeks in India, *Grand Union Dreams* and *Numerous Frames;* in 1972, *In the College, Performance,* and her first long film, *Lives of Performers.* Members of the Grand Union appeared in her performances, but the division of labor by director and performers was clear.

7. "Editors' Forum," *Dance Magazine* 46 (October 1972): 100.

8. Leo Steinberg, "Other Criteria," *Other Criteria: Confrontations with Twentieth-Century Art* (London, Oxford, New York: Oxford University Press), p. 90.

9. See, for instance, Robb Baker, "Mary Hartman, Mary Hartman," *Dance Magazine* 50 (August 1976): 20–22, 24–25; Elizabeth Kendall, "Grand Union: Our Gang," *Ballet Review* vol. 5, no. 4 (1975–76): 44–55.

10. Erving Goffman, *The Presentation of Self in Everyday Life* (New York: Doubleday, 1959).

11. Ibid., p. 128.

12. Erving Goffman, *Frame Analysis: An Essay on the Organization of Experience* (New York: Harper and Row, 1974).

13. Ibid., pp. 123–155.

14. Scott Bartell, "Eccyclema," *Minnesota Daily,* June 3, 1971.

15. I sent three questions to each of the Grand Union members in January 1979 and asked them to send me answers, as long or as short as they wished. The questions and answers appear here, except for Lincoln Scott's. Yvonne Rainer had undergone surgery that month and her answers here are not direct answers of my original questions but extracts from a taped conversation she had with David Gordon and me on February 15, 1979, in New York City.

Index

Boldface indicates pages on which illustrations or photographs appear.

About the Author

Sally Banes is associate professor of dance history and theater studies at Cornell University. She was graduated from the University of Chicago (B.A. 1972) and New York University (Ph.D. 1980) and has taught at Wesleyan University, the State University of New York at Purchase, Florida State University, and the New York City School of Visual Arts. Banes has received Guggenheim, Mellon and The American Council of Learned Societies fellowships. She has been editor of *Dance Research Journal* and performance art critic for the *Village Voice*, and she was formerly a senior critic at *Dance Magazine*, a contributing editor to *Dance Scope* and *Performing Arts Journal*, and the dance editor of the Chicago *Reader* and *Soho Weekly News*. Her books include *Democracy's Body: Judson Dance Theater 1962–1964; Fresh: Hip Hop Don't Stop*, with Nelson George, Susan Flinker, and Patty Romanowski; *Our National Passion: 200 Years of Sex in America*, with Sheldon Frank and Tem Horwitz; *Sweet Home Chicago: The Real City Guide*, with Sheldon Frank and Tem Horwitz; and *Amazing Grace: Images in the Avant-Garde Arts of the 1960s*, to be published in 1990. She has edited *Footnote to History*, by Si-lan Chen Leyda, and *Soviet Choreographers in the 1920s*, by Elizabeth Souritz. She lives in Freeville, New York.